OTHER PEOPLE

OTHER PEOPLE
Something You Should Know

Jonathan Coppin

LEVERTOV PRESS

First published in Great Britain in 2021 by The Levertov Press
www.thelevertovpress.com

Copyright © Jonathan Coppin 2021

Jonathan Coppin has asserted his right under the Copyright, Designs and Patents Act 1988 to be identified as the author of this work

All rights reserved. No part of this publication may be reproduced or transmitted in any form or by any means, electronic or mechanical, including photocopying, recording, or any information storage or retrieval system, without prior permission in writing from the publishers.

The Levertov Press does not have any control over, or responsibility for, any third-party websites referred to in this book. All internet addresses provided were believed to be correct at the time of going to press. The publishers and author cannot accept any responsibility if addresses have changed or sites have ceased to exist.

A catalogue record for this book is available from the British Library

Hardback ISBN: 978-1-7399290-0-8
Paperback ISBN: 978-1-7399290-1-5
eBook ISBN: 978-1-7399290-2-2

Designed and typeset by Studio Monachino

It turns out you were right all along, the problem is other people but probably not in the way you imagined.

CONTENTS

1 It's a Mad Mad World   9

2 Inadequate   65

3 Resentful   119

4 Lonely   145

5 A loop   173

6 Why?   179

7 What We Talk About When We Talk About Mental Health   215

8 Other People   257

9 The Rest   301

   Acknowledgements   326

   Notes   327

   Index   364

1

IT'S A MAD MAD WORLD

Alongside the widely recognised transformations of the last two or three decades – globalisation, the digital revolution, climate change – whatever you consider the really significant developments to have been, something remarkable has been happening. We appear to have been going mad.

According to the World Health Organisation, depression is now the leading cause of ill-health and disability worldwide.[1] Not cancer, not heart disease, not even lower back pain – the biggest disease in the world is depression. In the UK, the NHS tells us that one in four adults experience mental illness.[2] The same one-in-four figure has been quoted for the US.[3] And the WHO has said that 25% of the European population suffer from depression or anxiety.[4]

Things seem to be getting worse, fast. In 2001, the WHO was reporting that mental and behavioural disorders accounted for more than 10% of the total lost years of healthy life caused by disease or injury worldwide.[5] By 2013, it reported mental health problems as accounting for more than 21% of years lived with disability worldwide, with depression as the second leading cause globally and the primary driver of disability in 26 countries.[6] In 2017, it identified depression as the leading cause of ill health and disability worldwide and reported an 18% increase in estimated rates between 2005 and 2015.[7]

In 2018, doctors in England issued more than 70 million prescriptions for antidepressants.[8] At the time, the estimated adult population for the whole UK was 44 million.[9] Those 70 million prescriptions (which is actually a significant underestimate since it excludes hospital and private prescriptions and people in prison and other institutions) were nearly double the 36 million prescriptions in 2008.[10]

Ominously, young people seem to be particularly affected. One third of young people in the UK have been reported to be suffering from mental health issues.[11] The problem in England is reported to have got six times worse in the 20 years to 2014.[12] The number of children being treated for mental health problems by the NHS increased by one third in just the two years to 2018.[13] And there was a 73% rise in students reporting a mental health condition on starting university in the four years to 2017.[14]

These are startling statistics, but the moment you begin to examine them, serious problems appear.

'One-in-four' is the most widely reported statistic about mental health in the UK, but no-one knows where it comes from and we can't agree what we mean by it. It has been applied, by the most reputable sources, to time spans of over a lifetime (Department of Health),[15] during any given year (Independent Mental Health Taskforce)[16] and at any point in time (the Royal College of Psychiatrists).[17] Clearly, saying one in four of the population will suffer from a mental health condition during their lifetime and one in four of the population is suffering from a mental health problem at this moment are very different things.

It's sometimes suggested that the confusion comes from the 2007 edition of the Adult Psychiatric Morbidity Survey, which has been carried out on behalf of the NHS every seven years since 1993. The 2007 APMS reported that nearly one person in four surveyed met the criteria, or screened positive, for at least one of the psychiatric conditions covered in the survey.[18]

On the face of it, that seems clear enough. But the survey used different time periods to evaluate different types of condition (some over a week, others six months or a year and some over a lifetime). That makes sense: some conditions, like alcohol dependence, require a pattern of behaviour over time to diagnose. Some, like psychosis, are so serious that any incidence over a year might be considered significant. Others, like depression or anxiety, fluctuate.

However, the consequence is that you can't use these results to draw any conclusions about the overall level of mental health issues at any point in time or over any particular period. Because the survey only measured symptoms of depression and anxiety over the previous week, it might not include a very large number of people who had experienced depression or anxiety earlier in the year and recovered – that figure could be much higher than one in four. Equally, the results could include people who had met the criteria for other conditions earlier in the year and since recovered – so if you tried to use the figure as a measure of people suffering from mental health issues now, it could be grossly overstated.

Saying one in four people in that survey tested positive for a psychiatric disorder might be an entirely accurate statement, but it doesn't give much insight into the incidence of psychiatric disorders in England at any point in time. You can't even draw any conclusions about the number of people who suffer from a condition over their lifetime – the figures for far and away the most common conditions, which are depression and anxiety, only cover a week. Over a lifetime that could be one in two,[19] it could be all of us.

The 2014 APMS (which is the latest available) did focus on a fixed period for its headline conclusion, which was that one in six adults in England was suffering from a common mental disorder in the week prior to the survey.[20] One in four and one in six are quite different. The 2007 APMS refers to psychiatric disorders and the 2014 to common mental disorders, which aren't the same thing. The NHS has stuck with the 'one-in-four' formulation and charities, action groups and other commentators tend to take their lead from that.

There's another disconnect between the APMS and that one-in-four figure for the UK. The APMS is restricted to England – there's a question mark about how far it can support statements about the UK population. Research has indicated quite striking differences for mental health statistics between England and Scotland and Wales.[21] The APMS itself suggests significant variations even between different regions in England.

In any event, it turns out that 'one-in-four' was being used a long time before the 2007 APMS. The WHO was already using it as a global figure (for mental or neurological disorders over a lifetime) in 2001.[22] In the UK, it's been traced back as far as 1980, when it was used in relation to a restricted range of psychiatric conditions occurring outside the care system over a period of one year.[23]

'One-in-four' is the banner headline for mental health in the UK but we don't appear to have any real idea what we mean by it or where we got it from. If we don't know that, what do we know?[24]

If your experiment needs a statistician, you need a better experiment (Ernest Rutherford)

Most of what most of us read about mental health comes from statistics and that's how this book has started too. Producing reliable statistics about health is not straightforward. The results are rarely as robust as we'd like to believe. The conspicuous difficulties experienced by the world's leading epidemiologists, backed by all the resources of nation states in crisis, in tracking, reporting and modelling Covid 19 infection,[25] determining preventative measures,[26] treatment,[27] vaccine effectiveness[28] and side effects[29] may have made that a bit more apparent, but it's always been true.

The problems are much worse in mental health because the underlying conditions – what you're trying to measure – are much harder to identify, define and differentiate than in physical medicine. We know what meningitis looks like and we know what rubella looks like. Physicians don't have much difficulty in telling them apart. We'll see that's not the case for mental health.

An important element in collating health statistics is consistency in the way data is obtained and treated – population samples, environmental conditions, collection methods, evaluation criteria and measurement, treatments, periods of time and statistical analysis. All those factors impact on mental health statistics but, in particular, there is a problem with lack of consistency in data collection and its accuracy or validity.

A plethora of different questionnaires and assessments has emerged to try to identify and measure various psychological traits, emotions or mental health conditions. And when they get used in research, it's not unusual for these questionnaires and assessments to be tailored and adapted in ways which might make good sense in the context, but undermine researchers' ability to compare different studies or extrapolate beyond a particular set of results.

It's also important to recognise that these statistics are estimates, not direct measurements. They are the product of extensive modelling from often very limited samples. The 2014 APMS relied on results from 7,500 participants. As these things go, that is a very large sample, but it's still a reasonable question to ask how firmly could you ever draw conclusions about an adult population of over 40 million from a sample of 7,500?

And whatever the answer to that is, the huge ratios between samples and target populations mean the results are extremely sensitive to the modelling techniques used. Variations in these techniques can have consequences for the results as far reaching as variations in the data collection. And there are, routinely, differences in the way these figures are modelled in different studies.

So, very often statistics which appear to be quite comparable, may not be. The 'one-in-four' figure in the US relates to diagnoseable mental disorders;[30] the European 'one-in-four' is talking about depression or anxiety.[31] Data in the US was collected using one (adapted) form of structured interview, in the UK another. US data related to the previous 12 months and the 2007 APMS covered a range of different periods for different psychiatric conditions. The tests and measurements applied in each of these regions were different and so were the conditions they were intended to include. Can you make any legitimate use of them together or do they just have to sit side by side? WHO figures often use a highly engineered concept called 'years lost to disability', which is a very different way of looking at the subject from the APMS, for example. How much can putting them together add to the sum of our knowledge?

It's sometimes argued that when results compiled using different methodology appear to converge, we can take it as evidence of enough consistency to justify using them with more confidence – whichever way you look at it, it comes out more or less the same. That argument has been made to support using 'one-in-four' as the banner headline for mental health but it needs care. Convergence of the wrong kind of data could mean exactly the opposite. If the measures for a fluctuating health condition appear to be the same at a single point in time, during a year and over a lifetime (and whether we include all psychiatric conditions or just depression and anxiety) that isn't suggesting consistency; that's telling us at least one of the measures is wrong, and probably by quite a long way.

Often there's very little correspondence between different statistics relating to the same area. Two pieces of research about children and young people in the UK caught the media's attention in 2018. There was the six-fold increase in reported long term mental health conditions amongst four-24 year olds in England between 1995 and 2014 already referred to, which came out of UCL.[32] And the charity Action for Children reported that one third of 15-18 year olds were suffering from mental health and well-being issues.[33] However, around the same time the NHS's Mental Health of Children and Young People survey reported only modest increases in mental health disorders in five-15 year olds between 1999 (9.7%), 2004 (10.1%) and 2017 (11.2%).[34]

What sense can we make of these results? Action for Children is telling us there's a problem with one in three children, the NHS says its one in 10 and the figure underlying the reported six-times increase (UCL) was actually one in 20! Well, they do apply to different age groups: four-24 (UCL), five-15 (NHS) and 15-18 (AfC). But if problems for four-24 year olds have got six times worse (UCL), isn't it surprising that there were only modest increases in five-15 year olds (NHS)? Can the massive increase in 4-24 year olds be entirely down to people over 15?

Maybe that would partly help to explain things: the age group with the biggest increase in the UCL study was 16-24, with an increase of 10 times. But how do we square the fact that those UCL figures still only showed problems for 5.9% of 16-24 year olds against Action for Children's finding of one third of 15-18 year olds? Well, they are still different age groups and the UCL analysis was looking at long term mental health conditions, while the Action for Children survey covered mental health and well-being issues. Could that make sense of things?

It doesn't seem likely but nobody knows. Nobody could know – at the moment there is no way to know what to make of the fact that these studies seem to present such different pictures of the mental health of children and young adults. They stand in more or less complete isolation from each other.

Sometimes the statistics simply contradict each other. The 2014 APMS indicated that people in England over the age of 65 experienced common mental disorders at about half the rate (10.2%) of those in working age and the rate dropped further to 8.1% at 75 and over.[35] That seems like quite a comforting thought and the report's authors thought so too, picking it out as one reassuring statistic in their executive summary.

But other statistics, also from the NHS, suggest the exact opposite – that the elderly are, in fact, significantly more vulnerable to mental health problems, with rates of depression for the over-65s as high as 28% for women and 22% for men.[36] And that's depression on its own, whereas the 10% for the APMS covered the range of common mental disorders. What sense can you make of that?

Some of the problem is what people do with these studies – how the results get reflected and reported in the media. The Mental Health Foundation's website presents an unambiguous picture of older people becoming more vulnerable to mental health problems and it cites those rates of depression of 28% and 22%.[37] But those figures came from a survey in 2005; there is no reference to the very different results produced by the 2014 APMS.

It's a similar story with that research on children. We have no way of reconciling the results from those studies and that ought to make us mistrustful of each of them. But each is a recognised piece of research in its own right and gets cited on a regular basis, invariably on its own, with no recognition of the confusion in the area.

That can be highly misleading. The more or less stable levels of mental health disorders in five-15 year olds over nearly 20 years shown by the NHS's Mental Health of Children and Young Persons survey didn't get anything like the same attention as the Action for Children report released in the same year – something hasn't changed, isn't really news. But the NHS report was a better resourced, more thorough piece of research.

The problems aren't confined to presenting results in isolation from other inconsistent or contradictory research; the way information about individual sets of results is presented can give a misleading impression. The more than 70 million antidepressant prescriptions in 2018 captured headlines. But that's the number of prescriptions; how many people were taking them? It turns out it was 7.3 million in England which was about one in six of the adult population.[38] It also turned out that there had actually been a steady decline in the number of new users starting antidepressants each month in the period since April 2016.

You can't make much sense of the number of prescriptions without knowing how many people they were prescribed to.

It took access requests under the Freedom of Information Act from a national newspaper to get that answer, but asking how many users was at least an obvious question. The questions that need to be asked about these highly emotive and widely reported statistics about mental health aren't always that obvious.

Alarming rates of self-harm amongst girls and young women have been one of the most dominant features of recent reporting on mental health. The most recent edition of the Good Childhood Report by the Children's Society, for example, found 22% of 14 year old girls in the UK self-harm.[39] That's a shocking statistic – how could self-harm become such a normal feature of life for teenage girls?

It depends what you mean by self-harm. The NHS treats admission as a result of alcohol or drugs use as self-harm. You can see why drinking yourself into a state where people are worried enough about your welfare that they have to involve medical professionals could, and perhaps should, be thought of as a form of self-harm, but it isn't what immediately comes to most people's mind when they're told someone has been self-harming.

And, in fact, alcohol and drugs represent the great majority of admissions for self-harm. In 2012, which appears to be the most recent breakdown provided by the NHS, 89% of overall admissions for self-harm were for 'self-poisoning, including drugs and alcohol'.[40] Analysis of published admissions data suggest a similar sort of breakdown applies for self-harm by girls under 18 – between 2018 and 2019, around 80% of admissions of girls under 18 for self-harm were accounted for by self-poisoning, including drugs and alcohol.[41]

NHS statistics feed much of the research in the area and researchers compiling their own data will often use the same definition of self-harm. The statistic for 14 year old girls in the Good Childhood Report was compiled this way and this report wasn't about hospital admission, this was children responding to a survey which asked them questions about their drink and drug use.

Once you know what it might include, the statistic doesn't necessarily seem so shocking as on first presentation. Most of us would feel quite differently about isolated episodes of reckless teenage drinking, even if they resulted in medical attention, to a teenager cutting themselves on a habitual basis. But most of the statistics we see don't make that distinction.

This isn't to say that things might not have changed and there isn't cause for concern. NHS figures show an overall increase in self-harm admissions amongst girls under 18 of nearly 60% between 2005 to 2006 and 2018 to 2019, with a significant increase in the proportion of more overt forms of self-harm, such as cutting and burning, over the same period (7% of the total in 2005 to 2006 against 20% in 2018 to 2019).[42] And, of course, alcohol or drug abuse are themselves capable of being very serious forms of self-harm.

But it would be easy to get a quite misleading impression. In England in 2018 to 2019 there were around 2,800 hospital admissions of girls under 18 for cutting themselves (which is likely to represent a lower number of individuals as the same person might have been admitted on more than one occasion).[43] The total admissions for the same group over the same period for self-harm by burning, drowning, hanging, jumping in front of things and unspecified means was around 470.[44] The UK population under the age of 16 was estimated to be 12.7 million mid 2019, of which you would expect roughly half to be girls.[45] These aren't figures to take lightly but they're likely to be quite different to what a lot of people would be led to expect when they read what's reported in the media about self-harm among teenagers.

Unfortunately, most of us encounter mental health statistics without much explanation of how the figures have been compiled and usually reported in isolation, without any reference to inconsistent or contradictory research. That's what informs how we think and talk about mental health. And it's not just us, this confused mass of tenuous and inconsistent or contradictory statistics is all the politicians and policy makers have to go on too. It's not as if anything's being held back from us, or isn't finding its way into the media, there just isn't anything better there.

It would be helpful if these things were more often reported in a balanced way including references to inconsistent or contradictory evidence. But there's a limit to what that could achieve – very often there is no way to reconcile inconsistent or contradictory results and often no sensible basis for differentiating between them and preferring one over another. The usefulness would consist of showing us how little we know and dissuading us from believing we know things when we don't.

The situation is not helped by the fact that mental healthcare is a highly fragmented field. We have lots of different experts pursuing their own approaches and, at least to some extent, competing with each other for attention and resources. It's hard to attract resources without evidence to back up what you're doing and there isn't much to be gained spending a lot of time trying to reconcile that evidence with other evidence which might suggest what you're doing isn't working or that something someone in competition with you is doing is working better.

That fragmentation is, itself, a compelling indication that this is an area we don't know much about – when we understand a subject you don't tend to get so many different sets of experts doing different things to each other.

Who's Who in Mental Health?

In the UK, mental healthcare is provided by medical doctors (GPs and psychiatrists) and nurses, psychologists (who, in a clinical setting, are generally required to take a doctorate in psychology and, confusingly, are also called doctor, but it's a quite different process and qualification) and psychotherapists (including counsellors and psychoanalysts).

GPs and psychiatrists are the people who prescribe drugs for mental health conditions. They will often also refer their patients for psychotherapy. Psychotherapy is usually provided by a psychologist or a psychotherapist. Psychologists come from a tradition of trying to apply scientific principles of measurement and standardisation. Psychotherapists come from a tradition more concerned with theory and clinical formulation derived from individual case studies.

There are many different forms of psychotherapy. The most common are Cognitive Behavioural Therapy (CBT), Psychodynamic or Psychoanalytic Therapy and Person Centred or Humanistic. Each has a different theoretical base and clinical approach. Psychologists, with their preference for measurement and standardisation, usually practice CBT and that's the form of therapy most commonly available in the NHS. There are also Integrative Psychotherapists who seek to apply different ideas and techniques from across the main fields of psychotherapy as they feel appropriate for the situation they're dealing with.

If you compare the situation to physical medicine, the GP plays the same role; you could think of the psychiatrist as equivalent to the consultant or surgeon and whoever's providing the psychotherapy as similar to a physiotherapist. Many people with a physical health problem go direct to a physiotherapist themselves – equally, people access counselling or psychotherapy themselves, without involving their GP or any medical services. Often people with a physical health problem go and see their GP and get referred for physiotherapy – and that's also a common route for people to find their way to psychotherapy (with or without a prescription for medication).

With a more serious or complex physical problem, the GP may refer to a consultant or surgeon for specialist diagnosis or treatment and there may be a referral for physiotherapy after. The analogy holds for mental health, except the surgery equivalent will invariably take the form of a prescription of drugs. And, in the same way that people can find themselves under the immediate care of a surgeon or consultant via an A&E Department, in an emergency, people can come under the direct care of a psychiatrist. Finally, as with physiotherapy, sometimes a psychotherapist may feel that there's a need for medical intervention and refer someone to their GP.

But there are important differences to physical medicine. In mental health, the doctors have a very limited toolkit. Well, one tool really: drugs and really just two kinds – antidepressants and antipsychotics, sometimes used in combination with each other and sometimes used with sedatives. In very exceptional circumstances, electroconvulsive therapy, and even neurosurgery, are still used for mental disorders. And doctors can arrange for people to be taken into care, which can be a very valuable short-term intervention.

But, in the vast majority of cases, all the doctors can do is prescribe their preferred choice of medication and be ready to try another if it turns out the first is having no effect, making the condition worse or has excessive side effects for this patient.

Medication is crude: these are not tailored, specialist drugs with a focussed effect on specific aspects of mental health. Antidepressants aren't just used for depression; they are also prescribed for anxiety disorder, OCD, panic disorder, phobias, bulimia and PTSD. These are powerful chemical interventions affecting the whole of the patient's physiology; they're not just used for mental health disorders. Antidepressants are also routinely prescribed for physiological conditions such as fibromyalgia, sciatica, chronic back or neck pain. They are even prescribed for bed-wetting in children.[46] Antipsychotic drugs are used to treat anxiety and insomnia, as well as to control psychotic symptoms. Anxiety is often treated with beta blockers, which were originally developed for high blood pressure and heart conditions, and sedatives, which are also used for surgical procedures. It's hardly robot-guided laparoscopic surgery.

Here's another important difference to physical healthcare. There are still GPs who will just prescribe antidepressants, but not many. NICE recommended practice is that treatment for moderate to severe depression should 'ideally' include psychological therapies.[47] And that recommendation (which is probably heavily compromised by recognition of the current difficulties in getting access to psychological therapies through the NHS) lags best practice. It would be unusual for a GP to prescribe medication for a mental health condition without at least exploring the availability of psychotherapy with the patient. And any treatment by a psychiatrist would invariably involve psychotherapy at some point.

The average consultation time for a GP in the UK at the moment is apparently 9.2 minutes and the Royal College of GPs has said it would like to see this increased to 15 minutes by 2030.[48] It only needs a few minutes to prescribe medication, particularly a repeat prescription. A therapy session is typically 50 minutes and anything up to 20 sessions would be regarded as short-term work. Given that the majority of users probably find their way to therapy without seeing a doctor at all, in terms of time and cost, a great deal more mental healthcare is being provided in the form of psychotherapy than by doctors. Most people would probably agree that, in terms of the value of the intervention, in physical medicine the main contribution is usually made by the consultant or surgeon – it's what they know or do that makes most of the difference. That's much less clear in mental health.

But the biggest difference between physical medicine and mental healthcare is that in mental healthcare we don't have an equivalent of an X- Ray, let alone an MRI. We don't have blood tests, biopsies or ECGs either. What we have are forms and questionnaires from psychologists, personal observations and subjective judgements from individual psychotherapists, a set of psychiatric diagnostic classifications going back to the 1890s and some embryonic brain-scanning technology. In terms of reliable, objective diagnostics, none of this even amounts to being able to take a temperature.

There is a fundamental problem with the quality of the information we have about people's mental health which goes to the heart of what we know, how we diagnose mental illness and how we try to treat it.

Ask me no questions, I'll tell you no lies

The difficulties with psychological questionnaires are obvious and well-known. But just because something gets talked about doesn't mean it's solved or gone away – that's going to be a recurrent theme (perhaps ironically in a book by a psychotherapist). Instead, the tendency is to acknowledge the technical problems and move on (because you have to if there isn't a better way of doing it) and the difficulties drop out of sight. It's like the health warnings in marketing material for financial services: you know there's something dull in small print at the bottom of the page, you know roughly what it says but it's hard to keep it in mind when you're looking at the headline information.

That's a common feature of psychological research. Professionals 'know' that these tests need to be used with caution, but if you only have one tool to use, what does using it with caution look like? And whatever caveats and limitations the researchers and professionals do manage to keep in their minds, they definitely get lost when these things are reported on or discussed in the media, which is how most of us will encounter them.

Questionnaires rely on self-reporting. Self-reporting isn't that reliable. How often in your life have you found you've misled yourself about what you think or feel or what you really want? And for questionnaires used in mental healthcare, we're relying on self-reporting by people who may be in quite disturbed states of mind. It's not a strong start.

On top of the basic difficulty of understanding ourselves well enough to answer accurately, we have a problem with answering honestly. A powerful reporting bias comes into play with any survey – we're acutely interested in how what we say is going to make us look. Comparisons between publicly available data and responses to anonymised surveys has shown, time and time again, that large numbers of people deliberately misrepresent themselves in entirely confidential surveys.[49] They claim to give more money to charity than they do, to vote more regularly than they do and to belong to libraries when they don't. When there is no possibility of their responses ever being traced back to them, and on entirely factual issues, they just straight out lie to themselves – that's how powerful this bias is.

How comfortable then would we feel saying 'I regularly fear being abandoned'? That's a question designed to investigate different forms of attachment. For many, it's just not a version of themselves they're likely to welcome or recognise, even (maybe especially) if it were true. Even if we tried to answer that completely honestly, could we?

The 'demand characteristics' of questionnaires are often self-evident. It's not difficult to see what the test is driving at and we're suggestible – we may try to fulfil the test and that may influence the outcome. It's not deliberate but if we see a question aimed at feeling unhappy, we may be influenced to respond in a way that reflects the aim of the question and we'll be unaware it's happened. Alternatively, we may try to manipulate the test – if we're trying to get treatment, we're motivated to emphasise the problem.

Demand characteristics are a particular issue with outcome tests – treatment effectiveness is often assessed by getting someone to fill in a scored questionnaire at the beginning and at the end and looking at the difference. The problem is, tell someone they should be feeling better, or create that mutual expectation, and some are quite likely to tell you they are. That might itself be a helpful therapeutic effect but it means your outcome form isn't necessarily telling you what you want it to.

The whole aim of questionnaires is to provide a measure of objectivity but the questions themselves are often highly subjective. GAD-7, widely used as a screening tool for generalised anxiety disorder, asks people how often they found themselves *worrying too much about different things* over the last two weeks. Different respondents are likely to have quite different ideas about what's too much. That may be revealing for diagnostic purposes – if the anxiety feels like it's too much to someone, that may indicate a problem whatever its more objective characteristics – but it doesn't really allow us to use the results as a standardised measure for comparison between different people. That's exactly what we do, though. All scores of 10 or more (the cut-off for moderate anxiety disorder) are not equal, but we try to treat them as if they are.

At the same time, one person scoring 18 on GAD-7 and another 10 might actually have similar underlying levels of anxiety but different ways of responding on a form. Some people put on a brave face; others may be less in tune with their own feelings. There is evidence that some differences in the way forms get completed might be cultural in origin.[50] The two different scores might still be telling you something interesting – they might be telling you how troubled people are by their anxiety (or they might not if someone's putting on a brave face) – but they're not necessarily telling you how anxious people are.

And wouldn't you expect answers to depend on people's circumstances at the time – if you have a family member who's seriously ill, aren't you going to be worrying more? Whatever variable you're trying to test, you can't control effectively for everything else that might affect the subjects. Researchers often attempt to control for potential extraneous factors they anticipate might affect the results: gender, ethnicity, age, education. That usually involves complicated statistical processes which can themselves introduce distortion and error – the weightings you apply might be exactly right for that study or they could be way off. But you can still never be certain that you have identified all the potential variables that might affect how people respond: what they watched on TV last night or whether they had sex. In fact, you can be certain that you haven't. There has to be an assumption those won't matter. By definition, that assumption is always going to be untested – it could be right, it could be wrong.

Diagnosing the World

Ultimately, the legions of different questionnaires in mental healthcare rely for their credibility on correlation with clinical judgements made by suitably qualified experts. But the experts do not always agree with each other – in fact, the reliability of diagnoses when tested between different clinicians is not at all good. It's reported that in the field trials for the current edition of the American Psychiatric Association's Diagnostic and Statistical Manual of Mental Disorders, only three of the 20 diagnostic categories tested showed correlation scores over 0.6 (traditionally scores of 0.7 and below were regarded as 'unacceptable') and the score for mixed anxiety-depressive disorder (which is a common and important diagnosis) was negative, indicating that trying to use the diagnostic characteristics actually obstructed clinicians from making a diagnosis.[51]

Even in the most high-profile cases, when there are no constraints on time or resource, the picture isn't encouraging. When Anders Breivik was put on trial in 2012, the Norwegian Court ordered a psychiatric assessment. Breivik had launched an indiscriminate attack the previous year which had injured more than 300 people and killed 77, 69 of whom he shot individually himself. Two psychiatrists interviewed Breivik 13 times and applied a battery of tests and questionnaires. They diagnosed Breivik as suffering from paranoid schizophrenia and concluded he had been psychotic at the time of the attack. That was controversial, because it meant, under Norwegian law, Breivik wasn't legally responsible for his actions.

Two more psychiatrists were appointed to carry out a second assessment and they concluded, largely from the same materials used by the original team, that Breivik suffered from narcissistic personality disorder and had not been psychotic when he attacked. Debate raged in the media and amongst the psychiatric profession. In addition to the two sets of court-appointed psychiatrists, several other psychiatrists and psychologists were called to give evidence by the defence and by the victims' legal teams. The trial ended with the prosecution itself pressing for Breivik to be confined to psychiatric care, whilst Breivik and his defence team were vehemently protecting his legal competence because Breivik didn't want what he'd done dismissed as the actions of a madman. The Court preferred the second psychiatric assessment: it didn't think Breivik was suffering from schizophrenia and sent him to prison. There's been a stream of articles offering alternative psychiatric diagnoses since.

It's a problem psychiatry has always struggled with and it's always been the subject of critiques and exposés – in the last couple of years books like *The Psychopath Test* [52] and *The Great Pretender*.[53] And you'll find the same concerns widely acknowledged within the profession. Here's a sample quote from just one academic paper researching the issue – 'However, the reliability of psychiatric diagnoses among practicing clinicians is still poor. A review of the inpatient admissions of a single patient will reveal multiple different diagnoses for the same patient'.[54]

The situation isn't helped by the fact that there are two quite separate classification systems for mental health symptoms and diagnoses. There's the International Classification of Diseases (currently ICD-10, though ICD-11 is already on the books and will come into force in 2022), which is produced by the World Health Organisation, and the Diagnostic and Statistical Manual of Mental Disorders (currently DSM-5), which is produced by the American Psychiatric Association. And they differ – so (returning to the analogy with physical medicine) in one world you could have rubella and, in the other, scarlet fever; in one world you could have pancreatic cancer and in the other you're healthy. After the trial, experts at Oslo University pointed out that, on the evidence presented, Breivik did in fact fulfil the criteria for schizophrenia for DSM but not for ICD.[55]

Both sets of classifications emerged shortly after the Second World War – though they include diagnoses that derive from the earliest days of psychiatry at the end of the 19th century – and have steadily evolved ever since. You can see how difficult it's been to develop these diagnostic systems by the number of people involved, the number of iterations each system has gone through and the inordinate number of articles, controversies and debates they generate (it's not like that with pneumonia). The classifications get adopted, reviewed and changed by committee – and they read like it.

The problems in trying to draw a line between normal human experience and mental illness are obvious and enormous (maybe they're insurmountable). DSM-5 defines depression, which is probably its most important classification, as exhibiting at least five from of a list of nine symptoms for more than two weeks. The previous edition, DSM-IV, contained an exception for people who had experienced a bereavement – bereaved people weren't depressed, they were sad.

This was always controversial – why just bereavement? If you accepted that those symptoms needn't indicate a mental illness in bereavement, why shouldn't that be the case with people who've just got divorced or received a diagnosis of a serious illness or been severely injured? The problem was obvious: everyone on the committee responsible for this classification must have seen it. Presumably they just couldn't find a way through it that the committee could agree.

There was more controversy when DSM-5 was published and, rather than being widened, the bereavement exclusion was removed. You can see an argument here: bereavement is quite a common trigger for depression. We don't always recover our normal balance when we lose people we're very close to – bereavement can tip us into long-term states of unhappiness. But, how much sense does it really make to say that someone who is suffering from low mood three weeks after the death of someone close, or for that matter, a divorce or a life-changing injury or diagnosis, is clinically depressed and in need of medical attention? Particularly if that medical attention might take the form of powerful psychotropic drugs and will involve a diagnosis that will be with them for the rest of their lives?

Both classification systems have been susceptible to powerful influence from prevailing social values, which isn't ideal for something meant to be as objective as diagnostic criteria for illness. DSM classified homosexuality as a mental illness until 1973 and references to association between homosexuality and mental illness weren't taken out until 1987. Homosexuality remained an illness in ICD until 1990. And removing a classification very much goes against the normal course of evolution, which has been expansion and multiplication. Each system now identifies more than 300 mental and behavioural disorders.

People have suggested a link between the proliferation of classified mental disorders and research funded by drugs companies – find a new disease and you find a new use for a drug. That idea too has been written about in several books.[56] It's not an example, because depression is hardly a new diagnosis but it is quite striking that PHQ 9, the principal diagnostic tool used in the NHS for monitoring severity of depression and response to treatment, is copyrighted to Pfizer (because Pfizer paid for the research which produced it). Others have suggested that the drive for, apparently endless, formulation and classification in psychiatry is the product of 'physics envy': an overcorrection in favour of formulation resulting from a sense of inferiority to the physical sciences.[57]

It's likely something more basic has always been involved too. It's not a pleasant experience feeling you don't know what you're doing if you're meant to be a highly qualified expert. One way to manage that feeling might be to get together with others affected the same way and agree a really detailed classification system – *look how much stuff we know, we've identified 300 different disorders.*

Strangely, they all seem to have the same treatment: a limited range of drugs and psychotherapy, without any clear mandate on which drugs or what form that psychotherapy should take. Perhaps though (people really do make this argument)[58] that may mean that, for immediate practical purposes, the confusion around diagnosis needn't matter very much. If the treatment is going to be the same anyway, how much does it matter if the experts can't agree what you've got?

Certainly, these diagnostic categories don't feel very useful when you're dealing with real people. It can feel like a paint manufacturer's colour chart – 300 different words for blue: turquoise, navy, teal, indigo, cerulean, cyan, azure, celadon, sapphire, ultramarine, cobalt. After a while, there's no reliable, consistent way of applying them to the person in front of you.

And the people involved in the front line of mental health care – the ones who spend the most time actually dealing with the people who've come for help – don't believe in them. When I started working in the NHS, I was told by more senior colleagues to pick my three favourite diagnostic categories and just stick to those for assessment and outcome reports, because that's what everyone else did.

That's another major weakness of the statistics used in much of the research on mental health – frontline clinicians aren't even attempting to use the diagnostic criteria accurately. So, the outcome reports on which much of the research is based are inherently unreliable and to a very serious extent.

Here are the diagnostic criteria for depression (depressive episode F32) in ICD-10: 'In typical mild, moderate, or severe depressive episodes, the patient suffers from lowering of mood, reduction of energy, and decrease in activity. Capacity for enjoyment, interest, and concentration is reduced, and marked tiredness after even minimum effort is common. Sleep is usually disturbed and appetite diminished. Self-esteem and self-confidence are almost always reduced and, even in the mild form, some ideas of guilt or worthlessness are often present. The lowered mood varies little from day to day, is unresponsive to circumstances and may be accompanied by so-called "somatic" symptoms, such as loss of interest and pleasurable feelings, waking in the morning several hours before the usual time, depression worst in the morning, marked psychomotor retardation, agitation, loss of appetite, weight loss, and loss of libido. Depending upon the number and severity of the symptoms, a depressive episode may be specified as mild, moderate or severe'.

In its equivalent classification DSM-5 adds excessive sleeping and weight gain as symptoms – so not being able to sleep or sleeping too much or losing weight or putting it on are all symptoms of depression. That's probably true, in so far as they are all things that can happen when people are depressed, but it doesn't tell us much about what depression is, how to identify it or how to treat it.

In fact, a striking thing about these symptoms is they don't say much about mental life at all. The only mental phenomena, the only 'ideas', mentioned are guilt and worthlessness (and the related reference to self-esteem and self-confidence) – the rest of those symptoms could be affecting someone with flu, measles or cancer. This is meant to be a mental illness – where's the mental?

The key elements of any medical diagnosis are validity and reliability. Are you correctly identifying the right condition, so it can receive the right treatment and can the diagnosis be used consistently?

Many psychiatrists are disarmingly frank about their scepticism over the validity of psychiatric diagnoses. That is, that they don't believe that at least some of the diagnostic categories they use genuinely exist. They don't think there really is such a thing as mixed anxiety and depressive disorder, in the same way there is a flower called a tulip and another which is a daffodil.

Conclusions like the one from a 2019 University of Liverpool paper that psychiatric diagnoses are 'scientifically worthless as tools to identify discrete mental health disorders'[59] aren't considered particularly controversial or even unrepresentative of the way many psychiatrists think.

There is a competing more 'dimensional' model of mental illness, according to which diagnostic categories might be better regarded as expressions of different symptoms associated with a continuum of underling disorder, rather than separate conditions themselves. It is quite an influential idea but even so, psychiatrists tend to argue, if the diagnoses lack validity, they do possess utility – they are helpful in allowing clinicians to communicate with each other and conveying information about symptoms, treatment and outcome.[60] Actually, since they absorb thinking, energy and resource, which could otherwise be deployed elsewhere, and they can inhibit alternative ways of thinking about situations, if the diagnoses aren't valid, it's questionable how useful that really is.

Particularly if they can't be used reliably – and we've already seen some of the problems in reliability, with the Breivik case and the field trials for DSM-5. Psychiatric literature is full of acknowledgements and concerns about the reliability of psychiatric diagnoses.[61] Here are titles of some recent academic papers on the topic: *The Reliability of Psychiatric Diagnoses: Point—Our Psychiatric Diagnoses are Still Unreliable, Diagnostic Issues and Controversies in DSM-5: Return of the False Positives Problem* and *Reliability in Psychiatric Diagnosis with the DSM: Old Wine in New Barrels.*[62]

This can all sound charmingly modest and well-grounded, but the categorical model – in which the diagnostic classifications are regarded as real discrete entities (at least in theory) to be considered and treated separately – still prevails. Psychiatrists and other clinicians go on reasoning, researching, analysing, arguing as if the problems with reliability and validity weren't there, as if these conditions were real things and could be reliably identified. If the concerns that get regularly expressed in the psychiatric literature were taken seriously, there wouldn't be a lot of point to many of these discussions – they just wouldn't make sense.

Psychology - the science that tells you what you already know, using words you can't understand (after Raymond Cattell)

A major problem for experimental psychology is that experiments need to take place under strictly controlled conditions. That leaves a persistent question – how far can you extrapolate from the very specific, often rather artificial, conditions created in your laboratory to the real world?

In the famous 'hot sauce' experiments subjects are offered the opportunity to 'get' someone by adding hot sauce to their food after they've been told that person doesn't like hot sauce. The person who eats the food and the other people interacting with the subject are part of the experiment and acting. The amount of hot sauce added is taken as a measure of aggression and willingness to inflict pain and the subject is manipulated in various ways to see how aggression levels are affected.

Researchers were surprised by subjects' willingness, under these conditions, to 'get' people if they thought they could get away with it and the apparent ease with which aggression increased if the experimenters arranged for subjects to be involved in a confrontation immediately beforehand. That is interesting but what does it mean for our lives outside the lab? What could it tell us about our important relationships or about our mental health?

It's tempting to say that it shows we are much less rational than we'd like to think and that we have a capacity to descend into hidden feelings of vindictiveness and indulge in small secret attacks much more often than we'd be prepared to acknowledge, even to ourselves. As a psychotherapist that feels like it would be an important proposition to be able to ground in hard, scientific evidence. People who come for therapy often spend a lot of time in these states of mind and are very disturbed by them – they think there's something very wrong with them.

If we could point at solid evidence that these are perfectly normal experiences and, of themselves, don't necessarily say anything significant about us or the state of our relationships, that might be very helpful. But we can't pretend that the hot sauce experiments are good scientific evidence for what happens between couples or parents and their children in the real world. At the same time, if you restrict them to their facts, what do these experiments tell us that's at all useful or important?

That's the trouble: to get to anything useful or important with this kind of evidence, you need speculation, a leap of faith. The literature of experimental psychology is full of bridges like 'this supports', 'this is consistent with', 'therefore it seems likely'. But the claim these experiments make – the reason we should believe them – is that they're science; they're backed by objective, measurable, repeatable evidence.

A conclusion that isn't supported by science isn't science – in scientific terms, it's no better than a guess. That doesn't mean speculations in scientific papers are going to be wrong (any more than countless perfectly good insights that don't come from science) but there's a serious danger of giving them more credibility than they deserve, by selling them to ourselves with scientific credentials they don't really have.

Another problem we've already touched on, is that subjects are living in the real world and it's extremely difficult to be confident you have controlled for all potentially relevant variables. Another famous series of experiments involved testing children's willpower by leaving them alone with a piece of marshmallow and telling them they could have another, if they hadn't eaten it when the researcher came back. It's quite entertaining watching a small child trying not to eat a marshmallow for 15 minutes but, otherwise, so what?

Except, the researchers carried out follow-up studies with the same children and found better outcomes in later life on a number of measures (including academic results, body mass index, ability to cope with frustration and stress) for the children who were able to delay gratification and resist the first marshmallow. That does sound important, if a little difficult to work out what to do with. And it feels intuitively right – yes, you'd expect the ability to regulate emotion and impulse to be associated with more successful outcomes. It makes sense and that's what we're always telling our kids.

But this kind of follow-up work over several years is laborious and tends to involve small samples. When the study was repeated with a sample size ten times larger and a number of additional controls introduced, the conclusion was quite different.[63] It turned out that whether children waited for the second marshmallow or not made no difference to the later outcomes once a number of socio-economic factors were taken into account, including whether their mother had a college education, household income and home environment. Once you took those factors into account, children who didn't wait, did the same in later life as the children who waited. What the evidence really suggested was that, statistically, children from better educated, more affluent and stable households tend to do better in later life on a number of life scores – but we already knew that.

Researchers are acutely aware of the problems they're up against. They review, test and critique each other's work robustly. And there are a lot of different ways to pick holes – sample size or composition, controls, statistical significance, effect size, weighting and other statistical techniques, as well as unsupported conclusions. The result is an enormous body of material, far too much for anyone to understand properly outside their own narrow sphere of expertise, much of which comprises research taking issue with other research.

It's not just new research being commissioned; old data can be mined again and again. There's been increasing use of meta-studies: researchers comb through the sprawling mass of pre-existing research, sometimes hundreds of studies at a time, and re-analyse them, sometimes applying different statistical methods, sometimes excluding some measures or factors in the original study, often without access to the underlying data. The same individual study might now feature in several different meta-studies re-interpreted and presented slightly differently each time. In some ways it shows what a shaky proposition for research this subject area is that the people involved in it find so many opportunities to re-interpret what's already happened. And there isn't much sign that it's adding much to the clarity of the situation.

Much of the work is so specialist and contentious that only those directly involved in it are competent to judge it. And the results, when confined properly to their facts, are often so trivial that it's hard for anyone else to care. Until, that is, some piece breaks out and the unsupported speculative conclusion, which often feels like it's been added, with suitable caveats and disclaimers, only to provide some veneer of potential significance to justify the research grant, gets reported in isolation as headline news.

In a theoretical sense, much of this evidence is falsifiable (which is generally regarded as one of the key hallmarks of science) but, in practical terms, it's almost impossible to do it. Whatever the flaws and limitations in one piece of research, there'll be flaws and limitations in the studies which are inconsistent: you can't get the knock-out and points scores depend on the referee. The result is people can use experimental psychology to support pretty much whatever they want because there's invariably evidence somewhere for it, an argument to be had about any conflicting evidence and usually plenty of scope to argue about what any given set of results might mean in the real world.

This is how science is meant to work – observation, formulation, testing and challenge; it's an investigative, iterative process. The trouble is that it just doesn't seem to accomplish much in this field. Remarkably little that's clear and useful has come out so far at the other end of the scientific method when it's applied to mental health. There used to be a regular newspaper column in the UK called *Bad Science*, exposing pseudoscience and the mis-use of science. Perhaps we need another category of *Useless Science* for impeccably motivated and meticulously prepared research which doesn't tell us anything we need to know and contradicts itself all the time.

The scientific approach may be our best hope of being confident in our theories about the world, but science isn't doing its job well here. All the controversy about the reliability and validity of psychological testing and psychiatric diagnostic classifications, and all the problems and limitations with experimental psychology, just get acknowledged and absorbed into the research juggernaut. It's like a peculiar case of the elephant in the room. The elephant does get talked about but people just go ahead with what they were doing anyway because you can't push the elephant out and you want to stay in the room. In practical terms, the result is the same – the issues presented by the elephant are ignored.

The problem is that the attempt, in good faith, to apply scientific disciplines in this area brings a credibility to the results which is largely borrowed from the physical sciences and often doesn't belong here. We instinctively reach for science for our views and for our solutions – even anti-vaxxers latch onto research to support their case and treat it as established scientific fact.[64] It's a very powerful halo effect and the availability, on a selective basis, of something presented as scientific evidence (and the methods of experimental psychology are usually scientific in nature) which appears, however tangentially, to support them, can just make people even more entrenched in what they wanted to believe anyway. Without science, it's all just opinion. Too often with this science, it's still just opinion but more entrenched.

Babel

Different schools of psychotherapy espouse quite different ideas about what's involved in mental health problems and how best to address them. That's not particularly reassuring – there's not much agreement amongst the people providing most of the mental healthcare, in terms of time and money, about how to do it.

In very simple terms, CBT tends to focus on specific problems and tries to provide strategies (in terms of how to behave and ways to think) to help manage them. Psychodynamic or psychoanalytic therapy tends to focus on unconscious processes and adopts a more developmental stance – in its purest form, issues deriving from childhood (which are considered inevitable since we're exquisitely sensitive and no childhood could leave us entirely unscathed) are best addressed by recreating a parental type of relationship in therapy. Humanistic or person-centred therapy holds that we have an innate self-righting capacity and, if provided with the right kind of opportunity, which comprises open-minded questioning in the right kind of supportive environment, will resolve problems of our own accord.

But there are many other approaches which regard themselves as separate disciplines – Gestalt, Systemic and Existential Psychotherapy, for example. In fact, the British Association of Counsellors and Psychotherapists currently identifies 30 different forms of therapy on its website. Most people using psychotherapy (and most GPs making referrals) probably don't have much sense of the different schools of psychotherapy and many using therapy probably don't know which clinical model their therapist follows. In fact, therapists often develop their own quite individualised approaches and one therapist watching another might often struggle to identify the theoretical orientation being applied.

Luckily that doesn't seem to matter very much. We'll look in a moment at research on the effectiveness of psychotherapy overall, but a great deal of research has been carried out into success rates between different forms of psychotherapy. It suffers from all the problems of psychological research, and it is typically inconclusive, but one thing it does seem to suggest fairly consistently is that broadly equivalent success rates are achieved between all the different forms of psychotherapy that get tested. Certainly, the evidence as a whole does not consistently show that any one form of therapy is more effective than any other.

This may not be that surprising: a lot of the ideas involved in different forms of therapy aren't mutually exclusive. In fact, looked at closely, a number of the themes seem very similar – they just use confusingly different terminology. It's sometimes hard to resist an impression that the wheel has been reinvented and called something new dozens of times. It's as if a number of people, who all think of themselves as doing quite different things, have accidentally stumbled across the same way of helping people but no-one can work out what it is.

People have tried: there's a stream of research aiming to identify the 'common factors' – the ingredients shared between the different psychotherapeutic approaches which might contribute to success. This research too suffers from the problems already identified, but involves the additional difficulty that the factors put forward as important contributors to success, like 'quality of relationship between therapist and client' or 'client's motivation and expectations' are themselves impossible to measure on any reliable, objective basis.[65] The results have been unwieldy – a well-known study claimed to have identified 35 different specific common factors contributing to successful therapy but the figure has been put as high as 89.[66] No single factor, or even a short list, has yet been convincingly demonstrated.

You can find evidence which, taken in isolation, appears to offer powerful support for just about any form of therapy you like. Making the claim, as each of these different therapies has learned to do, that they are 'evidence based' is a very low bar – it doesn't tell you anything about how much evidence, what quality and what other evidence is around. 'Evidence based' is like marketing a movie as 'based on a true story'.

But, evidence (even as patchy and incoherent as this) is effective in influencing policy – though probably not as effective as cost at the moment – because policy has to be guided by something. And if we don't even try to measure what we're doing, we're left with pure subjectivity. Anyone could claim anything they want without having to offer anything other than their own personal conviction.

It seems clear we shouldn't be attaching too much credibility to the science we have at the moment around mental health, but the total lack of connection to objectivity and measurement has always been a particular problem for the more traditional branches of psychotherapy.

We've now had more than 120 years of people talking one to one, or in groups, with people who are suffering, in an attempt to understand and help mental health problems, and sharing the results. In this world, the practitioners aren't paying much attention to research. Ideas get their authority from the fact that someone else – also working entirely subjectively with nothing in the way of objective validation – said the same thing or something similar.

The academic literature contains reams of completely straight-faced references to equally unsupported statements from earlier papers by other writers or even the same author. Sometimes these are long chains of 'authority' – how much weight should it add to an idea that Donald Winnicott said it in 1972 and cited Melanie Klein saying the same thing in 1945 and she cited Sigmund Freud saying something similar in 1913? It's hard to know, but it's also hard to avoid a sense of a group of people trying to pull themselves up by their own boot straps.

There's no reason to doubt the potential to gain tremendously valuable insights from all this time spent by dedicated, intelligent people talking to others who've come to them for help and sharing their experiences and thoughts. In fact, there's a case to be made that this is how we've learned most of what's worth knowing so far about what causes people trouble and how to help them. But, how far can we rely on intuition, deductive reasoning, ourselves as our own laboratories and subjective experience of others as guidance on which are the good ideas and which might be bad or dangerous?

You might assume over time, in that kind of free for all, the ideas of the most successful, most effective practitioners, would come to hold sway. Well, that seems to take a long time – it's been going on quite a while and it's still a very confused picture. It also might be a little naïve – perhaps it's as likely to be the most superficially attractive ideas, or ones that appeal to powerful impulses, or the ones put forward by the best communicators, that come to predominate, as the ones that are most accurate or effective.

Brain reading

It seems obvious what's missing – a reliable method that we can agree upon and use with confidence, to get past the subjectivity of self-reporting or (perhaps worse) second-guessing by a psychiatrist or psychotherapist, and see what's really going on with people. That's what many have been hoping for from neuroscience. The development of brain-scanning technology seemed to offer that as a real possibility for the first time. Armed with an MRI of the mind, you could see straightaway whether someone has, say, depression, like you can a torn ligament, and then test properly what makes things better.

It hasn't turned out like that yet: the science is embryonic and the results are piecemeal. To start with, there are serious limitations with what the technology can show us. Brain scans can show blood flow (Functional Magnetic Resonance Imaging), glucose metabolism (Positron Emission Tomography), electrical currents (Electroencaphalography) or magnetic fields (Magnetoencaphalography). Research in cognitive neuroscience has tended to focus on metabolic factors like blood flow and glucose absorption because electrical currents and magnetic fields are much less capable of localization and, from that information, researchers try to draw conclusions about which parts of the brain are involved when people have different experiences.

But, that's it, they're not actually seeing the brain in action – fMRI doesn't show nerve cells firing, it doesn't show what the different parts of the brain are actually doing or how they're interacting with each other – the neuroscientists are watching blood flow around. There's a very real limit to what blood flow can tell us about what is actually happening in the brain and we know that blood flow changes occur on a very different time scale to the underlying neural activity: seconds against milliseconds.

Research from the 1990s which appeared to show differences in activity levels in the same areas of the brain for depressed and non-depressed subjects,[67] for example, hasn't been able to live up to its early promise. These measures haven't been any use as a tool for diagnosing depression because the range of 'normal' activity levels in different individuals exceeds the apparent effect of depression. That is, there may be evidence that people with depression have lower activity levels in certain areas of the brain and higher in others but those same activity levels would be normal for many people who aren't depressed. It seems that blood flow just isn't giving a sensitive enough picture of what's going on.

Neuroimaging studies of people suffering from depression and other mental disorders, before and after different forms of treatment, have suggested a number of metabolic and physiological features which might be relevant to different situations, but the results are nowhere near consistent or complete enough to draw any kind of reliable conclusions about what these disorders look like in the brain or which bits of the brain might be responsible for what.[68] At the moment, brain scans can't even be used as diagnostic tools to identify conditions which are considered to be neurological in origin like Alzheimer's[69] or autism spectrum disorder.[70] For all the talk of neurodiversity, and the notion of a neurotypical majority, at the moment it isn't possible to identify consistent neurological markers or signatures for the developmental and behavioural characteristics clustered together as ASD (or for ADHD (Attention Deficit Hyperactivity Disorder) or OCD, which are also sometimes grouped together as neurodiverse).[71]

And neuroscience can't get away from a number of the problems confronting more traditional psychological research. Imaging needs behavioural analysis (second-guessing by observers) or self-reporting to interpret or corroborate what's being seen. That re-introduces the subjectivity, and the potential for reporting or observer error and bias, we were hoping to eliminate. Neuroscience can't escape the need for complex statistical analysis to produce results. In some ways the problem is worse: what you see – the image on the screen – is not the raw data that's been measured. There's far too much data to analyse without an immense amount of complicated smoothing, thresholding, selecting and filtering. All of that is susceptible to error and serious errors have been found.

In her book *The Gendered Brain*[72] Professor of cognitive neuroscience Gina Rippon spends a great deal of time picking holes in a lot of neuroscience. Commenting on the dangers of having to deal with the enormous amounts of data processing required to produce brain images, she quotes a 2009 paper which reviewed more than 50 fMRI studies to that point: 'We are led to conclude that a disturbingly large, and quite prominent, segment of fMRI research on emotion, personality and social cognition is using seriously defective research methods and producing a profusion of numbers that should not be believed'.[73] Gina Rippon's take is that this doesn't mean that all the 'exciting findings' in social cognitive neuroscience to that date needed to be binned, just that they now needed to be viewed with a 'very large pinch of salt'. The trouble is how do you treat evidence with a large pinch of salt? How do you rely on something a bit? In science? Isn't the point of science that you can rely upon it?

But the biggest problem with the results available from neuroscience at the moment is the same as the one with psychological experimentation. If you look at the actual results generated by the science, the overwhelming reaction is usually 'so what?' To get to any conclusion which appears at all interesting or important, you have to make a large speculative leap beyond the evidence. At that point, you're guessing. In scientific terms, you're no better off than a 19th-century psychoanalyst framing a theory on the basis of a dozen case studies. In practical terms, probably worse off.

One piece of research Gina Rippon calls out reported *higher* levels of activity in the prefrontal areas of women than men, when subjects were asked to try to regulate their reactions, whilst looking at images designed to arouse fear and disgust responses. The researchers had actually wanted to test their hypothesis that women would show *lower* levels of activity in the prefrontal areas, which they thought would indicate reduced ability amongst women to regulate their emotions. But this research could never have provided any meaningful evidence about the ability of the subjects to manage their emotions. That would be like trying to draw conclusions on how fast people run 100 metres based on the oxygen consumed or the amount they sweated.

The fatal lack of connection between the data and the entirely speculative conclusion they were hoping to reach is neatly demonstrated by the fact that, when the results showed that women actually displayed *higher* levels of prefrontal activity, the researchers were able to conclude this was evidence that men were more efficient at regulating emotion and so didn't need the same levels of prefrontal activity to do it. It appears they came to the conclusion they always wanted – the gleaming technology and complex statistical modelling were all a bit of a masquerade.

Neuroscience may still be the path that will lead us to real testable discoveries about the way our minds work, what causes problems and how to fix them. But, as things stand at the moment, it's hard to see that it can tell us anything important or useful for understanding mental health. Gina Rippon's book isn't about important or useful things neuroscience can show us, it's about what it hasn't shown us but we might have been in danger of fooling ourselves into thinking it had.

Still, some neuroscientists believe that, even if it can't yet help us understand what's happening to the brain when people are experiencing mental health problems, it's time to start applying modern neuroscience to the treatment of mental health.[74] After all, they say, we don't know how antidepressants work.

And that's true. For many years, the leading bio-medical theory was that depression was caused by low levels of serotonin and the most popular antidepressants were believed to work by maintaining serotonin levels in the brain. That's one of the things everybody 'knew' about depression and the most widely prescribed drugs are still referred to as SSRIs (selective serotonin re-uptake inhibitors). But evidence has shown that reducing serotonin levels (or dopamine or norepinephrine) has no effect on mood in healthy subjects generally[75] (though the authors did report evidence of a slight decrease in mood, with reduced levels of all three neurotransmitters, for healthy subjects with a family history of severe depression). There was evidence of lowered mood with reduced serotonin (but not the other two) for people who had suffered from severe depression in the past and weren't taking medication at the time, but the biggest effect was found in people who had recovered from severe depression and were still taking SSRIs – reducing serotonin levels had the most effect on people who were already taking drugs to manipulate their serotonin levels. The firm conclusion has been that depression is not caused by serotonin levels. But not knowing how antidepressants work hasn't held us back – 70 million prescriptions in England in 2018, remember.

New treatments inspired by neuroscience include Deep Brain Stimulation, which involves applying continuous localised electrical current through an implanted electrode, like a pacemaker for depression, and repetitive Transcranial Magnetic Stimulation, which involves using magnetic fields to induce electric currents to stimulate parts of the brain believed to be associated with depression. Both treatments are already in use, though only in cases where other treatment methods haven't been effective.

And maybe that approach is right? Maybe it's that kind of firm minded, pragmatic, 'can do' stance we need? Even if we don't know what mental illness is, in the end the most pressing question is going to be what we can do about it. What works?

What Works?

Straightaway, we come up against a familiar problem – a mass of indigestible research. Different samples, different measurement tools, all beset by subjectivity, validity and reliability issues, flaky diagnostic classifications, different methodologies, with obvious (often acknowledged) design flaws or limitations, different statistical analyses and a range of inconsistent outcomes. The problem with that pragmatic approach is that we're not actually very well equipped to tell what works. Previous incursions into mental healthcare by neuroscience (Electro Convulsive Shock Therapy and the 1949 Nobel-Prize-winning lobotomy, for example) haven't always gone well but sometimes it's taken a long time for that to become apparent.

We'll have to see – maybe some of these new innovations will help plug a gap, provide something for people who can't be reached by our existing treatments. Maybe one of them will be transformative but you might argue that the most valuable contribution for neuroscience, at this stage, would be to concentrate on trying to help us better understand what's happening to people when they develop mental health issues, rather than adding to our already extensive range of 'have a go' interventions.

We've just seen that we don't know how antidepressants work, the question is do they – are they effective? Medication in mental health is controversial – there are millions of pages of research. Because of the problems we've been discussing with research in mental health, it's too easy in a controversial area for research to descend into opinion, claim and counter-claim. There are hundreds of studies on the effectiveness of antidepressants with differing conclusions – you could find evidence to support pretty much any view you want to take, so where do you go? There's no definitive source, no single authoritative view.

This isn't definitive either but it seems like a useful reference point – in 2018, the results from the largest ever review of trials of antidepressants were published. It involved 522 separate studies, covering more than 116,000 patients, carried out by universities and hospitals in the UK, France, Switzerland, Germany and the US.[76] And we can get some guidance on how the results should be interpreted because they've been recognised and reported on by national health authorities.

According to the NHS, the conclusion was that antidepressants 'work better than placebos'[77] (previous landmark research claimed to show with great conviction that they didn't[78]). The NHS was careful to say this didn't mean antidepressants were 'highly effective' (as had been reported in relation to this research elsewhere) and that, in fact, the researchers had said the effects of the drugs were 'mostly modest'. What the results said was that people are more likely to see their symptoms improve if they take an antidepressant than if they take a placebo.

That doesn't seem to be a very big claim, particularly given the more than 70 million prescriptions the same year in England alone. But the NHS still had to add some important caveats. The research only looked at results after eight weeks of treatment – that's actually an enormous caveat: what's eight weeks when dealing with a potentially chronic illness like depression? Also, a meta-analysis can only be as good as the underlying trials it includes and this review wasn't able to access, and so take any account of, any information about age, gender, duration and severity of condition of the participants in the underlying trials. That's also very significant – in a number of crucial respects this research was flying blind. Finally, the NHS felt it was important to note that 78% of the 522 trials reviewed had been funded by drugs companies.

There is evidence that the placebo effect can be particularly powerful in mental health,[79] so this wasn't necessarily as small a claim as might first appear, though the researchers' conclusions that the effects of the medications were mostly modest isn't encouraging. But there are also well-known side effects associated with all psychotropic medications, some of which can be very unpleasant and have a dramatic effect on quality of life. Some of the most common include obesity, loss of sex drive and increased risk of diabetes.[80] There's also concern about the effect of psychiatric medication on the kidneys and liver and increased risk of stroke with long-term use.[81]

In order to help with symptoms, medication affects the rest of people's emotional life too – people sometimes complain of feeling numb, or not feeling themselves, or finding it harder to care about other people.[82] It can also affect people's attention and their ability to think clearly, which can make it harder for people to find solutions to their difficulties or to participate actively in therapy.

It can be very difficult for people to come off medication. Not only can they become dependent on the soothing physiological effects of the medication, patients can become dependent on the idea of the medication as the thing keeping them safe and very frightened about the consequences of coming off. These drugs have a powerful effect on the body and so does reducing or cutting them out. The powerful physiological effects people often feel coming off medication may themselves cause considerable anxiety – and that's easy to say without appreciating just what it's like. Our brains respond actively to physiological effects, in ways we find very hard to control, and unexplained experiences like heart palpitations, disorientation and vertigo can be terrifying. In the anxiety aroused in those circumstances it's easy for people to think their previous problems are returning when they had been feeling much better. That's often the most frightening idea of all. Not everyone has these experiences, some seem to be able to use medication and stop without difficulty.

The generally held view is that where it can be effective, medication only helps by relieving the symptoms rather than addressing underlying causes. That too, can be made to sound like too modest a claim. Very often distress is the problem and relieving distress allows people to get through a pinch point and time to take care of the underlying issues. One of the major problems in establishing the effectiveness of any treatment for mental health – medication or therapy – is regression to the mean: acute issues will tend to improve by themselves over time. How do you know what was successful treatment and what was just going to happen anyway? If medication – or therapy, for that matter – buys you time for things to improve, that might be very effective treatment.

When you look closely enough at the scientific evidence, the only honest answer seems to be that it doesn't really help us very much at all in understanding how effective medication is in treating mental health. At the same time, you can't work in this area for long without encountering large numbers of people who are convinced that medication has helped them considerably or even saved their lives.

The picture for psychotherapy isn't any clearer. Here's some evidence for. A 2015 review of 30 studies concluded that psychological treatments were effective in treating depression in primary care, although the improvements over 'usual care' were only small to moderate.[83] A 2017 study of the results of 247 meta-analyses of randomized controlled trials of psychotherapy reported that 80% of the studies it reviewed had reported outcomes in favour of psychotherapy. However, the authors went on, in their view, these reviews suffered from a number of serious problems and potential sources of bias. Once those were taken account of, they believed only 7% of those studies had actually supported the effectiveness of psychotherapy.[84] That itself looks like pretty good evidence of the fallibility of evidence.

Here's some evidence against. A 2011 analysis of nine trials indicated that, in the long term (over seven-36 months) human-centred counselling was no more effective than routine visits to the GP and failed to have any impact on patients' short or long-term social functioning (work, leisure activities or family relationships).[85] A 2013 study reported that counselling was no more effective than acupuncture in treating moderate to severe depression over three to six months and neither was more effective than 'usual' care at nine or 12 months.[86] In 2017 – consistent with a number of other findings suggesting broad equivalence in effectiveness between different therapies

– a study involving data for over 30,000 patients didn't find any difference in outcomes between CBT (which is generally regarded as the therapy most firmly based in evidence and recommended by NICE for the treatment of depression in the UK) and what the researchers referred to as generic counselling.[87] That's a potent piece of evidence for people who want to argue about the respective merits of different forms of psychotherapy (which is pretty much the entire psychotherapy industry) but the authors added a critical afterword, pointing out that in their results more than half of all patients didn't show any improvement from either treatment. They called this a 'salutatory reminder of the extent of work remaining to be done regarding the implementation and delivery of effective psychological therapies' and suggested that's 'where efforts might better be focused rather than on pursuing research into insignificant differences between the effectiveness of differing models of psychological interventions'. Yep.

And yet, 50% (if that were a figure we could have faith in) would not, actually, be such a bad success rate for a treatment. There's a lot of physical medicine we don't question that has similar success rates. In fact, often the evidence available for the effectiveness of treatments for physical ailments is similarly inconsistent and confusing. Atrial fibrillation (generally referred to as AF) is the most common form of heart arrythmia. It's not usually immediately dangerous but the symptoms can be unpleasant, may impact quite severely on quality of life, and AF can significantly increase the risk of stroke. It's a reasonably serious condition, affecting around one million people in the UK.

It appears to be increasing dramatically: it was reported to have more than doubled in the adult European population in the decade to 2014.[88] The increase can't be fully accounted for by ageing population or increased prevalence of cardiovascular disease.[89] The language of epidemic sometimes gets used as it does with mental health. And, as is sometimes the case with some forms of mental illness, AF is considered to be a disease of the developed world, with strikingly lower prevalence reported in developing countries.[90]

Links have been identified with a number of life-style factors but as these include binge drinking, smoking, stress and a sedentary life style, as well as long-term endurance or intense exercise, that doesn't take us very far forward. And, since it's also associated with non-life-style factors, such as age and heart disease, it's fair to say nobody actually knows what causes the condition. There are a number of different theories about what is happening to the heart in AF: how the fibrillation forms and develops.[91] Equally, the underlying bio-chemistry at a cellular level isn't yet understood.[92]

Like mental health, there are two very different principal treatment pathways for AF: medication or a surgical procedure called catheter ablation. Medication usually involves beta blockers to slow down the heart rate, and a range of different drugs to stabilise heart rhythm. Some of these rhythm-stabilising drugs are sodium channel blockers, some are potassium channel blockers. One route might work with a particular patient and another not or neither might be any good. As with medication for mental health issues, there's a degree of trial and error involved and it's not clear exactly how things work when they work.

Often the patient will also be taking blood thinners to reduce the stroke risk. All of these drugs involve the potential for unpleasant, and sometimes severe, side effects, particularly when taken in combination. It's not unusual for patients to have to swap medication or give it up because of side effects.

Here are some: fatigue, nausea, dizziness, headache, depression, memory loss, confusion, erectile dysfunction, constipation, diarrhoea and the risk of excessive bleeding.

Catheter ablation involves the insertion of a thin wire into a vein or artery in the groin which is threaded up and into the heart where the tissue considered to be responsible for the abnormal heart rhythm is destroyed by freezing or radiofrequency energy. That's quite an intrusive procedure affecting a critically important organ. Of course, it comes with its own range of risks and has its own psychological impact on the patient.

Published data suggests success rates for ablation (generally followed up only for one or two years) of 50-70%, which has been described as 'relatively favourable'.[93] That's quite a range – at the bottom end, the same as the findings that prompt critical comments on the effectiveness of psychological therapies. Other studies have put success rates after 5 years at just 29% (though this has been claimed to increase to 63% when repeat ablations are carried out).[94]

Flecainide is the drug generally used as the first line treatment for terminating an existing episode of AF and also for maintaining normal heart rhythm and avoiding further attacks.[95] It's had a chequered history – a 1991 study had to be abandoned after it became apparent that patients treated with it were dying three times faster than the control group.[96] Once it was established that it was 'highly likely' these results were due to a greater incidence of patients with significant left ventricular disease or coronary heart disease in the sample population,[97] it's use recovered. Studies have indicated that 65% of patients respond to short-term treatment, in terms of suppressing or reducing episodes of AF, and 49% in long-term treatments.[98] The side effects can be unpleasant – in one study, which showed a positive effect for Flecainide in suppressing or reducing AF episodes over three months, adverse effects were reported in 32 of the 43 patients and 19 of them chose to switch treatment before the end of the experiment.[99]

In some important ways this is looking quite a lot like the picture for mental health. Admittedly, you do have a clear diagnostic classification – detectable with an ECG – and a clearer, objective measure of the outcome. And, unlike mental health issues, it isn't thought that atrial fibrillation can get better over time by itself. But research doesn't present a very consistent patterns of results, success rates don't look very different and, in neither case, do we understand fully how treatment works.

And physical treatments (though this would be true for antidepressants and other psychotropic medication too) probably have a much greater potential to cause harm to patients. In fact, a 2010 study reported that 29% of 2000 consecutive admissions to a general hospital in the Netherlands were classified as possibly iatrogenic (that is caused by medical examination or treatment) and 19% were considered definitely iatrogenic.[100]

Yet nobody's questioning what the cardiologists are up to or suggesting they don't know what they're doing. We seem to accept that cardiologists have come up with treatments with reasonable success rates which very much justify themselves, after taking account of their potential for harm. Maybe we're being too hard on the mental health professions?

Retrieving the Black Box

In 2016, the World Health Organisation estimated that every dollar invested in treatment for depression and anxiety disorders worldwide would generate a return of $3.3 to $5.7

in terms of health-life years and economic productivity gains and the value of increased healthy life years, across different countries, according to income groups.[101] That's a fantastically elaborate piece of analysis; epidemiologists and economists could spend their entire careers arguing about the parameters and assumptions involved. But it does reflect an idea on which everyone seems to agree – we need to spend more money on mental health. Not just mental health charities and professionals: teachers, parents, politicians, everyone seems to be saying the same thing – we need to spend more money on mental health.

OK but more money for what? If you were responsible for deciding where to put resources, where would *you* put them? More antidepressants? More talking therapies? Which ones? Would you invest in online therapy and apps? (answer, yes, that is what's happening because it's very cheap). More research (even more)? In what areas? With what goals? Would you focus on children and young adults? Or the elderly? Or people of working age?

How could you sensibly decide? The evidence is so poor for what's happening, what works and what's needed, most, where. In fact, if you believe the headlines about a mental health epidemic are correct, you might treat that itself as evidence that none of the treatments we have at the moment are particularly effective.

An important aspect of mental health we haven't discussed yet, is what we mean by it. What is the connection between someone in florid psychosis and someone who's talking to a counsellor because they're confused and unhappy? How should we regard them? Are they part of the same thing? It's the same kind of people with the same kind of training and skill set treating each of them. How does illness fit into this?

Often, it's the route taken to reach help that determines whether someone is thought of as ill or not. You're unlikely to be able to access a counsellor on the NHS, or through private health insurance, without a diagnosis of illness. Go and see a counsellor on your own time and money and you'll probably avoid being labelled depressed. That's a fairly arbitrary way of getting what might be a life-defining diagnosis.

That diagnosis might be reached with the help of one or more of a large array of different standardised questionnaires – perhaps a score of 12 or more using the Clinical Interview Schedule – Revised (CIS-R), or 10 or more on the generalised anxiety disorder assessment (GAD-7) or a trigger score on PHQ-9, CORE-10 or HADS. In many ways that's a very unsatisfactory way of deciding what ill means. It's circular – these forms tell us who's ill because when we look at samples of the people who score above thresholds, enough experts say enough of them are ill. But, we've already seen, the correlations this process uses to support itself are unimpressive and the underlying research and classification is the same stuff everyone finds it very easy to pick holes in.

The experiences these questions are asking about - *how often in the last two weeks have you been bothered by trouble falling or staying asleep* or *sleeping too much* or *finding little pleasure in doing things?* – are symptoms and often very indirect ones. The questionnaires don't really try to get at what might be underlying or causing these symptoms. In physical medicine you can see a broken leg, in mental health we ask how much you're limping. The diagnostic classifications focus on behavioural and affective symptoms and more or less treat the mind like a black box.

Most of our research seems to be about studying the treatment of mental health (the classification and processing of patients and success rates defined on their own terms by the same questionnaires) rather than the mental health conditions themselves. It's almost as if mental health – the states of mind which are involved – is a separate subject that researchers and psychiatrists aren't actually that interested in.

We have theories (dozens) about what can go wrong in people's childhood to cause problems. We have ideas about what might be missing in people's lives or being done to them to make them ill. But we don't have a very good picture of how people's minds are affected when they suffer from mental health issues – what is it that has happened to them, what's behind the symptoms we're trying to grade?

What is interesting about questionnaires is that they seem to be telling us that mental health is a scale – score 11 on CIS-R and you're OK, 12 and there might be a problem, 18 and it looks severe. Until you get to very unusual and extreme situations like psychosis, tests don't work by looking for qualitatively different experiences to identify people who might be suffering from a disorder. It's the same experiences or symptoms being asked about again and again in different tests for different disorders. And they are generally experiences which, in themselves, are considered perfectly healthy – it's the intensity or persistence that makes you ill.

If people have symptoms in common, if standardised questionnaires are measuring the intensity of the same experiences again and again, you might expect there to be similar things going on in their minds to cause those symptoms – ideas they have in common. If we could look closely enough, might we find particular ideas or themes or threads turning up again and again in people's mental lives when they are in trouble? Not just the specific troublesome thought patterns undermining someone in exam situations or making them invest in magic beliefs to ward off harm to others or the echoes of early family history running on through their current relationships, broader ideas or themes which you could see affecting people again and again when they come for help, like a high temperature in someone with a fever?

If we did, you'd imagine that ought to be helpful in providing effective forms of treatment. That might help us to understand better where to spend money most effectively. And, if you could identify some key mental processes that seemed to underly illness, you'd presumably learn something important about wellness. If we could identify some of the themes that come up again and again in mental illness, we might learn some lessons on how to avoid being unhappy, or at least a particular form of unhappiness. There might be valuable lessons for when we're struggling with normal confusions – lessons on how to keep the mind healthy, balanced, to help us make better decisions, to maintain better relationships with the people most important to us. We might then be able to see some kind of connection between the florid psychotic and the 'worried well' struggling with confusion, and with the way we'd all like to live.

So, are there key themes, threads, ideas you find again and again when you talk to people who have come for help? Yes, there are.

2

INADEQUATE

Something becomes apparent very quickly if you listen to people who come for help – they don't like themselves. That idea can express itself in different ways but, most often, people are just very down on themselves. It's not self-deprecating, it's not humility, it's more attacking than that. They might be very angry with other people but, at the bottom of things, there's a deep dissatisfaction with themselves – a preoccupation with the idea that they are somehow, secretly, shamefully, worse than other people. The more serious their problems, and the more complicated and difficult their lives have become, the more dominant this theme tends to get.

When she wrote *Prozac Nation*, one of the earliest accounts in their own words by someone suffering from mental health issues, the title Elizabeth Wurtzel gave the prologue was *I Hate Myself and I Want to Die*. Apparently, she wanted that as the title of the book but was dissuaded by her publisher.

In a different tone and state of mind, here's journalist Moya Sarner talking about her experience in therapy:

> I am discovering more about these anxious feelings and where they might originate, about the unconscious rulebook I seem to have knocking around in my mind, telling me what is right and what is wrong. I am coming to see how punitive we can be with ourselves without noticing.[102]

Or, here's journalist John Crace (reviewing a TV adaptation

of Edward St Aubyn's novels from his own perspective as a recovering heroin addict):

> I was never sexually abused by my father (I somehow managed to hate myself enough without being forced to endure that horror)…I took them [drugs] because they were there. Anything was preferable to being me…My feelings of inadequacy and despair gave way to a warm embrace… Shame is the one that gets you every time because deep down you know how worthless you are. You know that every day is another testament to your failure. …Your anger turns in on yourself as the days turn into weeks turn into months turn into years. The self-destruction gets steadily worse.[103]

This is *Metro* newspaper talking to Michael, a 28-year-old charity worker diagnosed with depression and anxiety:

> He says his mental illnesses leave him with a general feeling of "absolute worthlessness" and an inability to find anything good about himself.[104]

Here's singer Will Young talking about his experiences with depression:

> When I was homophobically abused by a bus driver last year…I was like, wow, I've done a lot of work on shame and it's still coming up. The feeling of being "wrong", that it was all my fault.[105]

In 2019, actress Jameela Jamil, who has used her own experience of depression and eating disorder as a mental health advocate, published an open letter to her 'inner bully' cataloguing ways her own critical inner voice had undermined her and made her feel inadequate and describing the harm she felt this had caused her.[106]

Here's counsellor, Leigh Hale, talking about his own Tourette's Syndrome:

> In turn my feelings of inadequacy grew and grew, causing me to withdraw socially. I developed self-statements like "There's something wrong with me" and "I'm not good enough"...I also still get the self-defeating thoughts telling me I'm crap/rubbish, inadequate, ugly, boring/beige/vanilla, useless/worthless, etc, in comparison with my peers – and anyone else, really.[107]

This is Leonard Woolf describing his wife Virginia Woolf's depression:

> If left to herself, she would have eaten nothing at all and would have gradually starved to death. It was extraordinarily difficult ever to get her to eat enough to keep her strong and well. Pervading her insanity generally there was always a sense of some guilt, the origin and exact nature of which I could never discover.[108]

Here's psychologist Jordan Peterson talking about his personal experience of depression:

> like freezing to death on an endless stark plain, knowing that the reason that you got there is because you did everything wrong.[109]

And this is from the suicide note left by 14-year-old Molly Russel, who's death in 2017 prompted a campaign to increase awareness of the availability to children of dangerous material about suicide and self-harm on the internet:

> I'm the weird sister, quiet daughter, depressed friend, lonely classmate. I'm nothing, I'm worthless, I'm numb, I'm lost, I'm weak, I'm gone.[110]

You could go on and on. Remember the only reference to ideas or thoughts that might be affecting patients in the ICD-10 diagnosis of depression? 'Self-esteem and self-confidence are almost always reduced and, even in the mild form, some ideas of guilt or worthlessness are often present'. It's the same story with DSM-5: worthlessness and excessive guilt are the ideas identified, alongside behavioural and affective symptoms (recurrent thoughts of death and suicidal ideation are also mentioned in DSM-5 but they're really just extensions of worthlessness and guilt).

Depression gets referred to in a lot of other diagnoses. In ICD-10 they include phobias, anxiety disorders, OCD, PTSD, manic episodes, bipolar affective disorder (manic depression), schizophrenia, mental disorders from alcohol abuse (and other psychoactive substances), affective disorders due to physical brain damage and various somatoform disorders, including hypochondria and body dysmorphia. Sometimes this is because ICD-10 says depression very frequently occurs with that diagnosis, other times it's because the symptoms of depression are considered to be so similar that clinicians have to be told not to use depression as the diagnosis in that situation (because otherwise you would).

In fact, the only really significant diagnostic categories where ICD-10 does not also mention depression are eating disorders and personality disorders. Which is surprising because actually there is plenty of research to suggest that both groups of disorder are strongly associated with depression.[111]

Certainly, if you listen to people suffering with eating disorders those core ideas of shame and lack of self-worth seem to come up no less often. Here's journalist Tanya Gold talking about self-hatred and her relationship with food:

> I was ill with alcoholism when I was young, and the worst thing was my denial. I conquered alcohol by hating what it made me with such ferocity I was too scared to drink again. But I never got anywhere with food. I am stuck on food.[112]

Here's psychiatrist, Frances Connan, talking about how she thinks social media could be fuelling a rise in eating disorders:

> It does not help because of the ways in which it fuels low self-esteem and makes people feel bad about themselves. We know rationally that whatever goes on social media is the shiny part of someone's life and beneath that everyone has stuff going on…but when we look only we can easily feel inadequate and envious.[113]

Research involving brain scans has given rise to a theory that bulimia sufferers use the idea of food as an unconscious strategy to distract themselves from self-criticism in stressful situations[114] (which might make good sense if not liking yourself and liking yourself had got very caught up with body image, food and being thin).

And if ICD-10 doesn't link personality disorders and depression, the NHS is quite happy to state that they frequently occur together.[115] In fact, research suggests that they don't just go together, they can be treated together – studies have claimed to show that successful treatments of depression are also successful for comorbid personality disorders.[116]

So, there really doesn't seem to be any clear basis for ICD-10 not linking eating disorders and personality disorders to depression in the same way as it does for the other major psychiatric illnesses. And we've already seen, as well as depression, antidepressants are routinely used to treat anxiety disorder, OCD, panic disorder, phobias, bulimia and PTSD.[117] That also seems to suggest that all these conditions might have something important in common.

If the diagnostic framework identifies guilt, low self-esteem and a sense of worthlessness as the signature ideas associated with depression, and depression is associated with just about every other diagnosis you have heard of, surely that's telling us that guilt, low self-esteem and a sense of worthlessness are very important ideas for mental health?

Maybe it's telling us more than that. A 2018 study into the genetics of mental health reported significant positive genetic correlations between major depression and every psychiatric disorder it looked at.[118] Furthermore, the authors claimed their data strongly suggested not just genetic correlation but a shared biological basis and processes for depression and schizophrenia. And they said that, whilst schizophrenia was the only condition for which sufficient genetic data was currently available to allow a full comparison, they thought the same thing was probably true for other psychiatric disorders too. They added that their results indicated that the current psychiatric diagnostic categories don't fit what's known about the genetic basis for mental disorders. And they concluded that major depression, which is what they were investigating, isn't a discrete entity at any level of analysis.

Who knows? It's early days for this kind of research but what these scientists – the Psychiatric Genomics Consortium, which consists of more than 800 researchers in 38 countries and described it's research as the most comprehensive and best-powered evaluation of the relation of depression with other psychiatric disorders yet published – seem to be suggesting is that, rather than thinking of it as a separate diagnosis, we should think of depression – and so the ideas of guilt and worthlessness associated with it – as an experience that crosses borders in mental health and affects people suffering from a range of conditions.

This is similar (and perhaps closely related) to a debate in experimental psychology between the dimensional theory of emotion – which argues that all our emotions are fundamentally the same experience, varying only in quality and intensity – and the basic emotion theory – which argues that our emotional life can be analysed down to four[119] (or is it six[120] or seven[121] or eight[122] or 27[123]) basic emotions, which are functionally (and perhaps in neurological terms too) separate and distinct from each other. To date, brain scans haven't been able to allow us to diagnose depression, or any other mental disorder. In fact, what they have shown is that a number of the physiological features researchers claim to have identified, to do with both brain activity and size and shape of brain regions, seem to apply equally in common to depressive and anxiety disorders.[124] That's been taken as support for the dimensional theory of emotion.

This debate – for and against its own tendency to categorise and identify separate, discrete phenomena – seems to be becoming more central to psychology. And the sheer amount of comorbidity between different mental health conditions – it's been described as the rule, not the exception[125] – suggests our diagnostic classifications aren't working well. It's one body, and physiology is interconnected, but people with a torn meniscus don't also get skin cancer or pleurisy.

Perhaps one day we will find that what we think of as depression underpins all mental illness and it's the place where other conditions find their roots. Or maybe we'll decide that all mental illness is what we currently regard as depression – based in intense feelings of guilt and worthlessness – and the other diagnoses we use at the moment would be better thought of as more or less extreme symptoms which accompany or develop from the underlying problem.

In any event, that formula in ICD-10 (self-esteem and self-confidence *almost always* reduced and guilt or worthlessness *often present*) is understated. In clinical experience, those ideas are always involved in depression – though that might not always become apparent in a 10-minute consultation with a GP.

As depression is so closely associated with this range of other diagnoses, you would expect to find the same ideas implicated there too. And not just the diagnoses usually associated with depression (though that is, in fact, pretty much all of them). Spend enough time with someone diagnosed with hypomania or with unipolar mania – a rare and sometimes disputed[126] diagnosis where, on the face of it, the patient doesn't appear to present with any symptoms associated with depression – and it's blindingly obvious that there's something desperate going on. They may not be at all overtly self-critical but that doesn't mean sufferers aren't being affected by the same ideas. And the rampaging elephant in the room is that they don't feel nearly as good about themselves as they're claiming, and acting, but it would be catastrophic to admit that. These are extreme reactions to extreme feelings of lack of self-worth. Only the most superficial, one dimensional analysis would take what these people say about themselves at face value but that's what the diagnostic classifications do.

In a similar vein, one of the explanations psychiatrists have offered for mass shootings, like the one carried out by Anders Breivik, is that they are examples of a mechanism called 'narcissistic decompensation'. According to this theory, a major injury to self-esteem leads the perpetrator to paranoid withdrawal and ultimately to indiscriminate violence.[127] That may be an accurate description of mechanisms which can lead people to want to kill complete strangers. But what it's saying is that, whilst the outcomes, mercifully, may be very different to our more common notions of depression, the root idea – where it starts – seems to be the same: damage to self-esteem and an inability to tolerate being made to feel bad about yourself, in these cases coming out in lethal rage.

References to self-esteem are everywhere in the literature about mental health and – we've seen some examples – whenever people describe their experiences with mental health conditions. We seem ready to accept, without any real discussion, that mental health and self-esteem are somehow intimately connected. But we don't spell that out – it doesn't get the prominent acknowledgement you'd think it would deserve from the frequency with which the two get mentioned in conjunction with each other. It's not as 'known' as it should be.

This might actually be the most important thing that we do know about mental health but science hasn't got much of a grip on it. Experimental psychologists tend to approach self-esteem as a personality trait – they talk about complex relationships or associations between self-esteem and mental health,[128] and that's the kind of language which has found its way into charity websites and public information.[129]

As ever with a statistical association between two different things, it's difficult to establish causation – there's a debate within experimental psychology about whether low self-esteem is a vulnerability predisposing people to depression or a consequence of suffering from depression, a scarring effect.[130] And, as ever, the picture is thoroughly confused. Some researchers have claimed evidence that people suffering from depression in fact display quite high forms of 'implicit' self-esteem (whilst admitting they don't really know what it is that they actually measured).[131] Others have argued that the real relationship isn't between self-esteem and depression but that both of them are driven by underlying levels of 'neuroticism',[132] which is another personality trait employed in experimental psychology. Since there's little consensus on what gets included in neuroticism – anxiety, withdrawal, vulnerability, hostility and aggression, impulsivity and its sometimes considered to include inferiority and dependency and, indeed, depression – it's not very clear what any of this tells us.

What none of this research seems to want to explore is the idea of self-esteem as an active element in the experience of depression, part of what depression is. For example, in 2016 a review of research into self-esteem and depression in children and young people found a strong association with low self-esteem in children who were suffering from depression but, against expectations,[133] showed low self-esteem in childhood as a relatively weak predictor of mental health problems later in life.[134] That's hard to explain if you approach self-esteem as a personality trait associated with depression. An explanation, which wasn't considered, could be that, more than a predictor, self-esteem is a key constituent of mental health – when your self-esteem is low enough, you're ill, when it isn't, you aren't. People with low self-esteem in childhood are depressed, if their self-esteem improves in later life, they're not going to be depressed anymore.

There seems to be a determination in experimental psychology to treat self-esteem and depression as separate – as in ICD-10 and DSM-5, depression is a discrete thing, which somehow exists independently of the ideas which are causing sufferers distress. It's as if the people doing the research are working in their own silo, locked into the prior constructs from their own field, however uncertain the foundations might be. It's the same point made about the psychiatric classifications: these categories psychology insists upon matter – if they're wrong, they can limit the way people in those fields can think about a situation.

If we seem more or less prepared just to take it as read that self-esteem and mental health are somehow closely tied up with each other – obvious – what's less obvious and intuitive is why this seems to be such a weak link for us: why it seems difficult for people to maintain a healthy balance of self-esteem. That question has received a great deal of attention and the conclusion people have come to is quite startling. It can be a little difficult to take it as seriously as it deserves.

A mini-me on your shoulder talking crap

The answer is that it seems we have a perverse trait, a mechanism in our minds which is actively trying to undermine our self-esteem – to make us feel bad about ourselves. This idea, in different forms, is pretty much universally accepted across the different fields of clinical psychology and psychotherapy. Freud originally popularised the idea of a mechanism like this, which he called the super ego, and he made it one of the permanent structures in his map of the mind – central to the most important drivers of our emotional life and behaviour. These days it also often gets referred to as the inner critic and it's a key concept in CBT, person-centred therapy and, in one form or another, just about every other branch of psychotherapy. It's easy to see reflected in well-known phenomena like imposter syndrome or the inferiority complex. Some neuroscientists claim that they may have identified the location of at least some of its functions in the brain.[135] There's little compelling evidence to support that, but it does show how widely accepted the idea of a persecutory, self-punishing, internal critic is.

Everyone has direct experience of it in their ordinary lives on a day-to-day basis. It's responsible for the hot, confused reaction inside (on a bad day, at least) when we miss a train or a bus, that makes you tell yourself you knew you were being stupid leaving that late and that this type of thing just doesn't happen to other people. Those kinds of trivial, incidental reactions are the way we like to think about this characteristic, and to describe it, but they don't really do justice to the situation.

You can see it working in small children. How anxiously they latch onto ideas of 'naughty', 'good' and 'bad' and want to apply them absolutely to other people and even to objects. The catastrophic states of mind they can get into when they think they've done something wrong and they're in trouble. That doesn't change as much as we'd like to think as people get older. It's in the way we often find ourselves more upset by apparently trivial criticism than we let on, or feel we should be – a little burning flush of hurt and resentment which itself often generates a twist of self-dislike for being so over-sensitive.

One striking aspect of all this is that it's the same experience that comes back again and again – these are familiar feelings. We recognise them straight away as coming from the same place. It's as if there's some set of preconceived ideas – that we're useless, weak, cowardly, undeserving – standing by and waiting for confirmation at any time, to make us feel lousy about ourselves.

That seems like a strange situation. Why would nature equip people with an inner suspicion, which they can never seem to shake off entirely, that there's something wrong – with them? It doesn't feel necessary: it's not at all hard to imagine life without it. We get by very well when we're not feeling it. Would you try to build it in if you were designing an AI system? What's this form of self-torture for?

Perhaps the answer is that it's an effective motivator; it gets stuff done. We need to take positive steps to validate ourselves because we have a predisposition to feel that we're not good enough. It's not just that feeling not good enough is an unpleasant experience, and so we need to find ways to escape it when it strikes. This idea is dynamic – it has its own life and its own energy. That's very important – left to its own devices, it will find opportunities to surface and we need to take active steps to keep it under control. It's like trying to keep a spring compressed.

And it's restless: yesterday's triumphs don't work anymore – if we want to feel OK about ourselves, we're going to have to do something about it, constantly. Here's (seven times at the time of writing) Formula 1 World Champion Lewis Hamilton:

> Naturally you have the whispers [of personal doubt] in your ears and you have to block them out. But it is healthy to question yourself. You can't go around saying I am the best all the time. It also motivates you to push more and grow and be better. It's like having a mini-me on your shoulder talking crap in your ear.[136]

If money makes the world go round, you could say that the engine is really this strange human predisposition to feel that we're not good enough, because it's very tied up with money. There are any number of different ways you can think about worth but, in any honest account, it's pretty much impossible to keep money out of the equation. Money is pervasive – it affects every aspect of our lives – and it's highly visible. However else people think about what's important and valuable in life, their stance towards money, one way or another, is going to be intimately connected with how they feel about themselves. And people will usually be very reluctant to give this idea it's full weight (that doesn't make us feel good about ourselves).

Part of the desirability of things that cost more is precisely that they cost more: their exclusivity. An expensive sports car probably will have superior performance and attractive design features. Those are things to be enjoyed for their own sake and most owners would insist those are the only reasons they bought theirs. They'd know, obviously, that luxury branding is highly effective – manufacturers and advertisers wouldn't use it otherwise. They'd know it works, on other people – but (at least for a good portion of the time) they'll be able to maintain a (reasonably) genuine conviction that that hasn't happened here. The cachet of the expense itself wasn't important to them; their reasons for buying this thing were different, purer – solely to do with fun, speed, beauty, appreciation of the quality of the engineering and build.

That's never entirely true. In fact, it's nonsense – and somewhere, secretly, they do know that. Whatever else is going on, a distinct part of the appeal of a high-end car is always that you can afford it. If you've got one, it tells you something about yourself – you're doing OK, you *are* OK. Whilst that's working for you, without having thought it through, or deliberately set it up like this, you will be a little less susceptible to those shadowy ideas that there's something wrong with you, with your life. And there's no particular harm in that.

It's not just high-performance cars; a similar kind of psychological value attaches to desirable post codes, high-end art, designer brands, luxury resorts. And it's relative: it's not just outright luxury and conspicuous consumption, it's premium brands, it's more or less desirable post codes, it's being able to afford a holiday at all. Everywhere we turn, all the time, our sense of ourselves is intimately tied up with what we can, or can't, afford. It's a very powerful economic mechanism because, in order for it to work, things have to be just affordable for you – there has to be a stretch to make you feel good. The richer you are, the more you have to spend to achieve the same effect and the more other people have, the more you need. Capitalism thrives on it.

People don't always use money quite so simply and directly to feel good about themselves, though, one way or another, everyone has to make their own deal with it. Some people make a choice to use discount brands because, at least in that area of their lives, they want to celebrate economy. And they congratulate themselves for knowing the value of money, for their more discerning relationship with it – they feel good about themselves as a result.

Others may reject or discount money as a measure of personal sense of self-worth more completely. That stance, against greed, against shallow materialism and in favour of different personal values, itself becomes something they use to feel better about themselves – it's still to do with money and feeling OK about yourself. And it's a line that will be easier, or more difficult, to hold authentically, at different times, as they come under pressure to want things and to be able to afford them.

Our attitude to money is just one illustration of the challenge we face. It's why even the crudest flattery is often so devastatingly effective, even when we know it's being done to us. It isn't just about strategic social status or one-upmanship in ways that can get rationalised and manipulated in social psychology experiments, though that is one of the ways it shows through; it's a visceral need to find ways not to feel inadequate. Everything that touches us has some significance in relation to our self-esteem – it's a kind of tyranny. If we want to stay healthy, we have to find ways to keep in check the idea that we might not be good enough.

We may not have a particularly accurate picture of the situation ourselves. Looks, success, a sense of purpose and significance in our work, ideas about ourselves (funny, sporty, intellectual) or a reliable flow of affection and intimacy coming our way from someone we like and admire – we're likely to exaggerate or minimise how important different things are to us (not just money) because we do, or don't, like the idea of them being important to us. Even our ideas about where we get our self-worth involve us feeling better or worse about ourselves.

The system needs fairly continuous recalibration (of which we're normally only dimly aware) as we find we have to make compromises in what we value, and the terms we use to define success, in order to make them work for us. It needs updating as we get older; the things that matter to us change and some of the things we used to value aren't available anymore. It's a constant, fluid process and we don't have that much control over it, which is a shame because it's absolutely vital to our well-being and our happiness.

The dark side of esteem

There is a dark side to your self-esteem. The reason owning an expensive car tells someone they're doing OK is that other people can't afford it – otherwise it wouldn't work. If someone's physically desirable, it's because they're more attractive than other people. You're good at the things you're good at because other people can't do them as well as you. Whatever you're feeling good about often involves an invitation to other people to feel a little worse about themselves.

To some extent that's unavoidable – we can't be endlessly responsible for other people's feelings. But given what we've seen about self-esteem and mental health, this is an important point – people getting to feel better about themselves and other people feeling worse. It's going to come up again and again. More considerate people will try to be a bit careful how they handle themselves – and will probably be better company, better liked and happier as a result.

Modern life has transformed our opportunities to compare ourselves with other people. We've never had so much information about other people and it's never been so manufactured. We've been surrounded by the idealised images and lifestyles of mass advertising since the end of the Second World War. Part of what makes advertising effective is people feeling a little less satisfied with what they've got and who they are. It's not just the product being pushed at us, encoded in many of the images is the idea that you might somehow be as desirable, popular, carefree as the people in the advert seem if you owned this thing or went on holiday here or banked with these people.

From the outset there was concern on many levels about people's susceptibility to the subliminal messaging in advertising. Some are convinced it has had a direct effect on mental health. More attention is now being paid to diversity (gender, race, sexual orientation, body shape) to avoid the potential for causing harm to people who don't fit into the categories advertising has traditionally portrayed.

In his book about depression, *Lost Connections*,[137] Johann Hari includes a strong critique of the advertising industry and suggests part of the regulation of advertising ought to be to block adverts which are 'designed to make us feel bad about ourselves'. Leaving aside the difficulty in establishing whether an advert was designed to make us feel bad (we're perfectly capable of making ourselves feel bad whenever we see someone we think is better looking, funnier or happier than we are), there isn't much compelling evidence to support a causal link between advertising and increased rates of mental health problems.

Much of the focus in this area has been on girls and young women. The 2007 report of the American Psychological Association Task Force on the Sexualisation of Girls reported evidence of associations between exposure to sexualised imagery and narrow representations of female beauty and lower self-esteem, negative mood, depressive symptoms and attitudes and symptoms associated with eating disorders in adolescent girls and women.[138]

That's been very influential in the formation of a widely held view about the powerful effect of advertising and media on mental health in young women. In fact, what the underlying research looked at were effects on body satisfaction in questionnaires immediately after exposure to media images, an association of use of diet pills and skipping meals with self-reported frequency of reading beauty and fashion magazines and associations between eating disorder symptoms and exposure to media content (for which there was no reliable measurement or control). These studies suggest that exposure to idealised body images can affect how we think about our own bodies, at least in the short term, and how much food we eat. But none of that's particularly surprising – since when has regulation of food intake been mental illness (in a society in which 73% of the adult population are reported to be obese or overweight[139])? It's certainly not the same as showing in concrete terms that exposure to these images causes mental health problems.

If it was, we might be able to do something about it, but it's hard to see how you could justify disrupting the way millions of people earn their livelihoods on the basis of evidence that sketchy. It's not easy to see how you could ever test this kind of proposition to acceptable scientific standards. The lack of evidence doesn't mean it isn't true – it may be that mass advertising has affected the delicate balance we have to strike with the idea that we're not good enough and tipped us all – not just young women – towards a more precarious sense of self-worth. It means nobody knows.

More recently, concern has focussed on social media. Social media can be used like a personalised advertising campaign for users' lives. We get to present the images and the perspectives of ourselves that we would like other people to see. We even get to enhance them digitally if we want. And so do our friends and family.

Suddenly, the idealised versions you encounter aren't just strangers on hoardings, or from a separate dimension of celebrity – they're in your world, all around you in your daily life. The idealised got closer: there's the performed version of you you're putting out, the perfected version of your friends' lives you're seeing and, somewhere in between, the real life you're actually living, falling short of both.

Are people able to manage that reality gap comfortably or is it causing dangerous confusion? Mental health professionals often talk emphatically about a link between social media and mental health as if it was definitively established – it isn't.

Significant increases in rates of anxiety and depression and suicide and suicidal behaviour amongst adolescents in the US since around 2010 have been attributed to the emergence of an iGen, the first generation exposed to the smart phone and wide-spread social media in their formative years.[140]

The iPhone was introduced in 2007 and social media platforms began expanding rapidly over the next couple of years, but a lot of other things happened too which could have affected adolescents' mental health since 2010. Researchers have pointed out that these increases in mental health issues don't track to economic data like unemployment statistics or the Dow Jones index when matched by year. But why would they? Why would you expect economic metrics to have an effect immediately and only in the year they occurred? The global credit crisis in 2008 had ramifications on lives for several years. It would be strange if it didn't have some effect on this generation too.

And there are many other social issues that could be contributing to those statistics. Not least, changing attitudes to mental health – these figures on adolescent depression and anxiety are based on self-reporting; people are willing to talk about their mental health more openly than they were and perhaps that's particularly true of this generation raised in that changed culture. It's been argued that the higher rates of suicidal behaviour in the figures in the US show that this isn't just a matter of an increased tendency to self-diagnose mental health problems.[141] Perhaps, but suicide rates haven't changed in the UK (where there have been similar increased rates of self-reported issues) and there's been exposure to the same technology and social media platforms over the same periods. And, actually, if people really were 'talking themselves' into states of depression there's no obvious reason why a number couldn't talk themselves into suicidal behaviour too.

Family issues are generally considered to be a vitally important factor for children's mental health[142] and a great deal has been happening to the family structure over the last two or three decades. One aspect has been an accelerating trend towards smaller family units, single parenting, single-child families and disconnection from the wider family. Research has associated single parenting and single-child families, in particular, with increased mental health problems for children[143] (though, naturally, there is also research suggesting that neither single parenting nor only child status has any adverse effect on children's mental health[144]). It's entirely possible that effects of changing family structures could be showing through for the iGen adolescents.

Research has indicated that adolescents who spent more time on screen were more likely to report mental health issues and adolescents who spent more time on non-screen activities were less likely to report mental health issues.[145] Those are clearer associations and they're interesting results which could have a number of explanations and consequences. As ever, association isn't causality – could it be that adolescents experiencing mental health issues are drawn to, maybe even helped by, screen time? And as the data couldn't tell us what study participants were doing on screen, it's definitely not evidence about the effects of social media.

It feels very plausible that social media could adversely affect people's mental health, and in a number of different ways, and that so could screen time, and lack of off-line social interaction and physical activity. There's plenty of compelling anecdotal evidence – but we don't 'know' it and science hasn't shown it in the way often claimed. How could it? How could you design an experiment to prove it? You can show that cigarettes are bad for our lungs and why; how are you going to prove that fantasy lives on Instagram are bad for us? And if you can't prove it, what can you do about it?

Actually, it's hard to see what you could ever do about it. You can try to regulate sponsored content, you can try to control the material which algorithms push at people, but the intense connectivity and idealised presentation of themselves and their lives is how people want to use social media between themselves. No-one's making them, no-one's driving this train, so who could stop it?

And, hasn't it always been like this? Our practice of smiling in photographs has been traced back to a marketing campaign by Kodak, in the early 20th century designed to associate photographs with displays of happiness (up till then photographs had largely been quite staid, formal affairs like the traditional portrait painting from which photography took its roots).[146] People found that invitation to broadcast themselves as happy, carefree and joyful irresistible precisely because it helps to push away the less appealing ideas about ourselves we also have. Now we're busier than ever curating versions of ourselves on Facebook, Instagram, Linked In and in our blogs.

Society changes and so do the ways we communicate and connect with each other. We've always had to keep up, to adapt ourselves to what's happening around us and try to stay healthy. In this respect, why should social media be any different? They used to worry that cowboy movies were bad for us.[147] Perhaps they were; nobody could prove it and nobody could make them go away.

Denial

Of course, the idea that we're not good enough is not the only idea we have about ourselves. We can also feel competent and confident, purposeful, powerful, euphoric even, and maybe for much of the time we do. But those ideas about incompetence, inadequacy, weakness, failure, shame are always available. And they start exerting a pressure on us way before we're aware of it – we are always in reaction to the experience of having felt like that, of that idea of inadequacy being there.

The effort involved in managing all this depends on our state of mind at the time and our circumstances. The worse things are going (relationships, money, work), the more opportunity to feel bad about ourselves and the worse you feel about yourself, the harder it can be to find a way to make things better.

The things people rely on most to feel good about themselves (or to avoid feeling bad about themselves) – relationships, money, work, socialising, drink, sex, exercise, drugs – will be the most important things in their lives. Leaving aside the immediate benefit they provide in keeping away the idea that there's something wrong with them, the things people rely on might be good for them or they might bring their own problems. And over time, things that worked for people – drink, a relationship that's become destructive – might become counter-productive and become the cue for feeling worse about themselves. Because of the dependence that's developed – and it developed because this did work for them, it was successful – that can be very difficult to recognise and act upon.

The ways people respond to the pressure exerted by these feelings of inadequacy become key aspects of the way they think and behave, even traits of their personality. Our first reaction to anything we don't like or which frightens us is usually to deny or minimise it. People climb out of cars after crashes with legs like rubber bands saying they're absolutely fine or stumble into A&E after a heart attack saying they're sure it's all a lot of fuss about nothing.

Denial is a core aspect of human behaviour: we all do it a lot and it takes many different forms. Generally, in the sense used here, it's not deliberate; it's an automated process. We're not even aware it's going on, we just veer away from things we don't like the look of. But not being aware of something isn't the same as not being affected by it.

Some of the time denial can be entirely successful, so we'd be able to deny, flat-out, with complete honesty, that these shadowy ideas applied to us. We'd be wrong but that's how it feels to us in the moment. Very often though, denial isn't complete: we're left with a lingering sense of a shameful secret, something we can glimpse out of the corner of our eye but don't want to look at.

If the circumstances are right, and someone else directs our view to it, we get it straight away and we know it was always there. That can be part of what therapy is for. If the circumstances aren't right, or its too clumsy, we reject the suggestion out of hand (and generally we don't feel at all well-disposed to the person who raised it). It's a difficult area to get into because it involves telling people they don't really think what they think they think. For a start that can be very irritating and intrusive (that's part of the reason people don't like psychotherapists) and it's also very easy to be wrong.

And denying or minimising the importance of something may actually be the most constructive, practical thing to do in the circumstances. If there's something you have to do for good practical purposes and you don't want to, the healthiest response may be to push away the anxiety and doubt and just get on with it. We do have to get on with things, we have to be able to manage our feelings – they are just feelings.

But, at the same time not being able to recognise what we're feeling can cause trouble. How many times have you thought you wanted something and found out once you had it, that you didn't want it very much at all? You can meet people one day who tell you everything's great and come across them a week later distraught because they have to get out of their intolerable marriage. Being too disconnected from our real feelings and ideas is a major practical problem. If we don't know what we really think and feel, how can we know what's important to us? And if we don't know what's important to us, how can we make good decisions and act in our own best interests, let alone behave responsibly towards other people?

Denial is a complex mechanism which we're all involved in all the time, with varying degrees of self-deception. It can work for us or against us in different ways and in different situations. And the strategies and techniques which we use to push away the feelings we don't want to have – to achieve and maintain denial – have their own consequences in our lives. They can

Perfectionism

One way to avoid the feeling of getting it wrong, is for people to be very focussed on getting things right. The opposite of feeling not good enough is always being on top of things – no room for the inner critic there. And there is a balance to be struck (as ever): lives are richer for better decisions and poorer for worse ones. Not just ours, other people's lives too. There's nothing wrong with having expectations of ourselves that get the most out of us and success works – it can be a very effective way of feeling better about yourself. Surely a sense of achievement is a legitimate way for people to feel good about themselves? The problem is with the mind sets often associated with achievement – problems always occur when ideas get too entrenched, too intense.

There's an idea we all seem to live with – a belief in the availability of an idealised state in which it's possible to figure everything out and get everything right. The idea that there are people like that (and we should be one of them). It's seductive – we'd all like to believe our lives could be like that. But, taken too literally and given too much rein, it's a very judgemental, punishing way of thinking – you're only good enough whilst you're excelling. People become reliant on conspicuous success to feel OK and the longer they manage to avoid feelings of failure, or averageness, the more frightening the idea of falling short of outstanding becomes.

This is a common trait in all sorts of high achievers. It exists in the corporate world as a kind of communal myth of 'failure isn't an option excellence' which everyone pretends to buy into but no-one really feels applies to them. On that kind of narrow canvas this kind of thinking can be very effective. It's extraordinary, and admirable, what driven people can achieve – extreme aspirations and effort lead to exceptional results.

But it's never a comfortable way of living because it isn't actually possible to feel like we're getting it right all the time. Obviously enough, because we won't be – and there are always feelings of guilt, shame and inadequacy around a sense (however firmly pushed down) of getting things wrong. Those persistent feelings are hard to reconcile with the perfected version of themselves that people are trying to inhabit and that can be very confusing.

As a result, the successful aspects of themselves they've been relying on can start to feel unreal to them. A sort of false version of themselves they come to devalue and despise at the same time as they're depending on it. This is an aspect of imposter syndrome and it's rife amongst people who drive themselves hard. Achievements are being made to carry a psychological weight they can't bear. People aren't convinced by their achievements that everything is as good as they're trying to make it and, as a result, the achievements become deprived of some of the value they do really have. They end up feeling dissatisfied with themselves and fraudulent.

Perfectionism or dependence on high achievement isn't even a safe strategy on its own terms, since it involves flirting with failure – doing difficult things and succeeding against the odds. The effort of maintaining this level of performance takes its toll and eventually the odds usually win. That's always going to be a difficult experience but if there aren't enough other ideas around, if the reliance on being outstanding is too dominant, it can feel catastrophic.

In 2019, Olympic cyclist Kelly Catlin killed herself, aged 23. At 18 she won a silver medal in the team pursuit at the Rio Olympics and she went on to win three successive world titles in the same event. She had completed an undergraduate degree in biomedical engineering and Chinese at the University of Minnesota and begun a master's in computational and mathematical engineering at Stanford, whilst riding for a leading professional road-cycling team. In the months before her suicide, she suffered two serious injuries on her bike and her mental state spiralled very fast. Looking back, her coach said 'I can say that Kelly was the toughest person I've ever met, exceptionally tough. Being a high-performance athlete, toughness is a prerequisite, but she was the toughest. She was the most driven individual I have ever met as well, which again, comes with high-performance athletics but she set the bar'. According to her brother 'Kelly worked harder than almost anyone you are likely to meet. She could be an Olympian and a full-time straight-A graduate student. We idolize such strength, but in the end it was destructive'.[148]

This isn't an isolated story. More and more is emerging about the mental health troubles affecting professional athletes and sportsmen and women. Here's a short list of well-known figures from that world who have gone on record about their struggles with mental health: Michael Phelps (swimmimg), Serena Williams (tennis), Tyson Fury (boxing), Freddie Flintoff (cricket), Victoria Pendleton (cycling), Frank Bruno (boxing), Jonny Wilkinson (rugby), Mike Tyson (boxing), Paul Gascoigne (football), Joe Marler (rugby)[149]. Simone Biles and Naomi Osaka, probably the two highest profile athletes participating in the Tokyo Olympics, suffered their own well-publicised mental health related issues in the build-up to and during the games[150] and around the same time England cricketer Ben Stokes announced an indefinite break from cricket to prioritise his mental wellbeing.[151] In fact, the theme of mental illness and elite sport is so well developed, it prompted its own editorial in the British Journal of Psychiatry for the London Olympics back in 2012.[152]

And if you've become very hard and judgemental on yourself in some aspect of your life, as is likely to be the case if you've become dependent on exceptional performance to feel better about yourself, it's likely that will leach out into other areas of your life and it's also likely that you'll be harbouring quite judgemental views about other people, as well as an acute sensitivity to criticism. Hyper-sensitivity and a judgemental approach to others is an unfortunate combination – but they very often go together. It's an uncomfortable state of mind to be drawn towards and hard for others to be with but, by that stage, it feels better than what it's keeping off – the buried idea that we're getting it wrong, we're not good enough, there's something wrong with us.

Absolute

Everybody enjoys feeling clear about things, sure and confident in what they know and believe. Part of the appeal is what you're not feeling, what that gets away from. Not knowing, feeling unsure, is uncomfortable, makes us feel weak and indecisive, invites ideas around not being equal to the situation and inadequacy. So, one way to try to keep feeling OK about ourselves is to be very sure – to refuse doubts and take refuge in absolute certainty. When people are reacting like this, statements and decisions tend to get a little more emphatic and decisive than they really feel. The closer to home the things they're dealing with, the more emphatic their views become and the more threatening it feels if they're contradicted. And the more insecure they're feeling at the time, the more they may need something to be right just because it's what they've said.

This can get caught up in personal dynamics – you've got to be able to hold your own with the person you share a bathroom with. When this happens, in addition to the plain vanilla aversion to being 'wrong', you've got the complication of not being able to afford to lose a power struggle and being 'wrong' in a couple. You get immediate reaction and counter-reaction, it gets harder to hear what's being said and consider the possibility that it's right or how it seems to someone else. It's part of why we often treat the people we're closest to worse and behave more childishly with them. And at some level we generally know we're not behaving the way we'd like to and we dislike ourselves for that too.

Getting sucked into this pattern can contribute to a lot of unhappiness in relationships. But so far, so normal – most people aren't trying to reach a state of serene reflection on the universe. Anyway, they're probably keeping their mind more open than it might appear, so the next time they express a view on this topic, it will have shifted. And, in the meantime, they'll find a way to make up to the person who had to suffer their intransigence.

The determination not to be wrong, or shown to be wrong, can become more urgent. It can develop into an entrenched pattern of behaviour, a more or less permanent trait. Maybe, everything gets stated up front with a great deal of force and energy, to ward off the risk of contradiction. Or views may be abandoned immediately if challenged, because the prospect of feeling defeated is too much. Or they might be clung to too tightly, there may be an inability to let the subject go until people can feel they've prevailed enough. That's uncomfortable for them and tedious for everyone else, but everyone probably knows someone like that.

In extremes, uncertainty can become completely intolerable. Doubt can't be allowed at all or it feels like everything that's being maintained by absolute conviction would come crashing down. If being wrong is just too hard to bear, because the ideas it incites about failure and inadequacy are too ferocious, people can end up painting themselves into a corner where all that's left is a core of assertion, to which they have to adhere tighter and tighter, more inflexible, more absolute. Everything becomes more binary – black or white, right or wrong, all good or all bad. Thinking becomes more rigid, alternatives can't be entertained. We've all got pockets of that in our lives – sacred ideas that can't be challenged – but this is a real siege mentality pervading a life. It's a frightening and exhausting way to live.

Textual analysis is a promising new area of research in psychology. Because it avoids self-reporting and the artificiality of a lot of observational experimentation, it bypasses many of the problems we've talked about. It generates readily reproducible, objective results, it can be applied to text produced with complete independence from the research and software can analyse large samples very quickly and economically.

Research, using textual analysis of online mental health forums, has reported that the use of absolute terms in language ('always', 'nothing', 'completely') was significantly associated with depression, anxiety and a range of other mental health issues.[153] In fact, the research suggested that 'absolutism' was more closely associated with the severity of the disorder to which a forum related than the use of words describing negative emotions – a better marker than expressions of unhappiness for the severity of people's conditions. It also reported that higher levels of absolute language than in control groups were found in forums for people who had recovered from depression.

It's not clear what, from that, you could translate into treatment and how (does absolutism contribute to mental health problems or does it flow from them or are they both just associated with some underlying aetiology?) but it's an interesting line of investigation. In any event though, most forms of therapy have already been treating absolute and rigid thinking as a problem for many years.

Tough

We don't like the idea of being over-affected by things, being over-sensitive. For one thing, the most dependable element in how we react to what happens is some form of anxiety (we'll come back to this), and anxiety is an unsettling experience, so we'll push it away if we can. But also because it cuts across our idea of how we want to be, which is rational, capable and able to rise above our emotions.

There are good reasons for that aspiration but, even in its mildest form, it translates easily into a reluctance to acknowledge when we have been affected by things. Everything that happens to us, however small, has some kind of emotional corollary. If we can't recognise well enough how we're affected, we're back to that problem of not understanding what we really think and feel and what's important to us. Often a productive element in therapy is helping people come to terms with how they are affected by what happens around them, that there isn't anything wrong with that, that's how they're meant to be and that accepting that provides a better platform from which to make decisions about everything.

Nevertheless, there's an almost irresistible impulse to downplay how we've been affected by things which never goes away – the desire to diminish experiences which are frightening or disturbing is too strong. When people get too dependent on that idea of toughness, it can cause trouble. They try to push any sense of their own frailty and fallibility out of view. Strength, toughness, hardness become the key virtues; mistakes, anxiety, doubt have to be despised.

In this frame of mind, people can become hard and unforgiving and so does the world around them (though there are also often surprising pockets of sometimes quite extreme sentimentality). They may not have a lot of time for other people's mistakes or weaknesses either and they'll assume other people wouldn't have a lot of time for theirs – not really. To some extent that's going to feel confirmed and true. Generally, people aren't very good at feeling each other's predicaments, other people will usually be less sensitive to what's going on for us than we would like them to be and these ideas in people often have their origins in a sense of disappointment in the way their vulnerability has been responded to in the past.

The result is a hard, brittle state of mind whose counterpoint is the persistent, shadowy idea that they might be somehow inadequate, in the way they sometimes feel themselves to be. In their minds, the hallmarks of that inadequacy are their own anxieties and insecurities. This state of mind holds itself out as being about strength, unsentimental realism and getting through (all important virtues) but the truth is it involves a failure of courage. It's a refusal to come to terms with how things really are – an inability to acknowledge sometimes feeling scared, inadequate, overwhelmed, the possibility of things going badly and what that's really like. If it collapses (and, at some point, it usually will), there can be a tremendous sense of failure and abysmal personal defects.

In the meantime, it's a tough way to live, for them and the people around them. Hardness is very common in people who come for help; it's intimately tied up with the self-loathing we saw at the beginning of the chapter. A frequent theme in therapy is trying to put people more in touch with their own feelings of vulnerability to allow a softening, in order to enable a more rounded emotional life to emerge and a more realistic relationship with the world.

Being impressive

An obvious temptation, if you're not feeling good about yourself, is boasting – showing off, trying to impress other people. People get better at it as they get older, so it's not so easy to spot – humblebragging, fishing for praise, vicarious boasting through children, name dropping, casually letting slip incidental details we're very keen on someone knowing.

Harmless enough but, actually, generally counter-productive. Often other people can see through it, in which case we risk looking foolish. Even if they can't see through it, they may be able to tell that something's being done to them and react against it. And when it succeeds, when we do manage to impress, all we may do is make other people feel worse about themselves and drive them away. Impressing people is not a good route to intimacy – you may get a quick sugar hit but only at the risk of feeling isolated. And we'll see that loneliness is a major theme in mental health and itself closely connected to the idea that there's something wrong with us.

When people go down this road, they're usually blind to the vicious circle that results. They'll set out to impress in order to compensate for anxiety about not being good enough, which makes other people feel worse and pushes them away, which makes the people busy impressing feel excluded and isolated, which feeds the idea that they're not good enough, which makes them try to impress other people more. And on it goes.

Control

There are always layers to everything we do – usually several different ideas and reactions and impulses mixed up in our motivation. At some level, you can believe that politicians really do mean it when they talk about their sense of public service and desire to give something back. At the same time, exercising power over other people can be a very effective way of feeling good about yourself.

The same thing applies to management – there is a basic appeal to being in charge which never gets mentioned in the po-faced business school courses about the trials and burdens of leadership. And the same thing finds its way into personal relationships. Control is an important subject – we'll come back to it again. People tend to feel good about themselves if they have influence over a situation or other people, less good about themselves if they feel other people are exercising too much influence over them and worse if it feels as if it's being done in a way which is humiliating or damaging.

Demeaning

That last bit can be a problem – some people do get a boost from demeaning others. We've all come across snide characters who just can't seem to help putting other people down – and that's because they *can't*. They've come to rely upon it in order to feel better about themselves.

When it's blatant, it's easy to spot but disguises are available. Humour is a good one – who hasn't used a joke as a veiled dig at someone at some point? For some, that's more of a way of life. People have speculated for years about a link between comedy and mental illness – the tortured comedian is a trope. It's been researched, but results here are no more consistent or convincing than we've seen elsewhere.

One study investigated whether there was evidence of an increased tendency amongst comedians towards traits, such as impulsive or anti-social behaviour and avoidance of intimacy, which the authors associated with psychosis. They claimed to have found what they wanted but, as they recognised in their own paper, their results were always going to be fatally undermined by the fact that the same traits could equally be regarded as perfectly healthy manifestations of features such as introversion and lateral thinking.[154]

Another study claimed to show positive correlations between the subjectively assessed 'funniness' of 53 comics and early mortality – the funnier the comedian was found to be by the researchers' review panel, the more likely they were to have died early. The authors suggested the association they found between high funny scores and early death might be explained by mental health issues and personality characteristics which were responsible for both comedic talent and reduced longevity.[155]

That is one possible explanation for the findings but nothing's been demonstrated – it's about the loosest kind of correlation imaginable and from the most flimsily constructed evidence (everything turns on the subjective score awarded to comedians by the study's investigators). And the research didn't offer any clues about what those characteristics might be.

But if the research can't shed much light on the situation, most of the time with comedy it's pretty obvious there's a victim. When the crowd is laughing, someone's usually got egg on their face (whether they're in the room or not). And comedy operates by surprise, a subverting of expectations. Even where there isn't an obvious target, there's a challenge to the audience – *Can you get this? Are you as quick as me?*

The joker, the clown, they're often ambivalent figures; there's a menace, a form of quite aggressive self-assertion going on. Comedians spend a lot of their lives in an edgy, slightly hostile environment testing, teasing, challenging or ridiculing other people. That is a potential response to shadowy suspicions of not being good enough. And it's not only the professionals, we all have a tendency to do this. People do many things with humour, some of them very positive, but one is to use it to feel better about themselves by, however subtly, putting other people down. That's probably not something you'd want to become over dependent on.

Feeling superior

Humour isn't the only mask. One of the most common ways to respond to the idea we're not good enough, is to try to find ways to feel we're better than other people. That's unfortunate because the idea of our own inadequacy is so universal and so persistent and primed, it means there's a lot of trying to feel superior about. Which tends to have the effect of making other people (who are equally caught up in trying to feel OK about themselves) feel worse about themselves and they, in turn, are tempted to reach for feelings of superiority to try to make themselves feel better and on it goes.

This impulse gets everywhere and takes an endless number of different forms. Any kind of snobbism or exclusivity immediately springs to mind. Socially sanctioned ethical and social issues provide a less obvious opportunity (there are plenty of compelling ethical and social issues which haven't been sanctioned in the same way and can't offer the same visibility or the security of a well-established approved position). As well as a genuine concern about the issue at hand, people can get caught up in the thrill of the moral high ground – we do care about the planet, but we really like telling other people off too.

The more urgent and compelling the issue, the more important it is, the more important people's feelings about it are, the more important they can get to feel and the more justified in berating other people. Aside from the effect this might have on individuals' mental health, it's unlikely to help us respond effectively to the ethical and social issues facing us.

One problem is our need to be on the right side of the line is so strong, we can be too quick to think we've found a right side. Intensive battery farms for egg-laying chickens were banned in Europe in 2012 and more than half the eggs now sold in the UK are free-range. That seems like something to celebrate. But, almost all young hens in the UK still have their beaks burned off, without anaesthetic, to prevent them pecking each other. The living conditions which fit within the definition of free range vary dramatically – many 'free range' hens are kept in large, multi-tiered sheds which are so crowded that the birds are unable to find the exits that would allow them to get outdoors. They're often provided with a highly artificial, high protein diet including a range of antibiotics, growth hormones and other drugs to suppress parasites and they routinely live less than a tenth of their natural life span. Unless they're a male chick, in which case they're killed at birth.

As with 'free range', there's a good deal of controversy about how much reassurance about quality of life voluntary guidance codes and quality marks in meat production actually provide. But, however well they're looked after, pigs usually go to slaughter at 5-6 months old and lambs at 6-8 months. Left to their own devices, sheep can live for around 12 years and pigs 15. Very young animals just taste better. Marketing food as a premium product, on the basis of quality of care, has been highly successful. To the extent people's motivation has been to feel better about themselves (or for producers to increase margins), the job's been done well. To the extent it was founded in real concern about food production and animal welfare, that's much less clear.

If their primary motivation for recycling was concern about the underlying social and environmental issues, people in the UK should be feeling worse about themselves after it emerged just how much of the waste they've been putting out for recycling by local authorities over the last decade hasn't been recycled at all but exported to poorer countries and dumped, degrading the environment of more deprived people and threatening their health.[156] If they don't, it's presumably because they feel secure in the idea that they personally have been doing the 'right' thing, or trying to, and they feel exonerated from the consequences. The issue itself is outweighed by people's sense of virtue. And they need that sense of virtue because it's one of the things they've come to depend on to feel better about themselves.

We don't have much power to affect things through our individual choices and, in the scheme of things, criticism and protest may be the most effective steps people can take in terms of having an impact. But they also have their own energy which is quite separate from concern about the social and moral issues. Protestors get to feel better than other people who just don't get the issues or the seriousness of the situation. If we're too invested in telling other people they're doing it wrong, it's unlikely to help collaboration, innovation and adaptation. It's unlikely to help us find good solutions.

Global deforestation (logging, food production, biofuels and urban expansion), car pollution (and if electric cars reduce air pollution in cities, they will require more energy production which, as things stand, is predominantly going to be carbon fuels), non-degradable plastics (not just conspicuous single use plastics but many widespread uses embedded in our daily lives, such as micro-filaments in synthetic clothing), industrial pollution, the built environment and flood risk (paved driveways, artificial grass in gardens, out of town retail parks, car parks and swathes of new development to meet an acute housing crisis), the cattle industry, food waste, ozone depletion, aviation pollution, overfishing, massively inefficient glass and steel skyscrapers, shipping pollution, imported plants, pest infection and tree destruction, waste storage and contamination issues from the nuclear industry, mining and carbon fuel extraction, water waste (including milk-alternative production), fast fashion, rapid technological development and built-in obsolescence driving waste in white goods and electronics, energy-intensive data centres and server farms, population expansion and a global redistribution of wealth driving appetite for goods and resources – telling everybody that you're never going to forgive them doesn't seem that constructive.

Self-Sabotage

It's not always about trying to feel stronger, surer, more impressive and superior. These ideas about inadequacy affect us in other ways – they can limit or inhibit us. People talk themselves out of things, tell themselves they can't do them or that they don't really want to. Or maybe they'll give something a go, but make it clear (at least to themselves) that they're not really trying. Or they find some other way to undermine their own efforts because that feels less painful than risking investing fully in something, giving it your best shot, and failing. None of this needs to be known or done deliberately.

To be fair to ourselves, we all have to set our own targets and ambitions and adapt them all the time. It's important that they are reasonably realistic and achievable and it's not always easy to tell the difference between realistic expectation setting and self-sabotage. But if insecurities make people err too far on the side of caution habitually, they can become a serious hindrance or block them from things that could be very important. And they have a self-fulfilling quality – every time people undermine themselves in this way, it reinforces the idea that they're not good enough.

Self-sabotage isn't confined to career ambitions or job applications. An inner conviction that we don't deserve to be loved, and couldn't be if someone really knew us, isn't the poignant abnormality its usually portrayed as. It's an idea that every one of us carries around inside and it's an idea which probably *ought* to occur to us all from time to time. But if it gets too dominant, it can cause a lot of trouble. It can make people sabotage their relationships or test them to destruction or compel them compulsively to prove again and again that they are desirable and can make others want them.

Shame

Through a kind of perverse magnetism, attributes which we associate with inferiority or inadequacy become key features of our sense of identity. They influence how we're affected by just about anything that happens to us – an immediate part of the evaluation (which we'll often be unaware of) becomes how this relates to the things about ourselves we feel most uncomfortable about.

Those attributes might be purely personal like shyness or difficulty in expressing yourself. They may be aspects of themselves which people feel derive from something they're ashamed of, that they feel is 'wrong' about them, like a neglectful or abusive childhood. Or they might involve an association with transgression or inferiority which has been internalised from, or implanted by, society or by history.

Everybody takes in ideas about themselves from what's around them. Social attitudes concentrate and intensify around key divisions like race, gender, sexual orientation. Individuals will react in different ways but it's impossible to be unaffected. Any notion of, or association with, second-class status in society will interact in some form with the ideas everyone's carrying about around personal inadequacy. The bigger the idea in society, and the more significant the practical consequences, the more powerful the interaction is likely to be. And that will be the case however carefully those ideas of second-class status are negotiated – diversity policies, progressive movements, the most well-meaning supportive initiatives themselves have an effect of reinforcing the idea of discrimination, prejudice and histories of subordination.

That quote from Will Young again: 'when I was homophobically abused by a bus driver last year…I was like, wow, I've done a lot of work on shame and it's still coming up. The feeling of being "wrong", that it was all my fault'.[157] That's a common cycle – however many different ideas about it they may hold at the same time, something about themselves that (still) holds (however unwillingly and unconsciously) associations for people with transgression or shame, gains a sense of stigma in their minds, to which they become intensely sensitive. When it receives unwelcome attention, they feel painfully vulnerable and unable to protect themselves and then they may despise themselves for being so weak and not defending themselves adequately.

The sensitivity, the difficulty they feel in defending themselves (in fact, in objective terms their response might be very robust and effective, sometimes, perhaps, even excessive) connects directly to that hard-wired idea that there's something wrong with us. For them, in that moment, this is the confirmation, this is how their defectiveness expresses itself. It's the same process with anything to which we attach a sense of inferiority or shame – height, a big nose, a lazy eye, being adopted, it can be something as pervasive and neutral as gender – it acquires a dominant position in our sense of ourselves through a direct connection to the idea that we're not good enough.

Hyper-sensitivity

The more dominant the idea that there might be something wrong with us, the more painful anything that feels like criticism. Terms like 'painful' or 'difficult' get bandied about in connection with emotions all the time and it's easy to downplay the intensity and ferocity of these experiences – mental health professionals can be as guilty as anyone. A sense of being criticised, particularly by people we depend on, particularly if feelings of anxiety are already aroused, can feel sharp and raw and leave us feeling betrayed, abandoned and hopeless, with a burning sense of injustice and resentment. In the moment it really does feel like the end of the world.

Challenge, opposition, criticism are invariably a more unpleasant experience than we're prepared to let on – even to ourselves – but for some people it can be so intense that they become extremely avoidant. They're more likely to see criticism and slights where other people wouldn't and to experience any degree of challenge or criticism as out-and-out attack or character assassination. That hypersensitivity can be a problem in many ways. One is that if people can't entertain the possibility that they might be getting something wrong, it's more difficult to find a way to do things differently. And it takes its toll on other people, which is likely to have an adverse impact on all sorts of outcomes and provide more fuel for the idea that there is a problem with them.

To avoid being scorched by the idea that there's something wrong with us, we do have to be able to take seriously enough the possibility that we might be getting things wrong – that it might be us. If that idea only ever creates a reaction towards excuse, justification and blame of others, people may avoid it for a while, but it hasn't gone away and it hasn't lost any of its force.

Caring

Again, there are always layers of motivation – and there are generous and selfless reasons to become doctors, nurses, paramedics, social workers – but a steady consolation these situations offer is an opportunity for people to feel better about their own lives when they see up close the chaos and suffering in other people's. There are other powerful psychological benefits to be gained from helping people too, but one element which is always in the mix with dedication to care or very explicit levels of concern about others, is a sense of relief from our own difficulties by being absorbed into others people's problems. That can involve a sense of perspective on our own troubles, it can involve feeling purpose and competence and kindness and generosity and it can involve feelings of superiority.

Whatever shape it takes at any point in time, it does involve making a use of other people's suffering. That's unlikely to be a problem unless this aspect of motivation starts to get in the way of effective care or causes harm to other people. This is all as true of psychotherapists as anyone else, perhaps more so. And problems do arise if the therapist's need to feel better about themselves by being the 'well person' in the room, with people who are confessing their unhappiness and confusion, intrudes too much into the therapy. At some level, people can usually tell when a job like that is being performed on them and they don't like it.

* * *

There's no end to the examples you can find of ways people react to the idea of inadequacy because that idea is part of how we're affected by everything that happens to us. It's a complicated picture: people don't rely exclusively on any one of these stratagems. It's not uncommon to find toughness and intolerance combined with extreme sentimentality in the same person. At any time, we're probably doing several of these things to try to feel OK about ourselves and, over time, we might all use them all.

By and large, the things people do are quite successful in their objective, at least on its own narrow terms. That's why people keep doing some of them even though they're wreaking havoc in their lives. Everyone *is* familiar with the sense of inadequacy but when you don't feel it, you don't feel it and it can be possible to forget you ever did. And it's important these strategies *are* successful: when people get so bewildered, so unhappy that they come for help, it's that idea of inadequacy you find dominating things – too persistent, too intense, too punishing. And it's not as if the evidence suggests that our methods for helping work conspicuously well when people do come for help.

Whilst this is all working well enough, there may be nothing to see. Sometimes the best evidence for the idea of not being good enough is just the way it makes people behave to avoid having it. If someone is adamant they simply don't recognise that idea about themselves, look at all the things you think they might be using to keep it away. If you really think it doesn't apply to you, look at some of the ways you spend your time and money, and what might be lying behind them.

Pick a career

Another way to illustrate how these themes are woven into the fabric of lives is to look at how they might relate to an important feature of life, like work. For working adults, the job is how they spend most of their waking lives. It's going to be a vital part of how they see themselves, how others see them, how they might imagine others see them and the money and other practical resources that are going to be available to them. These dynamics will apply to any work and their negative will apply to not having work.

Law looks like something that ought to be a good career choice in a fairly uncomplicated way. You imagine that most parents would probably feel quite comfortable if they saw their child heading down that road (and, of course, seeing their children doing well is a very effective and legitimate way for people to feel better about themselves). Yet, according to a Law Society survey conducted in 2019, 48% of junior lawyers said they had experienced mental health problems in the previous month and more than 6% had thought about killing themselves.[158] It's not just juniors, the legal press is awash with surveys suggesting that lawyers of all ages suffer from mental health issues at significantly greater rates than other professions or the general population. And not just the UK, surveys in the US, Australia and New Zealand generate similar coverage. And it's not a recent thing, back in 1990 research was suggesting that, after adjustment for socio-demographic factors, rates of major depressive disorder depression in lawyers were higher than for any other occupation in the US, nearly four times the rate for the working population generally.[159] If mental health is so intimately connected to self-esteem, what could it be about working in law that might be pushing so many people's sense of inadequacy so hard?

It's not hard to think of aspects of a job like this which ought to be good for people's self-esteem. Most obviously, it's socially respected and well-paid. Feeling financially secure and providing well for your family are powerful cues for people to feel OK about themselves (financial insecurity is a whole other world of anxiety and opportunity to feel inadequate). Law is competitive – there's a professional qualification to be obtained and, to get to that point, people need to have a track record of success and achievement at school and university. As jobs go, legal work is often interesting. It requires absorbing levels of skill and expertise and it makes a difference to people; it can feel significant enough to provide a sense of purpose – all good ways for people to feel OK about themselves. It's also a very social occupation: there's a good deal of interaction with clients, other occupations and colleagues and the opportunity to form close working relationships. So far, that all sounds positive.

But if becoming a lawyer involved a sense of achievement, it also involved a risk. It is quite hard to do – it won't have worked out for some people and that will have hurt them. The successful candidates won't have emerged entirely unscathed either. They may have got where they wanted in the end, but the anxiety, the effort, the risk of failure they encountered along the way, will have fed their insecurities and doubts. Achieving their goal doesn't banish the idea that they're not good enough (because nothing can). It does help to keep it at bay but, at the same time, the anxiety and uncertainty they've experienced along the way will have given it some oxygen.

And the effort isn't over – this is a job that generally requires very hard work. Most lawyers charge by the hour, the money they make is a factor of the hours everybody works. In the big commercial firms, it's routine to work late into the night for weeks or months on end. These are very profitable businesses and people get paid very well but there are no short cuts. As people become more senior, the barriers between work and personal lives dissolve – they expect to be involved in work during the evenings at home, at weekends and probably most days on holiday.

To some extent, even that can provide a positive for self-esteem: a sense of validation from being in demand. And being intensely occupied can provide a solving formula, a distraction from anxiety and other concerns. People can build a dependence on busyness. But this work is technically difficult and usually has to be carried out under a great deal of time pressure. The stakes are high: the sums of money involved can be very large and the personal issues for clients can be very significant. If mistakes are made, they're generally easy to uncover and demonstrate.

We have a tendency to venerate hard work, as if it's an unqualified good – it isn't. Pressure generates powerful emotions around fear and aggression – that's what galvanises us, we respond to the situation, rise to the challenge. Too much pressure and challenge start to feel more like an emergency. Well-trained professionals continue to perform professionally but, over time, the sense of crisis takes on a more permanent status and starts to colour how they experience other aspects of the world around them. Feelings of unfairness, persecution and victimisation develop and life takes on a discontented, sour quality. That discontented experience feeds the idea that there's something wrong – they're getting life wrong.

It takes self-discipline to spend evenings and weekends working when you'd rather be doing something else. There's an idea involved in there that what you want isn't that important. Lawyers owe their clients strict professional duties – in many circumstances they're required to put their clients' interests ahead of their own. In the big commercial firms, there's intense commercial pressure to attract and retain the most lucrative clients. The result is unequal relationships – there's a tone of subservience in all lawyers' interactions with their clients. And personal plans and commitments to others – dates, birthdays, wedding anniversaries, holidays – are always at risk of being disrupted. Again, the message is what you want doesn't matter very much; in these circumstances, it's only natural for people to feel powerless and helpless at times.

In the 1960s psychologists discovered that lab rats and dogs subjected for long enough to stressful situations over which they had no control exhibit 'learned helplessness'.[160] The researchers reported that the experience changes the way the animals can respond to their situation. They stop being able to access strategies and solutions they would have been able to use before they were traumatised and they become depressed and anxious.

Something similar can happen to people if they can't get away from, or do enough to influence, a situation, and its unpleasant enough and happens often and for long enough. They get stuck in the same sense of helplessness – perspective goes, they become unable to think the way they used to, things that made sense, don't, things that shouldn't make sense, do; they feel trapped and become demoralised and anxious. Other experiences in life can generate this kind of response, but it's something of an occupational hazard for lawyers.

Another problem for lawyers is pretence. That communal myth in the corporate world applies here – a wholesale rejection of the idea of failure, or even struggling, but also an endless appetite for more deals, more work. That's not how anyone is actually feeling most of the time but they're expected to perform it and that can be very confusing. Imposter syndrome is an entirely natural experience – everyone will have felt it at some time but this kind of pointed reality gap (with its own business-orientated social media where people can circulate pointless thought pieces and post fake 'likes' to client initiatives) is a fertile breeding ground for powerful feelings of personal inauthenticity.

If careers develop well, over time people earn more and have more. That too can be a source of confusion – a sense of personal achievement, wealth, status can all go a long way towards alleviating a secret sense of inadequacy and humiliation: it works, to some extent. But when, despite everything, people still find themselves feeling unequal and unhappy, they can be thrown back to a difficult place and a stronger conviction that the problem must be in them.

Over a number of years, lawyers can't not be affected by these aspects of their work. How they're affected will have an impact on the people around them, including the people they care about and depend upon most. A defensive drift towards toughness and invulnerability, for example, feels the same as insensitivity for those on the other side of it. And those people will also have been affected directly by this job, by its capacity to disrupt family arrangements, to break commitments, and perhaps drawn some conclusions about their relative importance in the mind of their partner or parent (which will have impacted how they feel about themselves).

Living in a troubled relationship is a frightening state of affairs – if there are serious problems with key relationships, everyone's sense of something wrong amplifies. If important aspects of life outside feel threatened, work may become an even more important measure of self-worth, of people trying to feel better about themselves. And, however well rationalised, relationship breakdowns usually involve a powerful sense of fault and lack of worth for everyone – for being the unloveable one who got left, for being the one who couldn't make it work and stay, or for getting into the relationship in the first place.

The final challenge with any job is stopping. We've already seen, a problem with basing your self-worth on things which are hard to do is that there will probably come a time when you can't do them as well, or at all. If that comes too early (and a lot of lawyers do retire, or get retired, early) that can feel disastrous. Not only is one of the key things they've depended on to feel OK about themselves no longer available to them but, in the end, they can feel they failed at it anyway.

Even if it all ends on their terms, a major part of their identity and self-esteem – the productivity, the expertise, being sought after, the income, the status, the activity they spent most of their time doing – has gone. That's likely to be combined with normal experiences of ageing and declining physical health and a number of significant changes in family structure and lifestyle that could all contribute to, or against, feeling OK about themselves. With luck, there will have been enough sense of achievement so the loss of occupation doesn't take too much away from their sense of worth. But it isn't always like that.

It's a similar equation for any kind of work – anxiety and stress, unequal relationships and inauthenticity against purpose and competence, financial reward, social connection and a sense of identity. But maybe we can see better now what's behind those alarming statistics about lawyers' mental health. Despite the challenges, this job works for a lot of people. Much of how well it works will depend upon the other factors in a life which make a contribution to how people feel about themselves – the things they value, the luck they encounter, the quality of their close relationships. All of it engaged in a continuous (largely unconscious) dialogue with their self-esteem and the unshakeable, pre-set idea that somehow, somewhere, there's something wrong, about them.

***

That picture experimental psychology and psychiatry paint of low self-esteem as a personality trait affecting some people and pre-disposing them to depression or other mental health conditions, isn't very helpful. Not only in terms of its impact on sufferers – you have depression because there's a problem with your personality – but also in terms of making progress in understanding things. It smacks too much of laboratory-based smugness and superiority – the researchers are missing out the experience of their own lives. Everyone has a hole in their self-esteem; everyone is trying to feel OK about themselves.

Here *is* something that we can 'know' about mental health and if we can recognise that we know it, we might be able to do more with it. Everyone is living with the idea that they're not good enough and everyone is trying to find ways to keep that idea down. Often, people can't put the idea into words coherently or consistently (at least until there's a crisis) – it feels too perverse and too different to how they want to think about themselves. But they can feel the hollowness it causes inside and the more intrusive it becomes, the more trouble it causes. When this idea becomes too solid and too real, people can't get away from it because it's to do with the way they feel about themselves and they are engulfed by a sense of despair. That's a regular state of mind for people who suffer from depression and depression isn't just the most common form of mental illness, it seems to be inseparable from the idea of mental illness.

3

RESENTFUL

Something not discussed explicitly so far, but it's an obvious way to try to deflect ideas about inadequacy, is blaming others or circumstances beyond your control (which is often really about other people) when things go wrong.

Looked at entirely rationally, we might say the world is what it is and it's our job to understand it. If it doesn't behave the way we expect, the mistake is always ours. Since the world is too complicated to anticipate correctly, our expectations are always off to some extent. So, we'd have to go easy on ourselves but, nevertheless, the conclusion would be we'd got it wrong.

That's not how people generally do think – we can't go easy enough on ourselves. Because the idea that there's something wrong with us is there, and as powerful and punishing as it is, it becomes necessary to say *this* wasn't my fault. Otherwise, we'd all be crushed by ideas of inadequacy.

Part of that reaction is invariably that something unfair happened or someone else was to blame. Even a perfectly rational response like *I couldn't be expected to know* tends to acquire a note of injustice, like a child saying *I didn't mean to*. Everyone has this reaction in their repertoire, but overreliance on this way out may be the most disastrous strategy of all.

Something else you quickly notice about people who come for help is that they're very angry with other people. Many come specifically because they want to do something about their anger. Perhaps anger has got them into trouble and someone (maybe a partner, maybe a court) has told them they need to.

Or perhaps they've just grown sick of living with it – it's not a pleasant experience. When it's not the ostensible reason people have come, it may take a little while before it gets revealed, but it's always an important part of the picture.

A sense of injustice, grievance and resentment is part of our default setting. The idea that something unfair has happened when we encounter a serious enough set-back is inevitable – we feel hard done by, we feel like a victim. We might not let on that's how we're feeling, we may not be particularly interested in owning up to it to ourselves, and we may have all sorts of other ideas about the situation at the same time, but that idea is there.

If we haven't suffered too serious a blow, and we're in a reasonably robust frame of mind, a self-righting mechanism kicks in. We feel better as we get further from the event, we cool down, gain some perspective. If the injury has come from someone we care about, the natural springs of affection wash it away. We find our balance again.

There are some clear potential positives to anger. Probably most importantly, it's communicative – it's a real part of our human reaction to a situation and it allows other people to know what's going on with us and how we're affected by something. Hide it too much, suppress it, and we're in danger of cheating people – not giving them a fair chance to understand what we really think and feel. Our anger gives other people some insight into the consequences of their actions, and it allows them an opportunity to make good, and maybe avoid some kind of lasting damage to the relationship when they hurt us.

It gives us agency too: it motivates us to change things which could be causing us trouble or might harm us. It can be a way of asserting balance in a relationship: we all have a tendency to push our luck with other people and an occasional display of teeth can be an effective way of telling someone that's as far as you go, helping to maintain some kind of balance that works better for both people.

That isn't to say that there aren't other ways of achieving these objectives, but anger can be an effective tool.

Many of the less positive aspects to anger are obvious: most acts of violence and crime derive from a sense of grievance and resentment. At some level, people invariably feel some kind of justification for what they're doing, usually around a sense of injury and injustice. And anger often provides the fuel for the most destructive things people do in their lives – the lashing out, the disastrous choices, the making things worse.

But there are less obvious, and more pervasive, dangers with anger. One is that you can think of anger as a secondary emotion: it's a reaction to feeling something else, to being made to feel hurt or scared. When you say you're angry about something, what you really mean is that it's frightened or hurt you. Hurt or frightened don't feel good: weak, helpless – powerful cues to feel inadequate.

There are many ways to feel frightened which don't involve direct physical threat. It could be a sense of threat to your relationships, a threat to ideas about yourself which you value or the threat of an idea which you find frightening. It doesn't have to be directly about you – when people feel moral outrage about something happening to others it's partly because it's a frightening idea that the world could be like that. And, we're empathic creatures; we can feel hurt or scared for others. Though it's noticeable that our anger tends to increase the more we identify with the victims, the more they mean to us, and that often means the more they are like us or have become connected with our sense of ourselves.

Not knowing what to do can be frightening. If we're painfully confused about something that's close to us, we can become frustrated and impatient with the situation, and ourselves – it makes us feel inadequate. People can use anger as the engine to punch through to a decision.

So, very regularly, we'll take an escape route into anger. Sometimes we might have some sense of what we're doing – there's a deliberate element to it – but more usually it just happens, without any decision involved. It's empowering, exhilarating even, we feel stronger – which feels much better. In immediate terms, it's often effective too: we get our way. But it is another form of denial; it's not owning up to something – that we're scared or hurt – it's a retreat from real feeling.

On a purely practical level, that can lead to some dreadful decisions. It's the problem we've already met. If we're using anger to avoid experiencing what we really feel about a situation, if we can't tell what we really think and feel, how can we know what's important to us, how can we act in our own best interests? Of course, decisions made in anger can be very effective; however hot-headed, they might turn out to be just what was needed at the time. But when decisions fuelled by anger work out badly for us, it can be difficult to recognise what's happened, to admit our own contribution to the situation (because that's not going to make us feel good about ourselves) and there's a fair chance our way out is going to be more sense of unfairness, grievance and more anger.

Everyone gets angry. Hopefully, we don't take too many important decisions like that – or they're not irretrievable and, as the anger subsides, we can see the situation more clearly, get a more honest, complete, picture of how we really feel and make fresh decisions which reflect that, if we need to. Easy to say; impossible to resist every time, or even consistently. When we're angry, we're primed for action – it's extremely hard to stay with your anger without reacting and it can be difficult to retrace your steps afterwards.

That's the biggest problem with anger – that sugar-rush sense of power. It's such a seductive alternative to feeling frightened, hurt, weak, powerless, to blame, or any other variety of inadequate. And, it is like sugar, it is like junk food: it's a powerful state of mind. When people are angry, they can't feel much else – that's an essential part of its appeal. There's a danger people become dependent on it to avoid other emotions they don't want to feel. People use alcohol or drugs to feel better, stronger – it's the same with anger except there's no need to do anything deliberate or overt like order a drink or pop a pill. But anger is a form of unhappiness – people just don't generally recognise it at the time.

Unfair

One of the constant themes you find talking to people who have come for help is a sense that they have been let down – they haven't been treated the way they should have been. In fact, this sense of having been 'slighted' was one of the defining features identified in the first modern attempts to analyse depression.[161] But, as we saw in the ICD-10 and DSM-5 definitions of depression, it's lost its place in current diagnostic criteria – it doesn't get referred to at all.

Perhaps this is because anger and resentment are less appealing and sympathetic than low self-esteem, shame and guilt. It feels harder, punishing, to attribute these ideas to people who are suffering so much. But resentment is a major issue in mental health and we're missing something important if we ignore it.

At the heart of resentment is the idea of fairness. The desire for fair treatment appears to be absolutely fundamental, it seems to go right to our core. It's hard to know what to make of it in terms of thinking about or treating mental health, but evidence has been claimed of an innate sense of fairness in dogs,[162] monkeys[163] and rats.[164] Clips of extravagant reactions from research into a sense of fairness in capuchin monkeys have gone viral.[165]

When we hear about children with terminal diseases, young mothers with cancer diagnoses, couples killed on honeymoon, part of our reaction is how unfair it seems. It's not necessarily that we expect fate or the universe to behave fairly, to serve up just rewards. It's more about being singled out – outliers, things going against expectations.

It's the same when we're the wrong side of things; what seem to hurt most are things that don't happen to other people. If they do happen to other people, we feel better about it. Feeling treated differently, and worse, is a large part of unfairness. You can see the ingredients in this article about England footballer Danny Rose and his experience of depression before the 2018 World Cup:[166]

> Danny Rose revealed he has had depression which he believes was triggered by the treatment of a knee injury coupled with family tragedy. In an extraordinary interview days before he flies with England to the World Cup, the Tottenham left-back said he lost track of the number of times he was injected with blood-thinning and painkilling drugs.

The 27-year-old's mental health deteriorated as he contended with the triple trauma of his uncle killing himself, his mum Angela being racially abused and an assailant shooting at his brother inside the family home.

Speaking for the first time about the illness that he said left him unable to get out of bed and on medication for months, Rose described how his time inside the England set-up became an escape as he grew increasingly miserable and isolated at White Hart Lane.

"It's no secret that I've been through a testing time at Tottenham this season," said Rose, who is set to start England's final warm-up match, against Costa Rica, on Thursday. "It led to me seeing a psychologist and I was diagnosed with depression, which nobody knows about. I had to get away from Tottenham.

"I'm lucky that England gave me that opportunity to get away, refresh my mind and I'll always be grateful to them. I was on medication for a few months – nobody knows about that apart from my agent – but I'm off the medication now, I'm good again and looking forward to how far we can go in Russia."

Sitting behind a desk at England's St George's Park training base, Rose spoke freely and largely unprompted about his illness. "Nobody knows this either, but my uncle [his father's brother] killed himself in the middle of my rehab, and that triggered the depression as well," Rose said.

"Off the field there have been other incidents: back home in August my mum was racially abused in Doncaster. She was very angry and upset about it, and then someone came to the house and nearly shot my brother in the face – a gun was fired at my house.

"England has been my salvation and I can't thank the manager and the medical staff enough. It was really hard, and being referred to a doctor and psychologist by the Spurs club doctor helped me massively to cope. I haven't told my mum or my dad, and they are probably going to be really angry reading this, but I've kept it to myself until now."

Rose pinpointed the treatment of a knee injury suffered in January 2017 as the beginning of his strife. He was advised he did not require an operation but when he returned to training in May that year he experienced pain and was recommended to have surgery. In total he was side-lined for eight months and it took a toll.

"I was getting very angry, very easily. I didn't want to go into football, I didn't want to do my rehab, I was snapping when I got home; friends were asking me to do things and I wouldn't want to go out, and I would come home and go straight to bed.

"It all stemmed from my injury when I was advised I didn't need an operation. I don't know how many tablets I took to try and get fit for Tottenham, how many injections I took trying to get fit for Tottenham. I had cortisone and platelet-rich plasma injections trying to be fit for my club.

"I had to have an operation four months down the line – after all that football I missed, when the team was flying and I was playing really well, the team were playing really well. Seeing the lads beat Arsenal comfortably, seeing them beat Man United comfortably, it was hard. I'm not saying I've had worse treatment than anybody else. That's football. But it was difficult – that was the start of it".

Rose made only 17 club appearances last season because of injury and then failing to dislodge Ben Davies. "I think it's fair to say I'm the luckiest player to be in the [England] squad," he said.

You can see a series of powerful 'slights': racist abuse of his mother, potentially lethal violence, in his own home, against a close family member, the loss of his uncle through suicide and a career-threatening injury. And, specifically, the sense of being let down in his medical treatment – going through additional painful rehab that he might have avoided and losing a further four months of his playing career, because it turned out the wrong treatment option was selected. You can see references to his anger taking over, the pain of feeling singled out, excluded from what his colleagues were achieving at the time and the consolation offered by the idea that he hasn't had worse treatment than anybody else, even that he's been lucky.

Some slights are very real – surely someone who loses their legs to a landmine, or a woman encountering her third recurrence of breast cancer, are entitled to feel singled out and let down? There may be some rare individuals out there who could retain a sense of universal perspective in those circumstances, who wouldn't have the idea of being dealt with unfairly as a prominent part of their response – I don't think I'd be one of them.

Danny Rose is a professional athlete – a great deal of what he'd built in his life, everything he'd achieved in a career, which is always frighteningly precarious anyway, had been put at risk by something that looked like somebody else's mistake. And at the same time, people he cared about were being insulted and threatened and another had died in extremely distressing circumstances.

But not everybody who comes for help has experienced these kinds of objectively overwhelming circumstances. It can be expectations, of life, of other people, that drive a sense of being treated unfairly, as much as what actually happens to people. With some, their resentment may seem misplaced because the problems in their lives, which might be very real and serious, seem more of their own making. With others, perhaps objectively their difficulties don't seem very serious at all and are more to do with how they expect their lives to go or other people to behave. Unfortunately, that doesn't diminish their suffering in the least.

This is a permanent problem – how should we expect the world to treat us? What can you legitimately expect other people to do for you (and what should you be prepared to do for other people)? If it sounds trite, it shouldn't, because there really aren't many more important issues to try to resolve. There isn't a formula, there isn't even a 'right' answer – everyone has to try to work something out for themselves.

Where anybody is on it at any point will be the result of how they grew up – how they were treated, how they saw other people treating each other – and what they've managed to learn since. That last factor can be very significant, or very significant in relation to some aspects of our world view but not others, or not very much at all – some people escape the gravitational pull of their childhood better than others. How all that works for people will be largely determined by the social attitudes and people they encounter, particularly the people they form close relationships with and what those people's expectations are (which will have been shaped by the same kind of influences for them).

Once you take all that into account, a moment's thought tells you it's never likely to be a perfect match. Human nature being what it is, in practice, in our most honest feelings, it's rare that we entirely feel other people are doing everything they could for us. There's usually a little voice somewhere inside us wanting more – it's just a question of how insistent and loud that voice gets. When things are going OK, it's a voice we can usually find a balance to and resolve into genuine feelings of appreciation and gratitude.

The trouble is, the less realistic our expectations of other people, the more inclined we are to feel quite strongly that they aren't doing enough for us. Feeling that other people are being self-centred isn't a very reliable guide: the more self-centred your frame of reference, the more we tend to think other people are self-centred. When you have a couple calling each other self-centred (which is probably true of just about every relationship that breaks down), it doesn't get you very far.

But if there's no perfect formula, there are certainly positions likely to involve greater or lesser degrees of difficulty. If our expectations are too unrealistic, we're going to run into disappointment and frustration on a nearly constant basis and we're going to experience a great deal of resentment.

It's frightening and hurtful when our expectations collide with reality, particularly if those expectations concern the people we're closest to. Everyone has a way they want to be loved, an expectation of what love looks like, derived from their personal experience, their childhood and their imagination, which no-one else could be expected to understand and which is inevitably going to be disappointed at times. That's easy to say, and write about glibly, but these disappointments are about our closest, most important relationships, the ones on which we depend most for our emotional security and happiness, and they're going to happen repeatedly over a sustained period of time.

Everyone struggles with this and it's easy to slip into anger and resentment. It's easy because it's natural – it's how our minds work, automatically, without us deciding or even registering that it's happened. The resentment may only play out in our heads, in little secret vignettes of revenge, or we might become withdrawn and sulk, we might indulge in a few sideways, coded digs or we might explode in rage. It's going to happen, it's just a question of how much time you're going to spend living with that feeling of being hard done by.

It's not just disappointed expectations of other people, it's also a question of expectations of life and what happens when people get unhappy. One of the most troublesome set of expectations is how happy we should expect to be because there are always going to be things to make us unhappy. If the picture we have of how our life is going to be – how it ought to be – is very unrealistic, we'll struggle more to come to terms peacefully with these cues for unhappiness. We'll need something to keep at bay the idea that there's something wrong with us, that we're getting life wrong. We'll be more inclined to feel victimised, to feel something unfair has happened and our resentment will need something to attach to.

Without meaning to, without even knowing what's happened, in the absence of anything else to blame, we're likely to locate the problems in others – we'll blame other people for our unhappiness and it'll be the ones closest to us. In the end, even our most abstract expectations of what our life should be tend to turn into expectations of other people and rebound on them.

Ambivalence

It is inevitable to spend a certain amount of time feeling acutely let down and disappointed by the people you care about most. And for this to take surprisingly mean, petty forms that aren't at all how you like to see yourself – ideas of punishing, getting your own back or leaving. All of this secretly playing out in your head whilst you're doing the dishes.

This is called Ambivalence – it doesn't mean not knowing what you feel about something, it means having sharply contrasting feelings about something at the same time. It's the thin line between love and hate. But just because it happens all the time, doesn't mean ambivalence isn't a very disturbing experience – these are the people we care about and depend upon most. We're supposed to love them and we're furious with them and filled with resentment.

That doesn't feel good; we feel lonely, abandoned, betrayed – it's traumatic. We may wonder what kind of person we are to be feeling this petty and vindictive – how weak and spiteful. And that feeds right into the idea that there's something wrong with us, with our lives, with our relationships.

It's not a fair reaction. These experiences are universal – we just don't know that because they feel so shameful, they don't generally get talked about honestly or realistically. These thought patterns do seem mean and childish, they probably do derive from 'childish' parts of us, but we have other parts, perhaps more developed, more mature, certainly more open minded and generous spirited, which can look at these impulses and draw different conclusions.

Our feelings aren't the test of us, the test is how we behave and treat other people. Your mood and ideas this afternoon are different to this morning and you'll think and feel another way this evening. These feelings come and they go, it's up to us what we do with them and how we live.

OCD is frequently associated with difficulties in dealing with our own ambivalence. Sufferers are often troubled by ideas of harm coming to the people close to them. It's made a more distressing experience because they sense that they are somehow responsible for these ideas in their heads. In some cases, it's them directly hurting the people they care about themselves in their imaginations.

These are secret ideas and they play out in secret parts of the mind where peculiar things make sense. People resort to investing in ritualistic behaviour in an effort to ward off the harm to the people they love – secret rituals in response to secret feelings of resentment surfacing in ideas about people close to you being hurt or hurting them yourself. The problem isn't so much the entirely natural occasional feelings of resentment towards the people around them, it's the way sufferers react to their own ideas.

The brain can generate all sorts of fleeting ideas and impulses, and it's a frightening experience for a new mother to imagine in her own head shaking her own baby. But if that experience is too traumatic, the momentary thought assumes a significance and force it needn't have. So, it comes back and the mind grasps at ideas to oppose it – *if I touch my baby's cot it'll be OK.*

The idea that caused the problem, which was originally isolated and fleeting but has now become recurrent, is suffused with shame and guilt and the ritualistic behaviour also takes on a shameful self-punishing quality. All that attaches readily to the idea we're all carrying around that there's something wrong with us, and we fall into a pattern of increasingly desperate attempts to ward off the idea we feel so guilty about, with increasingly intrusive and disruptive rituals, which only entrench things further with shame, humiliation and guilt.

This is an important theme: we get disturbed by the ideas we find in our own heads, because they feed our sense of inadequacy, our sense of something wrong with us. We attach too much significance to our own thoughts and react to them too strongly.

People who come for help are often caught up in intense ambivalence – stuck between blame and resentment of the people closest to them and guilt and self-loathing for the way they feel. That's a very uncomfortable way of living and it triggers another difficult emotion: envy. People tormented by intense feelings of resentment and ambivalence find themselves envying others' apparent peace of mind. That too, feeds the idea that there's something wrong, that they're somehow worse than other people. And it triggers more resentment because they understand that others are somehow implicated in what's happened and it's the way other people are (or appear to be) that's making them feel worse about themselves.

A rabbit hole

These thought patterns around disappointment, unfairness and resentment may be natural, they may be in all of us, but the more ingrained and persistent they are, the more unhappy people are. These ideas make us more thin-skinned, more likely to feel affronted. Disagreements and conflicts assume a greater symbolic value beyond their practical significance. Things becomes more emphatic, more urgent – too much is at stake. Beliefs, values, impulses have to be asserted against the world or it feels like a slight.

Resentment towards the people we're closest to is destabilising – it generates powerful currents of anxiety because it makes us contemplate losing key relationships, question whether the people we depend upon love us, whether we love them. All of this feeds the idea that there's something wrong with us, with our lives, makes us feel dramatically worse about ourselves. The people who should, don't seem to love us and we must be horrible people because we're filled with horrible thoughts so much of the time. That makes it harder to take pleasure in anything. The worse we feel about ourselves, the more we resent others who don't seem to be afflicted like this.

And the worse we feel about ourselves, the more preoccupied with ourselves and more self-centred we tend to become. The harder it gets to see other people clearly and the easier it becomes to have unrealistic expectations which get disappointed and cause resentment. Depressed people often live with a lot of guilt, not just because of the unpleasant, resentful ideas they have in their heads, but because they know quite a lot of the time they don't behave very well, they cause trouble to other people. They're often acutely aware of their effects on other people and it adds to their pain and their self-hatred. But it's somehow not enough – their concern for others doesn't mean that they can stop inflicting that pain because, right in the heart of their world is the idea that in some fundamental way, things are different for other people. That idea persists even though they can also think quite clearly that their circumstances aren't worse than other people's, and feel powerfully that they aren't justified in the way they're feeling, which just increases their sense of shame, guilt and inadequacy.

But at the same time all that's going on, resentment, blame and complaint can bring some immediate practical benefits –

they have their rewards. Being dissatisfied, fretful, discontent is a good way of exercising power, of controlling other people. If we're the unhappy one, other people get pulled into trying to make things better for us, they do what we want. Unhappy people can become quite dependent on that. Of course, it's ironic that complaint and resentment can confer power and control in relationships because they have their origins in feelings of weakness and grievance, of things being done to us, of not being dealt with fairly. The result is the sufferer still feels like they have very little influence over situations whilst others are actually spending a lot of time dancing to their tune. That is, if they can find people prepared to dance to their tune.

The term co-dependency describes relationships where one person is considered to have become dependent on someone else's problems – they need the other person to be ill so that the ill person will depend upon them for care. The concern is that in these relationships, without having any conscious intention of doing so, the carer becomes an obstacle to the ill person improving their situation.

Like a lot of psychological concepts, it's often difficult to know exactly what different people mean when they use it. How do we safely draw the line between 'legitimate' levels of care and pandering, when all our relationships involve a complex mesh of mutual dependence and need? But co-dependency is a particularly tricky term because it can be employed with dubious motivation and that can include professional settings. Most species of 'tough love' have chequered histories and you can mask some fairly unpleasant impulses by labelling more caring behaviour as co-dependent.

At the same time, you see a lot of relationships where one person is more volatile, quicker to feel disappointments and slights, and the other is busy trying to keep things OK for them; it's quite a common pattern for people to fall into. If being the unhappy one is a good strategy for keeping the whip hand, at least for certain purposes, in a relationship, it's a bad one for avoiding depression. And if personal relationships may be susceptible to this kind of pattern (though it's also very easy for people whose lives are spent in blame and complaint to be alone), relationships outside the home tend not to be.

Unrealistic expectations and a predisposition to resentment and complaint are likely to be a real impediment at school, work and any other dealings with the external world. That can mean people become more dependent on the control they can exercise at home to keep anxiety within tolerable levels and it becomes increasingly difficult to engage with the outside world. All that will inflame further the sufferer's sense of resentment and the idea that there's something wrong with them.

Accumulate enough sense of grievance and people can get stuck in bitterness – it can come to feel like the world is permanently set against them and resentment becomes the stock response. Their sense of agency becomes more severely threatened, they feel powerless, everything that happens is being done to them. Getting their way becomes even more important, but also more precarious – it gets harder to feel they're ever getting their way enough. They may become hyper-sensitive, moving from quick to feel slights to hair-triggered, and prone to sudden explosions of rage, or flat, sullen and withdrawn.

Sufferers become less capable of recognising other people's experience and more insensitive to other people's predicaments. The world becomes a harder, more defended place: views get more entrenched and rigid. They may lose touch with softness altogether, beyond the heightened sense of their own vulnerability.

Sometimes it retreats to sentimentality – reserved for kittens or whales and babies that can't make them feel bad about themselves, but harder and harder to find in the real world with people who can make them feel let down or rejected or criticised.

Hurt tends to make us all feel vicious; somewhere in the mix there's invariably an impulse to lash out. In these circumstances people may be largely oblivious to their own aggression and cruelty, but feelings of shame for the way they behave still persist and have to be suppressed. States of mind become less stable as they oscillate between extremes of guilt and self-justification, resentful toughness and self-pity, hopeless rejection of expectations of other people and secret, extravagant fantasies of care.

There can be a perverse impulse to spoil things more, to make it worse with the half-buried idea that someone will see how bad things are and do something or at least feel guilty and sorry. They may become reckless, more extreme in their actions. If it goes far enough, they might become seriously self-destructive or a danger to others.

In the worst cases, states of mind become so fierce and unstable that people start to lose control of these cycles altogether – their own states of mind happen to them like external events, which is terrifying, and their sense of reality may start to break down. At the heart of it is hurt and resentment. When walls talk to people, they're not generally calm, whimsical conversations – it's invariably about grievance, threat, fear and violence.[167]

Souring

But the threat of full-blown psychosis isn't the most serious risk presented by resentment. We all have some kind of encounter with desperate states of mind at some point or points in our lives, but most of us manage to avoid these extremes most of the time. The biggest problem with resentment – what affects most people, worst – is the flavour it can lend a life on a long term, maybe even permanent, basis.

Resentment sours things. It's like having a foul taste in your mouth – it's hard to enjoy anything properly like that. It deprives people of the ability to take enough pleasure in the things in their lives which should give them pleasure. And it feels horrible, like there's something wrong inside us. This is the great ailment, this souring of life. Millions of people go and see their GP or a therapist because their lives are being spoiled in this way. It would make perfectly good sense to call depression 'resentment' and talk about prescribing anti-resentment pills.

We are fretful and restless by nature, we become discontented at times. Many aspects of our lives will feel unsatisfactory but this kind of creeping, low-level resentment is different. It's not just dissatisfaction with ourselves or our circumstances, it's the persistent idea that we're being treated badly, we're being short-changed. Self-esteem fluctuates, circumstances can change, resentment blocks the way out.

Privileging Anger

We can't make our minds up about anger. On one hand, there are thousands of anger management courses up and down the country. At the same time, anger is often treated as a therapeutic virtue – some kind of touchstone for people to approach, a connection to authenticity. That can seem odd – very often what's bought people to therapy is an entrenched sense of resentment, of their circumstances and the people around them. They rarely need much help getting in touch with their anger, it's bubbling up through the cracks of everything they say and do.

There's a vague idea, rarely spelt out, analysed or explained, that anger that gets expressed is good – it's internalised anger that's the problem. There isn't a great deal to support that – certainly, there's plenty of therapy going on in prisons and young offenders' institutes with people who have been spectacularly effective at expressing their anger. Bottling up anger may well cause us all sorts of issues but so can expressing it. It's anger that's the problem, or more precisely, the cause of our anger, which is hurt or fear. If we're spending too much time hurt or frightened there's a problem and it's either the world around us or it's us.

Are we getting angrier? Is modern life making it worse? It's a popular idea.[168] People have argued increasing levels of anger and resentment are having significant effects on society and that's what lies behind apparent global shifts towards more polarisation, populism, nationalism and identity politics, challenges to confederations and alliances like the EU and NATO, and climate accords, culture wars – even the idea of a snowflake generation, primed to feel slighted and dealt with unfairly.

We have experienced massive increases in population density in modern times – even as resources grow, our sense of people around us and competitiveness grows too. And we're not just more crowded together physically, connectivity has also increased dramatically. We are much more aware of a much wider range of people, what they have, what we haven't, the views they hold, how they're different to us. And we can talk to them, or about them, and publicly, we can air our views in a way we've never been able to before.

In particular, we can express grievance and aggression without much in the way of immediate practical consequences – we can say what we like, we can grandstand and our targets can't reach us. Outrage has always been an effective tool in mass communications. This may be even more true of social media – a well-known piece of research in China suggested that anger is significantly more effective than other emotions at spreading across the internet.[169]

There's been a significant shift in the way we buy products and services which are integral parts of our daily lives. We depend on multi-national corporations which have become largely unaccountable to individual customers and we deal with them online. Those companies depend on process, increasingly automated, for the efficiency they require to manage businesses that size. When we, as individuals, encounter problems with these services, we're often quite powerless – there's no-one to appeal to, often there's no-one even to talk to. If you have 10 million customers, it would be an absurd business practice to devote time to looking with care into the concerns of an individual customer. So long as your service levels aren't discernibly worse than the handful of competing businesses left – all of whom share a similar scale and business model to you – all you need to take care of is price and marketing. It wouldn't be surprising if all that had quite a powerful effect on our sense of how the world was treating us, offending our innate sense of fairness and self-worth, on a daily basis. There might be a very significant indirect cost we'll never be able to measure for all those synergies and savings driving cheaper consumer prices.

We're never going to know whether we really are angrier than we used to be. How could you test anger levels against different points in history with any degree of credibility? And there was enough grievance and resentment around last century to fuel two world wars. But we might be able to see signs that we could be treating anger differently, or at least certain types of anger. Rage has recently become respectable – socially approved, applauded (for the right people, in the right setting), something to be claimed, a source of personal pride.

You can see it in book titles – *Rage Becomes Her: The Power of Women's Anger, Eloquent Rage: A Black Feminist Discovers her Superpower.* In early 2020 the *New York Times* ran *A Female Rage Reading List: 16 Books That Scream To Be Read.*[170] It's not just female and black writers: titles like *The Subtle Art of Not Giving A F*ck* and *Everything is F*cked*[171] convey the same kind of take-no-prisoners, back-to-the-wall and coming-out-swinging mentality (the books themselves aren't actually much like that but somebody thought it was smart to market them that way). It was the dominant note, from both sides, in the 2018 Senate Judiciary Committee hearings on the appointment of Brett Kavanagh to the Supreme Court. You can see a kind of socially sanctioned outrage in celebrity red-carpet activism (we've had celebrity protest and support for counter-cultures before, but this indignation seems different, more mainstream, almost a required element of the celebrity package). Righteous anger seems to have become a ticket to work and all sorts of people are ready to jump on board.

Is this kind of anger coming more to the fore because there's actually *more* inequality and injustice now? Or is it that there's more awareness and intolerance of inequality and injustice now? Maybe there's a sense that now is a time to make a push, an opportunity has come to level all sorts of things and the tipping point requires the biggest shove? Maybe we've become less prepared, or able, to live with inequality as an idea;

maybe all the connectedness has made it feel too painful, too destabilising? Maybe we've got quicker at translating hurt into anger, more attracted to the idea of expressing our anger and resentment, maybe we've got more used to stamping our feet?

In his book *Spite...and the Upside of your Dark Side*,[172] Simon McCarthy-Jones makes a case for our readiness to go out of our way to punish people who have offended our sense of fairness as an important positive social force. Of course, he concedes, it can be destructive, it can generate atrocities but also, he suggests, it functions as an essential stabilising force, bringing balance to society, and a powerful agent for social progress. That's an interesting and plausible idea – our predisposition to grievance and resentment helping to keep us all safer from exploitation and oppression. Certainly, anger and outrage have been potent tools to drive change. Maybe it's wider than that, not just reactions to our personal circumstances, maybe the fuel tank for progressive movements invariably includes at least equal parts of aggression in the mix – we're as interested in getting someone as we are in doing any good? It's not love that will save us but resentment – a *via negativa* driven by spite? But that presupposes we might eventually run out of other people to hate and, in the meantime, it's easy to miss the personal cost these ideas can exact from the individuals caught up in them, and the people around them. One of the themes Helen Lewis explores in her book, *Difficult Women – a history of feminism in 11 fights*,[173] is just how unhappy some of the very effective activists she writes about were and how much trouble they caused other people.

We've seen the long-held theory that depression is caused by reduced levels of serotonin couldn't be maintained – the link between serotonin levels and low mood wasn't found.[174] But other well-established lines of research going back many years have suggested firm links between serotonin levels and aggression.[175] More recently, people's willingness to inflict harm on others, and to retaliate against perceived unfairness in laboratory scenarios, were reported to be affected by manipulation of serotonin levels. Increasing serotonin levels, using SSRI antidepressants, had the effect of reducing the intensity of people's reaction to unfairness and their aggression to others.[176] We may not know how antidepressants 'work', but there is evidence that one of the effects of the drugs we most commonly use to treat depression is to reduce people's sense of grievance and resentment – to modify how they react in situations designed to stimulate feelings of unfairness – and their willingness to hurt other people.

A righteous cause can provide a license for self-assertion, a cover for lashing out, for taking out our own resentment and hostility. You can mask a lot of aggression with a *Be Kind* hashtag – it's always other people who are the unkind ones and ripe for attack. And the people who are uncaring are the ones who don't care about the same things we do. You can turn your own life into a righteous cause – a determination not to put up with it. But how far is the absolute determination not to be a victim preceded by a predisposition to feel like a victim?

Are we just getting better (or worse) at expressing anger? Do we 'learn' to be angry? Does expressing it make us angrier? We don't know any of these things. But something that is clear is that when people come for help, one of the things pushing them there is anger – a sense of unfairness and resentment which spoils the way they think about themselves and other people and gets in the way of them being able to take pleasure in their lives. There is a risk here. If we are privileging anger in this way, it's likely that we have lost sight of its very important connection to mental health.

4

LONELY

Something else you notice about people who come for help – which seems like two things, but they're very closely connected – is that they are often very anxious and feel very isolated.

Anxiety is another one of the major topics in psychology which you come across in every branch. Evidence has been found to suggest that we're programmed to prioritise threat, trauma and negative outcomes.[177] Researchers investigating memory and emotion have claimed that we remember events associated with negative emotion more clearly than non-emotional events[178] and even suggested that negative emotions we experience now can actually re-write the way we remember things that happened in the past.[179] Evidence that our fear of loss outweighs the value we put on potential gains[180] is one of the most influential contributions psychology has made to market economics and investment theory and won the Nobel Prize.

All of that seems intuitively plausible but, at the same time, this being experimental psychology, there's also research supporting a widespread bias in the general population towards optimism.[181] Other researchers investigating memory and emotion say they have found evidence that, in fact, we remember positive events better and for longer than negative ones.[182] Evidence suggesting optimism is associated with more positive outcomes in all sorts of walks of life, including physiological health – such as the incidence of,[183] and recovery from,[184] heart disease – and that pessimism is a predictor of depression,[185] has led to the foundation of a whole branch of 'Positive Psychology' devoted to trying to teach people to be more optimistic.[186]

But there's contradictory research to that too: for example, denying any effect for optimism or pessimism on recovery rates for cancer and HIV.[187] And suggestions that pessimism itself (rather than life stressors once properly controlled as a variable) may be overrated as a predictor of depressive symptoms[188] particularly with age.[189] Even that optimists, or the wrong kind of optimists, might be at greater risk of depression than pessimists following negative life events[190] or that optimism, in the form of positive fantasises about the future, is itself a predictor of depression.[191] Psychologists have even produced evidence to argue that in many situations a less optimistic expectation actually produces a better outcome,[192] and that this extends to fundamental aspects of life like primary relationships[193] and earning capacity.[194] Others have associated optimistic illusions of performance with high levels of narcissism.[195]

Whatever that tells you (or doesn't) about optimism or pessimism, none of it comes anywhere near the way we actually live with anxiety and the way it affects our lives. All of us are constantly affected by anxiety and much more powerfully than most of us would like to think. And the reason we don't want to think that is, of course, because that doesn't make us feel good about ourselves. It feels like weakness and cowardice and, because we can't so readily see it happening to other people, inferiority – and we're busy trying to feel OK about ourselves.

In fact, we are anxiety machines. Anxiety pervades our whole experience, in one form or another; it's a continuous backdrop to our lives – it's like the water fish swim in. Everything that happens affects our anxiety levels and, when nothing is happening, that affects us too. We're scared, we always have been – the motor is running all the time. It seems to be a feature shared by all sentient life – dormouse to chimpanzee to astronaut, it helps to keep us alive. Our ancestors were the ones sufficiently alert to threat to survive long enough to reproduce – the more relaxed citizens never made it that far.

But it's not much fun. It dominates us, the quiet moments we celebrate are the ones we manage to subdue it – in the snow in the mountains, the sand between our toes and the sea curving beyond us on the beach, the immensity of space mitigating the things we feel anxious about, making them seem trivial. We constantly pursue distraction and a big part of what we're trying to distract ourselves from is anxiety. But even when we're not aware of our anxiety, it's still affecting us.

You can analyse anyone's life by how they manage their anxiety (or don't). Work, sex, TV, screens, social media, exercise, all get recruited and so does pointless activity for the sake of it, empowering rage, nagging, control, criticism, irritability, the pursuit of wealth, autocratic bluster and pomposity, domineering, dependency, people pleasing, trying too hard or studied casual indifference. Humour gets in here too – the tortured comic. A mind which can't stay with itself, which has to undermine the situation and whatever it's feeling and find it ridiculous. As compulsive and evasive in its own way as alcohol abuse.

Alcohol, and that includes moderate social drinking, is a conspicuous response to anxiety. We know that really – we acknowledge to ourselves that we do it to relax but we don't generally admit what we're relaxing from. People talk readily about stress (which is just another word for anxiety but feels more acceptable because it sounds like it's more directly attributable to something outside us) or say it's to get over inhibitions (which come from anxiety) and oil the wheels of social interaction or just to have a good time (as if it wasn't possible to do that without dealing with something that's in the way first). And in the short term at least, alcohol can be an effective way of managing anxiety – clinicians refer to it as 'self-medicating' for a reason.

Alcohol's prevalence round the world is a very good illustration of how pervasive anxiety is and how much it affects people, even when we're largely unaware of it and it's not causing any particular trouble. And in parts of the world where alcohol isn't allowed, or widely used, there's usually some form of alternative mood-altering substance which is sanctioned or tolerated – hashish, opiates, nicotine, shisha, coca, khat, betel – and carries out a similar role. Again, part of the attraction, the justification, for these substances is usually explicitly stated to be relaxation.

It makes sense to imagine that the opioid crisis in North America owes some of its power to the same anxiety-quelling properties – certainly research has suggested an association between opioid misuse and sensitivity to anxiety[196] and it's reported that more than half the opioid prescriptions in the US are to people with mental health issues.[197]

In the last decade or two, we have enthusiastically embraced yoga and mindfulness, often explicitly as ways of managing anxiety (or stress or well-being as we'll prefer to call it). We're prepared to spend an awful lot of time, and money, and to recruit all sorts of substances and activities, trying to relax.

We may not be alone in finding chemical assistance. Researchers have found that various primates are tolerant to, and regularly eat, fermented fruits and other food sources which contain alcohol.[198] Some have claimed evidence that at least some primates, given a choice, will actively select food sources with a higher alcohol content over alternatives with equivalent nutritional values but with lower alcohol levels or none.[199]

The scientists so far have confined their speculation to potential evolutionary advantages conferred by a tolerance for fermented food stuffs providing a wider range of source and one which might be easier to find (because fermentation tends to produce a strong smell). But these are anthropologists and zoologists and approaching their research from a very different perspective. The idea that these animals might be using alcohol for pleasure or relief, to manage anxiety levels, in the same way we do, isn't one that they're likely to follow, at least in a professional context.

Even in the happy state of having anxiety under control – running at low levels so they're largely unaware of it and it isn't making them behave in dangerous or destructive ways or cause trouble to other people – it isn't difficult for a careful and astute observer to detect the way someone's anxiety fluctuates from moment to moment from the way they behave and react to what's happening around them. And unfortunately, it doesn't stay like that, all the time, for anyone.

There is always plenty to worry about – work, money, relationships, health, other people we care about. At times everyone will feel overwhelmed and like they can't cope, even if only momentarily, and that's always a deeply unpleasant experience. Few of us won't have encountered at some point, maybe waking in the early hours, a sense of gloom and despair which is all the more disturbing because we can't immediately find any reason for it.

For many though, the way they experience anxiety is much more intense and debilitating. Many people who come for help, come specifically for help with anxiety. And the most common forms of anxiety people come for help with are to do with other people. We are intensely social creatures and a great deal of our emotional life has to do with how we see ourselves relative to other people.

Social situations where we feel exposed to unfamiliar people or we're expected to perform can become the focus for acute anxiety. Sufferers may try to avoid those situations altogether or they may be able to endure them but experience extreme distress and only after they've gone through periods of intensely anxious anticipation.

The anxiety around these situations, and the anticipation, introduce an element of performance where there may not have been one. Sufferers often come to feel they're being scrutinised, even in situations where no-one is watching. People scared of flying, or confined spaces, will imagine they're being watched, whilst the people around them are usually entirely oblivious to what's happening.

Even when they're on their own, they might imagine people they know judging them as they struggle with their situation. And they don't need to invoke any external critic – we've seen that we're always primed to feel inadequate and sufferers are usually ready to judge themselves ferociously for being in this predicament in the first place and how they're handling it on this occasion.

Where anxiety attaches to specific kinds of situation like this, it is usually an expression of a wider anxiety about the self and how others see us and think about us. It may be possible to reduce the anxiety associated with the specific situation – by devising coping strategies or controlled exposure to the triggering situation – and sometimes that can be enough. But often, the underlying ideas about the self and others will continue to generate distressing levels of anxiety – which is unpleasant enough anyway – and that anxiety will find an outlet by attaching to some other specific trigger which might be equally or more disruptive or debilitating.

And the ideas about the self and others which cause the trouble are the ones we've been talking about around inadequacy – the vague shameful sense of not being good enough, of being unworthy. The idea that we are covering up some peculiar defect which carries with it the fear of being exposed – no-one could love us if they knew what we were really like. As well as attaching to the specific situations we find to be anxious about, these ideas involve a deeper sense of unease, a fear of something unspecified and awful happening.

Here's journalist Moya Sarner talking about the 4.a.m experience when you wake up and feel a vague, generalised anxiety you can't find a reason for (and notice how her immediate reaction was self-blame – she's doing it wrong):

> I would regularly wake up with a pain at the back of my throat and a vague sense of jittery doom that sucked all the peace and pleasure from my life. I blamed myself for these feelings. I told myself they came because I had not done enough exercise – so I did more exercise.[200]

The vague sense of jittery doom has a link to the same underlying fear – the fear of being inadequate and rejected. The unspecified awful thing that's going to happen is exclusion and isolation, being completely alone. Perhaps waking at 4.a.m in the wrong frame of mind, in the dark when everyone else is asleep, gives us a taste of what that might be like.

In the worst cases of breakdown, that's all that's left. The mind shuts down, there are no other ideas – just a sense of extreme isolation and a huge petrifying fear with no clear ideas attached. Sometimes referred to as 'primitive agony', 'unthinkable anxiety'[201] or 'nameless dread',[202] it's a terrible experience brilliantly described by Andrew Solomon in *The Noonday Demon*.[203]

Exclusion

Fear of being rejected, excluded, abandoned is one of the most powerful ideas in our heads. Maybe that shouldn't be at all surprising. Membership of the group seems to be essential for survival in many areas of the natural world: starling murmurations, sardine shoals, prides of lions, troops of baboons. And, after all, we are just very sophisticated monkeys – why wouldn't we still have this echo of our early evolutionary history in our heads?

In fact, people working in this area suspect our sociability goes much further than anything we might have inherited from our primate ancestry. Researchers believe that early human brains went through a period of explosive growth in size – an increase of more than 250% in less than 3 million years and much of it in the last half million years.[204] They argue that this massive increase, in a very costly organ in terms of physiological resources, can't be explained by ecological demand.

The argument goes, we didn't need a brain that size to compete effectively with other species (other primates have been able to do that perfectly well) and, as the brain requires so much energy, there must have been another good reason why we developed that way. Leading theories hold that most of what the brain developed into as modern humans evolved, developed specifically for the purpose of enabling more sophisticated social relationships.[205] That is, we didn't develop that brain to achieve ecological dominance – we did it because we'd achieved ecological dominance and, more than anything else, we needed to get along with each other.

Relationship formation, membership of groups and communities, these researchers suggest, is primarily what the modern human brain is for. If that were the case, no wonder that we'd be so vulnerable when social relations feel threatened or break down. Rather than an evolutionary hangover with no modern purpose that we can't shake off, in an age of hyper-connectivity anxiety about exclusion and abandonment has never been more relevant.

We need to be careful here – the only scientific evidence is some data (a very small number of very old skulls) indicating that the human brain developed massively over a short (in evolutionary terms) period of time: the rest is pure speculation. It's always so easy to get carried away and try to get the evidence to do more than it can.

Neuroscientists claim that they have found that some of the same parts of the brain which are believed to be involved when we process physical pain are activated when we experience social rejection.[206] At some level, they suggest, we really do feel rejection or betrayal with a similar intensity to a knife in the guts – our nervous system treats exclusion and abandonment on a par with survival-threatening physical injury. Separate research has indicated that painkillers can be effective to treat the pain of social rejection in the same way as a bad back.[207] Remember too, we've already seen that antidepressants are routinely prescribed for fibromyalgia, sciatica, chronic back and neck pain.

It's tempting to see all this as pointing, however tentatively, towards some kind of overlap in the neurological basis for psychological distress, like exclusion and rejection, and physiological pain. But, judged, on it's on terms, as science, that's not very convincing or conclusive. It's not just that many other explanations other than the ones put forward would be available to explain the facts, the facts themselves really aren't sufficiently coherent to demand an explanation. And, anyway, in practical terms none of it adds anything to what we do already know – loneliness and isolation tend to make people extremely unhappy.

We are tremendously attuned to groups. Responding to those punishing internal ideas about inadequacy doesn't just get stuff done on an individual basis, it helps to organise us into groups and societies, which gets even more stuff done. We are fixated on membership, who's in and who's an outsider, who is like us and who isn't. We can draw more or less impermeable boundaries around any area of difference between us and other people: race, nationality, gender, religion, class, sexual orientation, and these boundaries can very easily fuel aggression and conflict.

You can see the dynamic in the merciless way children (and not only children) turn on the one who can't seem to pick up on the right cues for acceptance in the same way as the others. That ruthlessness is partly driven by a ferocious anxiety about belonging – we're so anxious about it not being us that gets the wrong side of the group, that we feel actively better, relieved, if it's happening to someone else. If we see it starting to happen there's a pull to join in (and certainly an aversion to getting in the way of it) because, if it's happening to them, it can't be happening to us. Horrible but standard and, however well we may sometimes manage to behave, we're all probably less innocent here than we'd like to think.

For the victims it can be absolutely traumatic – particularly for the serial or persistent victims in childhood. For them it can create lifelong scars – it can be lethal. But it's not all passive suffering, exclusion can generate powerful feelings of resentment and aggression. Researchers have produced evidence using social manipulations in laboratory settings[208] but that victim's impulse to hit back is obvious and it's all around us.

Confusing ourselves and other people

People hate being alone when they don't want to be. Everybody knows that about solitary confinement or the loneliness of the elderly, but the idea of being abandoned is always with us – we never get over it. It goes right to the heart of our closest relationships and it takes any number of forms in our everyday experience. When people aren't physically there, we need them in our heads. Our basic reaction to anything we don't like remains to deny it and that's how our minds operate at a deep unconscious level in relation to feeling alone.

This denial mechanism is called Narcissism and it has to do with blurring the distinction between us and other people. It's not, as commonly believed, only about being egotistical and grandiose and dominating other people. For our purposes, the point about the myth of Narcissus isn't that he was in love with himself, but that he couldn't tell the difference between himself and someone else. There's an equally prevalent form of 'thin-skinned narcissism' in which people feel dominated and taken over by other people. Both processes are usually going on in us at the same time.

Narcissism is a term which gets used rather unkindly and labelled dismissively (probably because of the narrower meaning it's acquired in psychiatric classifications). In the sense in which it's being used here, that's not really fair. It's a powerful natural bias and it's not something any of us can be immune from. Neuroscientists have claimed evidence that the part of our brain which we use when we think about ourselves is activated in the same way when we think about the people we're closest to.[209] That conclusion requires a familiar kind of speculative engineering from the data but if it turns out to be valid, maybe that's part of why it's so hard to take on board how separate these people really are – we use the same part of the brain to think about them and ourselves.

Whether neuroscience has found a physical locus or not, the confusion between us and other people is real and rooted deep in our minds. We have to wrestle with this issue all the time and one reason it's so hard to overcome is because it's unconscious – it takes place in thought processes over which we have very little influence. Another is that overcoming it involves coming to terms, at some level, with the very unpleasant reality that, in many ways, we are much more alone than we want to be.

The result is that often we may be able to acknowledge the situation rationally – we can say all the right things about how we know we ought to think – but, in our unchecked imagination, our unconscious processes and fantasies, we tend to go on treating other people (and particularly the ones we depend upon) as if they were extensions of us, our creatures. That makes it more difficult to allow them the separateness and independence they deserve.

Deep down, we expect them to do what we want them to do, when we want them to, we assume that they can read our minds and anticipate our needs and we feel let down and resentful when they don't. You can see this fantasy of union coming to the surface in the language of romantic love – look at Valentine's cards: 'You're Mine', 'I'm Yours', 'We're One', 'Together For

Ever'. We can have other ideas at the same time, we can know – more or less – that it's not entirely true, but we can never see through it entirely. It's like a trompe l'oeil and (part of) the eye is always taken in.

The problem is a kind of existential fear about loneliness and isolation that we do not want to acknowledge. We didn't want to go up to bed to sleep alone in the dark as children and we don't like this idea either. We can feel it even when we're with the people we're closest to – underneath it all, we're still, at some level, alone. So, we convince ourselves of an unconscious desire, that the people we need will think like us, see things the same way, want the same things we do, and understand us, and that we understand them – more completely than can be the case. Why not, we depend upon them?

Most of the time the illusion holds and most of the time it pays to live like that. We often develop an unspoken pact with the people that are most important to us and we try to help each other sustain things. Through countless compromises, modifications of what we say and do, even what we think, most of the time, without knowing it's happening, we try to be what we believe the other person needs us to be. And they do the same for us. There's nothing wrong with that in itself, there probably isn't another way to do it.

When the ways in which the people we depend on most don't really think like us become more starkly clear, at the times this illusion breaks down, it's alarming and we can feel acutely alone, even if they're physically in the room or beside us in bed. When it breaks in that they are separate people, alien, with their own desires and agendas, they don't always think and feel the way we want them to – we have to confront the fact that, in the end, there is a risk we can't completely depend upon them.

Divorce statistics, friends' experience, newspapers, films, novels, our own relationship history and, perhaps, previous experience in this relationship, may all suggest to us that it is quite possible that there is a limit to how far we can depend on even the people we're closest to – but none of that penetrates readily into our deepest thoughts. And it's impossible to know because people are complicated and unpredictable – they can be astonishingly thoughtful, selfless and generous. They can make immense sacrifices for us – people give their lives for other people. But they can't think like us all the time, they can't read our minds and always do what we want them to do and from time to time everybody will feel disappointed, let down and alone.

We can't eradicate narcissistic thought patterns – you can't expect to hold clearly in mind all the time that other people are separate and independent and conduct your whole life like that. Anyone who thinks they have is deluding themselves. And, in fact, imagining people are (like) you is a very convenient and effective tool for navigating the world – it's a good short cut for working out what's happening and at some level it's true.

But other things are true too and there are other ideas which need to be involved to get a healthy balance. Other people have their own lives, their own motives, fears and insecurities. How much should we expect them to be there for us, to do what we want them to? We've talked about this already. It isn't something you can get 'right', like solving an equation – everybody struggles with it their whole lives. We can do it better or worse and, hopefully, we gain a more realistic and benign view of ourselves and other people as we go through life – it's certainly an important part of growing up. When the illusion is too strong, if people can't see clearly enough that other people aren't them, expectations become unrealistically demanding and they're doomed to disappointment, and a more permanent and intense sense of grievance and resentment.[210] We've seen some of what that can do.

A degree of confusion between us and other people isn't limited to our closest relationships, it's more fundamental than that. It's widely believed that an important part of the way personality develops is through a process of identification. Most of us probably recognise that idea – without knowing we're doing it (at least most of the time) we attempt to borrow and assimilate qualities we admire or envy in other people. The idea is that, at least to some extent, we become the people we are because we want to be like other people we come across. If that's right, the divisions between us and others are blurred right from the beginning, our own sense of self is assembled from fragments of other people.

And we do the same thing the other way. As well as taking aspects of other people into us, we cannot help but put ourselves into situations we come across, as if they were happening to us – our imaginations run riot. Marie-Therese Walter was 17 when she met the 45-year-old Pablo Picasso who was married with a child at the time. They became lovers, their relationship lasted about eight years and they had a daughter. Marie-Therese was an inspirational muse for Picasso at a time of dramatic development in his art. She features in a number of his most prized works and many regard her as the most inspirational figure in his career. The relationship ended, after a great deal of pain to everyone concerned, when Picasso started a relationship with another woman much younger than himself. Picasso supported Marie-Therese and her daughter for the rest of his life. After her daughter was grown, and a few years after Picasso had died, Marie-Therese killed herself.

How you respond to this story is dictated by who you are and what's happened to you. It's as if you see yourself in it and respond accordingly. Your reaction is likely to be affected by your gender, age, whether you're married, whether you've ever been an interloper in a relationship, perhaps whether you're a creative yourself, and innumerable other factors from your personal history.

This kind of identification of yourself with a situation affecting other people – as if it were happening to you – is the way we think. It's natural, it's how we experience things, how we process them at first blush. There isn't anything wrong with that in itself – in fact, again, we don't have another way of doing it. But it can be a trap. If that's too much of what we bring to the situation, it can lead to experiencing too many things too powerfully, as if they were happening to us, an extension of our lives. When too much that doesn't really bear on us at all feels personal, there's too much skin in the game.

Whenever we find ourselves upset by something that doesn't directly affect us, it's because at some level in the mental processes, we are imagining it's happening to us. We've already talked about how noticeable it is that the causes and social issues we're likely to feel strongly about tend to be closely connected to us: things happening to people we feel are like us or ideas which have become very tightly bound up with our sense of ourselves. This is why. It can produce a sense of community and support, which helps mitigate the idea of being alone and isolated, but it also creates a sense of shared injury, even though we haven't actually been affected at all.

You could call this empathy, which it is, but taken to extremes there's also a confusion, an over-identification. These situations aren't happening to us, we're not involved in them, we don't know these people, there's a limit to how much we really care about them or they care about us. That kind of over-extension of ourselves can lead to an over-developed sense of expectations that too much of the world will behave the way we want it to and an over-developed sense of injury when it doesn't. There's always plenty to feel disappointed and angry about in the world but it's a different kind of disappointment and anger when people are struggling too much to tell the difference between themselves and other people.

Groups are powerful things – not only in terms of what they can achieve but also in terms of how they affect the individuals who belong to them. There are whole branches of psychology, organisational dynamics and business consulting looking at the way experience and emotion get intensified and distorted in groups.[211] We feel things differently when we go through them with other people – it's why you have crowds at football matches, mass religious events and stadium rock.

It can be a subtle, pervasive effect, capable of applying in a wide range of situations where we might never suspect it – research has claimed the flavour of chocolate, for example, may be intensified simply by eating it with someone else.[212] It can be much more overt, though equally difficult for those affected to detect. There's been a stream of research since the 1960s investigating group polarisation[213] – the tendency for people to get drawn into taking up more extreme positions in a group. A clip of the Nuremberg Rally shows you what this kind of intensification of experience can do on a mass scale.

A sense of disappointed expectations, of not being treated fairly, is a more powerful experience in a group. And our sensitivity to exclusion creates a particularly strong impulse towards mutual recognition and affirmation when people feel they have that experience in common. Researchers claim to have shown this in the laboratory – a visceral sense of oneness, which they call 'identity fusion', based around a perception of shared suffering in a group.[214] But when the foundation of the group is itself a sense of injury and grievance, the dynamics of membership – the blurring of the distinction between self and others, the tension between exclusion and inclusion – can become amplified. Groups necessarily entail boundaries between members and outsiders – when membership is based on something as personal and emotive as an experience of inequality and injustice, those boundaries can easily become disputed and unstable. The result can be a hot house of grievance and confusion between who's you and not you. You can see this breaking out periodically on the borders between gender, race, sexual orientation, gender identity and disability.[215] A series of unstable coalitions and people finding themselves the wrong side of a line.

A spirit of community, a sense of like-mindedness and a shared sense of outrage are effective agents of change. But that doesn't mean this kind of group dynamic isn't capable of having an adverse impact on individual group members and, in particular, how they're affected by the ideas that dominate people when they come for help – grievance, resentment, a sense of exclusion and the consequences they hold for self-esteem. Those ideas can become enlisted under cover of a righteous cause and they can become magnified and more entrenched through participation in a group.

At extremes, these unconscious group processes can also pose a threat to other people. Solidarity in a shared sense of injustice is how the Suffragettes succeeded and the Velvet Revolution, but researchers in this area argue that the results from their questionnaires and predictive models will help us better understand gang related violence, holy wars and suicide attacks.[216]

Our susceptibility to confusion between us and other people tends to increase as soon as we start to gain influence or power over them. And any relationship of significance involves a degree of mutual influence and power. In some situations, it can be a necessary warping or distortion of reality – leadership or management roles involve an expectation that people will do what you want them to. When we take up that role, we take up that idea. Within that setting it may be appropriate, at times, but it's always a distortion – other people aren't real enough, not wholly, at an emotional level whilst you're in that role. They're there to do things for you and it's necessary to disregard their feelings, needs and agendas. That's a powerful, intoxicating idea and some care is always going to be needed to stop it leaching out into other situations.

In fact, an enthusiastic receptiveness to the idea that people are your creatures and there to do your bidding, can be a useful practical tool in business. And in other situations, at least in the short term – personal relationships too. An expectation that people will do what you want is quite a good way of getting them to do what you want – don't ask and you don't get. But leadership positions, wealth, fame, beauty, being spoilt – any situations which distort and manipulate people's readiness to do what we want – are potential traps, even for the most self-aware.

As ever, the confusion is mainly unconscious – whilst it's happening, we'll be able to say all the right kinds of thing about respecting other people's independence, our rationalisations for what we're doing will be impeccable, but what we say to others, and what we tell ourselves, isn't what's really driving our expectations, how we see things and how we're behaving. People *are* separate and independent – forget that too completely and we're in the grip of a serious misunderstanding which is likely to end up in powerful undercurrents of grievance and resentment.

Every dominant partner in a relationship pays a price and every CEO ends up feeling betrayed. It's an old truth that getting our own way too much isn't good for us and this is why. Maintaining a healthy respect for other people's independence and a realistic set of expectations of what they should be prepared to do for us, and an appreciation of what they are doing for us, is never easy. Get it badly wrong and it can cause a lot of trouble.

Loneliness

Because anxiety has so much to do with other people, exclusion and isolation, other people can be a very effective way of reducing anxiety, particularly the vague, formless variety. But because anxiety has so much to do with other people, exclusion and isolation, being with other people generates its own anxiety too. We agitate each other a little just by being with each other. There is always, however residual, however deeply buried, an anxiety about being criticised, judged, found unworthy, rejected, left.

We are stuck between agitation and loneliness. When we're in a relationship, and we feel better – an ease and contentment like something missing has been supplied – we sense that this feeling is dependent on the other person. We could lose it if we lost them and that would be terrible. We sense it would cause us a great deal of pain and might do us a great deal of damage.

So, we fear it, and we fear the other person a bit, and resent them for the power they hold over us. That can get inflamed when we find them disagreeing with us, taking a different view – it can feel like a betrayal and a warning. Of course, we can rationalise it, rise above it, but that little qualm is still there. You can't think it away entirely because it's how you're meant to feel. One of the most disturbing things for couples who are getting on badly is premonitions of splitting up. Even whilst they're furious with each other, and fantasising about being on their own, one of the things that frightens and angers each most about the other is that they're not getting on and the idea of parting. The sense of inadequacy can cause immense problems between people but it's also what makes us vulnerable, part of what makes us need each other and how we can help each other. It's a large part of what intimacy is – we can feel better about ourselves because other people are there.

It's disorientating, giddy stuff; people who claim to be immune from that kind of insecurity are bull-shitting – themselves, if not you. Loving someone brings immeasurable risk – they could get harmed, they might die, they might stop wanting you. There is no way of protecting yourself from that risk but it can destroy people.

To be comfortable enough in a relationship, we need to be able to keep this agitation in check enough. Close relationships play themselves out in themes of intimacy, loneliness and feeling overwhelmed by other people. We need the right balance of company or intimacy and independence and solitude – it's never settled and it's different for different people.

It's unrealistic to expect that to feel right all the time. If we're not occasionally affected by feelings of being oppressed, dominated and in danger of being engulfed in our closest relationships, with the people we care about most and depend upon most, something's probably wrong. And what's wrong could well be the other person *is* feeling like that a lot of the time. It's something perhaps we ought to be prepared to feel for the people we depend upon most and share our most intimate life with.

It can be too much – if the way anyone feels in a relationship becomes dominated by grievance and intense ambivalence, it may be less painful to leave. Loneliness isn't just a matter of having people around or not: the worse we feel towards other people, the more isolated we feel; the more resentful we are, the more cut-off and anxious. Leaving might be an opportunity to reboot, to approach situations with a greater sense of other people's separateness or to find someone better accommodated to our appetite for intimacy. Or it might just be easier to be alone. For some, it's very difficult to trust the situation enough. Maybe the feelings of anxiety about dependence are too much. Maybe the claims and demands inherent in other people's separateness feel too overwhelming. Either way, being alone can become a refuge from the way that being close to other people makes us feel.

We have a tendency to talk about relationship breakdown quite forensically, even approvingly, in books and articles. That's misleading – in the real world, relationship breakdowns are more often extremely disruptive and damaging events. More damaging than the parties are usually prepared to recognise or admit, even to themselves. They change people, not always for the better and they can be catastrophic – they can kill.

That's true for living in abusive or dysfunctional relationships too. But none of us like the idea of being the kind of people who are needy or over-dependent (that's a very good way of making ourselves feel inadequate). Since we're all reluctant to recognise our own complicity in relationship issues, it can feel altogether easier if it's all the other person's fault, or we've just grown apart, or it's time for a new phase in life and the only, or best, option is to leave. The result is a bravura tendency to underplay the impact of relationship breakdown, even extol it, in the way we think and talk about it, at least in the public arena.

The trauma of relationship breakdown will change the ways we relate to other people and many of those changes are likely to be permanent. It will invariably undermine to some degree our sense of faith in relationships and faith in ourselves in relationships. Whatever we may like to think about our ability to learn valuable lessons from difficult experience, as often, it prompts a retreat into more rigid self-justification and more determination that others will do it our way. That's only likely to lead to a deeper, more wide-ranging sense of grievance and resentment. Every break-up can jeopardise our capacity to attach to other people and our chances of avoiding a particular form of unhappiness.

There is a huge irony here. The reason it is so difficult to live with a full acknowledgment of other people as separate, independent people, with their own view of the world and their own agendas, is because it invokes feelings of abandonment and loneliness. But if we can't do enough to treat others as real, separate people, if we can't respect and cope with their independence enough, in the end it's equally isolating – we are the only person there.

That's more obviously the case if our difficulty with independence takes the form of trying to control other people. It's lonely dominating other people, being the boss, being the dominant partner in an unequal relationship. All those unhappy celebrities and rich people calling the shots, feeling alone and still left feeling aggrieved because the world can't do everything they want it to.

But something similar is going on for a dominated partner. If we can't recognise our own separateness fully enough to avoid feeling engulfed by someone else, there's a failure to take responsibility for our own requirements involved, an implication they will get taken care of by someone else. Those expectations are likely to be similarly unrealistic – no-one else can read our mind – and the likely response to those disappointed expectations is a resentful sense of being overwhelmed, taken over by other people's separateness and agency. It's a similar confusion about where other people end and we begin. And when we retreat to a private inner space and withdraw ourselves, we're the only person there – it's the same experience of loneliness arising from other people's separateness and the same grievance and resentment from expectations not being met.

Most relationships, in fact, involve both people taking up more or less dominant or influential and dominated or compliant roles in different aspects of the relationship and at different times. So, both will have both these experiences at different times. The more people can see each other as separate and independent, the more they can see those roles alternating and the more they can see each other as they really are, rather than figments in each other's heads. And it's only in those times when we can see other people as separate and independent enough – see them better as the people they really are – that we have a solid basis for connecting with each other and a genuine potential to share experience together. That kind of connection makes us feel very worthwhile – it's a powerful, healthy counterweight to ideas of inadequacy.

Being close up and paying attention to other people as separate and independent expands our lives. It can show us things about the world which we couldn't see otherwise – ways to think about or see things our minds couldn't come up with but that seem as natural and automatic and right to them as ours do to us. It's almost like a magic mirror in a story or a portal – glimpses available into other worlds. This is on offer all the time but it can be disorientating and frightening. Maybe the person we're doing it with can't be gentle and careful enough, maybe we can't be. Often it is too much, we can't expect to be able to live like this all the time. But the more clearly we can see other people as separate and independent, the more potential there is for this to happen. To do that involves passing through a kind of loneliness first and somehow managing to trust and give yourself into the relationship whilst all the time living with the possibility of being disappointed, or disappointing, and left.

Anxiety again

Anxiety isn't just an abstract philosophical concept or an existential insecurity about us and other people, it's a real, daily practical issue, for everyone.

For one thing, anxiety, remember, converts easily into anger. For another, it's contagious – anxious people make other people feel more anxious (which is probably, at least partly, to do with it being the lit fuse paper for anger). Feeling anxious is an unpleasant experience – we don't need to catch it off other people. That can be difficult enough when we come across anxious strangers, it's harder to be involved in close relationships with people who suffer badly from anxiety.

It's a profound influence for children when a parent can't contain their anxiety. To a small child, relying on its parents for protection, an anxious parent is the most frightening thing of all. That's not just a matter of specific incidents and triggers (you don't just inherit a fear of heights because your mother had it) or even living in fear of outbursts of anxiety-fuelled irritability, it's a subjective quality like a flavour affecting everything. An over-anxious parent is a powerful lens through which to be introduced to the world.

Anxiety makes it harder to bear other people's problems – empathy goes out the window and quickly turns into solution finding, exasperation or nagging or diminishing the issue. These are all serious deterrents to being with anxious people.

Anxiety can get tied up with controlling others. We've talked about trying to get people to do what we want as a response to our fear of separateness, a type of denial. It's also an unconscious strategy to manage anxiety, either generalised or aroused by specific situations – we can feel better if it seems other people are doing what we want, we gain a sense of control over the situation. People who become dependent on it may start barking instructions, or manipulating people, when they start to feel anxious. Or they may need to get people to do what they want enough on a continual basis in order to feel OK at all. Neither is likely to endear them to those around, but it feels so natural and compulsive to them that it's likely they'll have very little idea they're doing it. This can become a spiral – the struggle to control others becomes ever more desperate the more people come to rely upon it because, when it feels like it's failing, that itself provokes intense anxiety. Everybody depends on this mechanism in childhood, people who don't get a fair opportunity to learn that other people are separate and independent as they grow up will find it harder to give it up.

Crucially, anxiety makes us feel bad about ourselves – we feel irrational, scared and weak, and we feel inadequate. That's the main engine of anxiety disorders – not the anxiety itself, but the reaction people have when they find themselves feeling anxious, the way that makes them feel about themselves. It's a similar mechanism to the one we saw in relation to OCD – it ignites the idea that we're not good enough, there's something wrong with us. Anxiety symptoms get exacerbated and reinforced by judging yourself for being anxious and concern about being found out and judged by others for being anxious. That's why the worst anxiety triggers are so often about elements of performance and scrutiny by others, like public speaking.

And anxiety makes people feel resentful towards other people who seem to have less anxiety. Sometimes, people aren't particularly aware of their anxiety and to sufferers that may seem a very enviable situation. Maybe – but everyone *is* anxious and *is* affected by it. It's true, people do a better or worse job of managing and containing their anxiety, but nobody wants to feel anxious and no-one particularly wants to think of themselves as an anxious person. Sometimes it's a matter of people signing up to a version of themselves they'd like to be and trying to stick to it, like when people say they don't care what other people think about them. It's a decent working hypothesis that when we aren't prepared to admit that we are affected by what other people will think of us, it's because we are so affected by the idea of what other people think that we don't want to be thought of as the kind of person who cares what other people think. Denial on this kind of scale isn't necessarily a blissful escape from anxiety, it's a potential trap.

Quite often, these can be people for whom the idea of things going wrong is so difficult, so threatening that they can't really let their minds take on board the possibility of it happening. They actually aren't capable of feeling their own anxiety – at least in relation to particular situations or settings – it would be too much for them, intolerable. That may have its practical benefits but it doesn't always go well when things do go wrong - and at some point, things go wrong for everyone. Anxiety is going to be affecting us all, all the time and we're going to be reacting to it. From time to time, it is going to be making us feel agitated, unsettled and unhappy. If we can't see, or own up to it, it might be causing us a deal of trouble we can't admit to. It isn't an option not to care what other people think and it isn't an option not to be affected by anxiety.

Anytime people are 'too much' of anything, anytime reactions are out of proportion and there's an excess going on – too angry, too emphatic, too concerned about money or status, or looks or age, laughing too much, too loud, trying too hard, drunk – anxiety is part of what's driving it. Most of us are going to do a better job of living with our anxiety if we can accept the reality that it's going to be there, that it's meant to be there, and see past it. That way, we have a better chance to avoid it compulsively directing our behaviour, without us knowing about it, and to avoid inflicting it on others (which, since anxiety is so intimately tied up with other people, will only increase our reasons to be anxious).

And to the extent we do manage to fool ourselves, we'll probably fool other people too. That may feel gratifying because we've managed to come across as the person we'd like to be, but we've deprived other people of the opportunity to see us as the person we really are. We've made it that much harder for them to come to terms with us as a complete, separate, independent person. And we've made ourselves that little bit more lonely as a result. And since we never manage to fool ourselves entirely, we'll feel fake as well which will make us dislike ourselves. And, whether we can recognise it or not, that creates anxiety.

5

A LOOP

What we've been talking about are the ideas which dominate people when they come for help – inadequacy, resentment and isolation. Here's writer Chris Brock describing the difficulties he was struggling with before he found a way out through meditation. Words expressing these key themes have been emboldened for emphasis – you can see how they thin out as he gets into the second half and starts to talk more about recovery:

> Meditation helped me drag myself out of **self-loathing** and **failure.** I spent my 30s **angry**, confused and depressed – until my wife suggested I try listening to my breath. In my 20s, my career escalated pretty quickly. I started out in London as a reporter on a magazine writing about design. Before I knew it, I was living in Manhattan, working as an editor and loving it. I felt like I was living the dream. But by the time I was in my 30s and living back in the UK, things had changed. After a bullying boss crushed my **confidence**, I chose to try a freelance career instead. I was good at what I did. I won a few awards and gained plenty of recognition, but I couldn't make ends meet. After 10 years of slogging away, I found myself working shifts as a driver for a supermarket just to pay the rent. I was getting up at 3.30am to deliver groceries to people all over the south of England. My **self-esteem** was in tatters and I was **broke, bitter** and confused. I couldn't figure out how to get along in life. It was as if I had **missed that day in school when they** tell you the **secret** to making it all

work. No matter how hard I tried, it always seemed to be the **other guy** who had the car, the house, the holidays and the happiness. No matter how hard I worked I never seemed to get **my big break**. My CV was awesome, my LinkedIn profile on point, and I was applying for job after job after job. Yet it felt as if life kept **passing me by**. I was wallowing in **self-pity**. I **resented** everyone who had, in my head, found the **secret** to life and **stolen it from me** in the process. My mind constantly raced with **negative thoughts**. I was filled with **self-loathing**. I would lie awake at night **cursing myself** for not being as good or as clever or as capable or as qualified as **the next person**. I **cursed my life decisions**. And I **blamed the world** and **everyone** in it for my problems. I had, after all, followed all the advice and done **everything I was supposed to do**, and here I was, stuck in a rut. **Angry**. Confused. Depressed. It was my wife who suggested I try meditation. I don't know what persuaded me to give it a go. Perhaps it was because I'd tried everything I was supposed to do on the outside, and all that was left was to try to look inside. And so, one day I closed my eyes, focused on my breathing, and when I noticed my mind drifting into that **self-loathing** internal dialogue, I simply brought it back to focus on my breath. I did this over and over again. For weeks. And things began to change. When the chaos inside my mind began to quieten, it became apparent very quickly that it was no-one's **fault** but my own that I was where I was. I had allowed the things that had happened to me on the outside affect me so much on the inside that I had adopted a **victim mentality** and spiralled downwards. Suddenly I saw that if my failings were due to my own actions, then my successes could be, too. I began to change my perspective. I focused on my strengths, all the things that I had rather than all the things I didn't have, and I suddenly found that I was surrounded by beauty, by wealth, by an abundance of joy. Don't get me wrong, it didn't happen overnight; it took a couple of years. But as my mental outlook improved, my real-world results changed, too. Job offers started to come my way, and before long I found my career back on track and my confidence along with it. Financially, things improved, and my social skills began to return. My life turned around almost completely. It's not all a bed of roses. I still have bills to pay and debts to clear. I still get **angry** on a regular basis. But these days, while depression lurks in the background and pops up occasionally, I have the tools to manage it. Staying positive is like going to the gym. For me that centres around meditation. It gives me a chance to slow down, to gain perspective and to take a break from my **ego**, my **anxieties** and my **self-doubt**. Meditation enables me to cut through the chatter and see the beauty in life. It allows me to choose who and what takes up space in my thinking, and to choose happiness and joy over misery and rumination. If we could all spend a couple of moments every day to concentrate on our breathing and look around at the world, we might find there is a lot less to **complain** about than we think.[217]

These patterns are in all of us but they are right at the forefront of people's experience when they come for help. You find a different balance in different people, and in the same people at different times, but whenever you talk to patients or clients, and in any case studies or accounts by anyone who's needed help, it's the same ideas in action.

These ideas are connected, magnetised – if you're feeling

one, you'll be feeling something of the others too. If you go to therapy to talk about not feeling good enough, you'll end up talking about anger too. If you go to therapy to talk about anger, you'll end up talking about not feeling good enough. And you'll always talk about feeling alone and wanting more from other people.

Feeling anxious makes us feel inadequate and weak and ideas about inadequacy make us anxious – about not being equal to the situation, about being found out. Anxiety is always quick to tip into anger and anxiety about exclusion leads to grievance and resentment – about the circumstances which made us feel inadequate (because the idea of unfairness offers relief from feeling inadequate), about the idea of exclusion, about the people who don't seem to be affected in the same way. Feelings of grievance and resentment make us, and our lives, feel defective and inadequate. So does feeling excluded and isolated. Isolation makes us anxious. So do grievance and resentment. It's a tight loop. We go to strenuous efforts to avoid these ideas, or to avoid being aware of them, and we react strongly against them when they affect us. The things we do in the course of those reactions – to try to escape these ideas – are most of the things we do to make life worse for ourselves and other people. Ideas about inadequacy, grievance, exclusion and rejection are undercurrents to everyone's lives, below the surface level where we try to live – rational, collected, saying and doing the right thing. They're always there and if they get too strong, people go under.

Studies into bereavement have described how these ideas are implicated in some of the most painful aspects of losing a loved one. Famously – an integral element of the Kubler-Ross grief cycle [218] – people who have suffered a bereavement often experience powerful anger and guilt. The anger or resentment often finds several targets, including other people who haven't been struck by this blow and the person who died. It's unfair – we've lost someone we loved and depended upon. It hasn't happened to other people – their lives are still carrying on normally. Why wouldn't we feel resentful? Maybe the person who's died could have done more to take care of themselves, maybe they've died in avoidable circumstances. Why shouldn't we feel angry – they've left us and they allowed it to happen? It's often the same thing at the end of a relationship: even if we're the one who left – *we had no choice, they made it so we had to* – we feel resentment and we blame someone else for something that happened to them. The feelings of guilt are to do with not having been good enough: an irrational sense of responsibility for not having been able to save someone, or not having done enough for them when we could, or not having resolved some outstanding issue between us, or for having hurt them in the past – any number of different ways of somehow having failed.

Anytime these ideas get too strong a grip, people fall into rumination – intrusive, punishing thought patterns they can't break, round and round the same themes: self-blame, inadequacy, shame, guilt, grievance, resentment, self-justification, isolation, anxiety. When it happens, they live too much inside their heads – they're distracted and pre-occupied. It gets in the way of concentration, blocks kids being able to learn, affects our performance at work and affects us at home.

It's not just the major life events: the great losses, the obvious blows – everyone lives with this gravitational pull all the time in their daily lives. How we feel about everything we do or that happens to us – elated, frightened, frustrated, contented, calm, sad, hopeless – is to do with how it makes us feel about ourselves.

Most of us will experience it getting too strong, getting caught in this loop, at times. Some live like it for years at a time or pretty much their whole lives. No-one's immune.

There's no need to just write these aspects of ourselves off and just say everyone's crazy underneath, everyone's a bit mad. We're not mad, there's more dignity, more endeavour, more courage in it than that. We're intelligent, rational, resourceful, competent, but these are our wildest parts – there's not much balance, not much nuance, in these ideas and there's not much balance or nuance in us when they're in control.

6

WHY?

If these are ideas and patterns which affect us all, there's an obvious question – why is it that for some people things get to the point that they need help? What is it about people or the things that happen to them, that push them to that point? By now you shouldn't be surprised by the answer – we don't know.

We've seen a lot of good reasons to be extremely sceptical about data on mental health. However, it is there, in industrial quantities, and simply ignoring it seems as wrong-headed as cherry picking the bits you want to suit your personal convictions and treating them as gospel. But, if we are going to try to use it, where do you start? How do you differentiate between a mass of inconsistent and contradictory data?

Stats again

There are three main sources of evidence at the moment: government, academic research and research from charities. Though, as more private healthcare providers move into mental health, we're seeing more research from them. When you compare them as sources, government data has a number of clear advantages. It's usually professionally compiled to the highest standards – generally outsourced to academic institutions but often better resourced, in terms of depth and sample size, than purely academic research could manage or evidence from charities or the private sector. Very importantly, it tends to be the only research which gets carried out on a regular basis over extended periods of time, allowing comparison and evaluation of trends.

Crucially, it's also independent, in the sense that there's no obvious axe to grind. The interests of private businesses in persuading us there's a problem which needs to be addressed by buying something from them are self-evident. But, equally, the amount of money charities can raise is in direct proportion to how urgent and acute their cause is seen to be. The more money they raise, the more secure the jobs of the people working in them, the more significant and important their work appears and the bigger the empire for the people running them.

Maybe it's a selective process (as has been reported with academic research funded by drugs companies[219] - the research that doesn't fit what you wanted, doesn't get finished or never gets published) but, for whatever reason, what comes out of charities always seems to lend itself to reporting at 'the Aliens are coming' end of the spectrum. In chapter 1 we mentioned a survey conducted by the charity Action for Children in 2018 which suggested that one in three teenagers were suffering from mental health issues. It was widely reported, though the affected age groups in some reports varied between 13-15[220] and 15-18,[221] and taken up enthusiastically by political organisations[222] and individual politicians.[223] It's no longer on Action for Children's website[224] but it's left an impression. We also saw in chapter 1 that the NHS's own survey carried out at the same time found that one in 10 five-15 years olds were suffering from a mental disorder and the NHS's figure for five-19 year olds was one in eight.[225] That's a startlingly different picture from one in three – and significantly less than the one in six reported for the adult population.[226]

The best resourced and most in-depth research into mental health in the UK (though confined to evidence from England) is the Adult Psychiatric Morbidity Survey, which we've already met and which has been carried out every seven years since 1993. Even with the resources available to the government, sample sizes in the APMS can start to get quite small and unreliable as you drill down into different population characteristics. The results still suffer from many of the problems discussed – issues to do with self-reporting, difficulties in managing samples and controlling for extraneous factors, poor correlation between questionnaires and independent diagnosis and the problems with the diagnostic categories themselves.

In addition, the APMS may involve underestimates relative to the population as a whole because it applies only to private households and so excludes institutions like prisons, care homes and students in communal accommodation, all of which you might expect to be at higher risk from mental health problems. The authors believe that these excluded samples would be too small to make a difference to the national estimates but we can't be sure.

According to the 2014 APMS[227] (the most recent available) the highest rates of common mental disorders are associated with:

- young women
- people who live alone
- people who are unemployed or in receipt of benefits
- Black women
- women in large households
- smokers.

The authors also found a positive link between chronic physical illness and mental disorders. The survey indicated that people over working age have a much lower incidence of mental disorder than people in working age. And the authors reported that, with the exception of Black women, there was no evidence of significant variations in rates of mental disorder between different ethnic groups.

In their summary the authors said their findings were compatible with increased social disadvantage and poverty being associated with increased risk of common mental disorder. They also pointed to the possibility of exposure to social media as having a role to play in the higher (and recently increased) rates of disorder found in young women.

It's important to note that the authors weren't saying their results were evidence that social inequality and poverty cause mental health problems, they were saying their findings were consistent with there being an association between the two. That's as much as anyone can say at the moment. Statistics can show that two things tend to go together but it's much more difficult to show that one causes the other. ESA (Employment and Support Allowance) was the benefit paid at the time of the last APMS to people who were unable to work because of a disability. How much does the fact that 66% of ESA recipients were reported to be suffering from a common mental disorder reflect that poverty and unemployment make you ill and how much that a great deal of disability that prevents people working takes the form of mental illness?

But the careful way the evidence has been worded is not how it's received – by journalists, commentators, politicians and even mental health professionals. Many people regard it as proven fact that mental health problems are caused by social inequality and poverty (other potential causes tend to fade out at this point) and the evidence is statistics like those revealed in the APMS. From that it follows that reduce social inequality, and we will improve mental health. That simple (if it were simple to reduce social inequality). In the meantime, there's no need to think too hard about the causes of mental illness or perhaps even treatment – you can't expect too much from the mental health professions, it'll all have to wait for a more equal society.

We've seen this before – highly granular data, rigorously compiled and responsibly caveated, treated as established scientific fact to demonstrate a conclusion it can't support. There might be half a dozen other potential explanations which are also consistent with that data. There might be a couple of papers from rival university departments which critique the methodology and come up with quite inconsistent or contradictory findings. The 'science' is out there, it's been published and its available for people who want to use it as 'proof' of what was only ever tentatively conjectured or even, as with the APMS, scrupulously avoided. And other science is out there for the people who want to disagree with them.

The higher rates of common mental disorder found amongst the unemployed and people in receipt of benefits *are* compatible with an association between mental illness and social disadvantage and poverty but (if this is science) that's not the same as a clearly established link (let alone causation). Social inequality and poverty are not the only aspects of unemployment and receipt of benefits that could plausibly be associated with mental health problems.

Unemployment involves financial disadvantage, but it can also bring a sense of exclusion and potentially difficult issues around purpose, identity, use of time, distraction from anxiety. Benefits involve severely restricted financial resources but they also involve difficult ideas around care and sufficiency, dependency, control and power. To what extent might those be the factors associated with mental health issues? Social disadvantage is a broad term; which aspects of disadvantage might be most associated with mental health problems? Get this wrong, we get the response wrong (if we were going to be making a response). More money might not, of itself, be a very complete or even effective solution – we might need to think harder than that.

Certainly, other factors highlighted in the APMS have a less clear association with social inequality and poverty. Should we connect living on your own with poverty or social disadvantage? All other things being equal, it is generally more economical to live with someone else, so people living together should have more money than they would living alone. But perhaps that also shows that it can often take a degree of financial independence to live on your own and so perhaps we should expect that a good number of people who do that might be better off financially?

Do poverty and social inequality fit with people over working age, who are no longer receiving a salary, having (much) lower rates of disorder than people of working age? And, if social inequality and poverty were, at least in statistical terms, the main drivers of mental illness, wouldn't you expect to see a much greater variation between different ethnic groups? And, actually, that's a good question we'll come back to.

It would certainly make sense, in terms of the ideas talked about in this book, for mental disorders to be very strongly associated with social inequality and poverty. We're all primed to feel bad about ourselves, to feel unfairly dealt with and resentful and to feel anxious and excluded and lonely. Those are the ideas you find again and again in people who've come for help. Ideas of inferiority, inadequacy, shame, guilt and exclusion are entrenched in inequality – and so is resentment. So, you would expect any group whose experience might be more likely to stimulate those kinds of ideas, more often and more intensely, to show higher rates of disorder. But social inequality and poverty, of themselves, are looking like quite incomplete explanations.

It would hardly be surprising to find that people living on their own are more likely to feel lonely and isolated and that this might have important consequences for how they feel about themselves and other people and their mental health. In addition, many of them may be on their own as the result of divorce, relationship breakdown or bereavement, which may have taken their toll in terms of how they feel about themselves and levels of resentment and isolation. Though, of course, relationship breakdown may itself have been the result of pre-existing problems.

Unemployment presents some serious challenges for mental health but so can work. The workplace generally involves complex relationships of power and reliance on others, providing plenty of scope for unfair treatment, abusive behaviour, resentment and anxiety about performance. Perhaps that might explain why the APMS results show much higher rates of disorder for people of working age than people who've reached retirement age. Or perhaps (statistically at least) we just mellow as we get older.

Similar issues to do with workload, stress, self-esteem and resentment might contribute to the increased levels of disorder found in women in large households. You might also expect that struggling with chronic physical illness could make people feel worse about themselves, prone to resentment and isolated.

Could the higher rates of disorder found among smokers (surprisingly significant statistically and more so for heavier smokers) be due to higher levels of smoking among socially disadvantaged groups? Could it be people who have high levels of anxiety using smoking as a self-soothing tool or perhaps down to low self-esteem breeding a reckless disregard for their own health? Could it be related to the direct physiological effects of nicotine? Or something of all of them? Who knows? It begins to feel like we're grasping at straws but the truth is we always were. We don't have clear evidence to support the belief, which we all surely share, that poverty and social inequality are drivers of mental illness.

And it's always been obvious there must be other causes, because not everyone who becomes mentally ill lives in poverty or under obvious social disadvantage. The 2014 APMS refers to a number of factors, other than the ones they identified from their own results, which the authors feel have been demonstrated by research elsewhere to be associated with mental illness. They include work stress, social isolation, being a member of some ethnic groups, poor housing and fuel poverty, negative life events (bullying, violence, bereavement, job loss), childhood adversity, including emotional neglect, physical and sexual abuse, institutional care, low birth weight, poor physical health, a family history of depression, poor interpersonal and family relationships, a partner in poor health, being a carer and problems with alcohol and illicit drugs. That's looking pretty comprehensive but a little difficult to know what to do with.

If we go to the Mind website it adds to this list, experiencing discrimination and stigma, severe or long-term stress (which could be wider than work stress), significant trauma (including military combat or being involved in a serious accident) and physical causes such as a head injury or neurological condition.[228] The net is now cast so wide it doesn't feel like it can tell us anything very useful. It feels like this whole line of enquiry is failing – it's not making a lot of sense anymore to ask what it is that happens to people to cause them mental health problems, because the answer seems to be pretty much anything.

And we're not done yet: researchers have also suggested associations between the bacterial population in our gut and depression,[229] between inflammation and depression and a range of other mental health problems[230] and, of course, genetics.[231] Evidence has even been put forward to suggest toxoplasma infection (a common and usually asymptomatic infection most people won't know they have, which is caught from infected meat or the faeces of infected cats) has a role to play in depression.[232]

To round things off, if there's evidence that social and financial disadvantage are linked to mental health problems, there's also evidence that wealth and privilege are too. Studies of upper- and upper-middle-class students in the US reported they suffered twice the rate of depression, anxiety, suicidal thoughts, loneliness and somatic symptoms (physically unexplained headaches, stomach aches etc) as the national average. The highest levels of alcohol abuse and drug use were found amongst students with the highest family socio-economic status. Narcissistic exhibitionist scores of boys at elite private schools were almost twice as high as the averages among more diverse samples. Affluent girls were found to be almost twice as likely to base peer admiration on physical beauty than girls of lower socio-economic status. Wealthy girls were also apparently more likely to 'externalise' emotional upset, through emotional displays, rule breaking, delinquency and alcohol and drug use.[233]

It seems at this point it might be more useful to shift the focus back to the ideas that seem to be associated with mental illness rather than what may have happened to people to get them into these states of mind or, for now, the physiological phenomena (neurotransmitter levels, bacterial composition in the gut, infection from cat shit) or genotype that might (or might not) go with them. A sense of inadequacy, lack of self-worth, grievance and resentment, exclusion and isolation – it seems these tracks are so well laid down in our minds that there's a limitless number of different ways of getting on them.

Of course, there will always be circumstances, experiences and conditions that will make it more likely that these ideas will become more exaggerated, intrusive and cause trouble but they're not confined to inequality, deprivation, abuse or neglect. The problem isn't always not being loved or not getting enough. A seam of research into 'Expressed Emotion' in family relationships suggests that 'over involved or intrusive' relationship styles, including excessive self-sacrifice and protectiveness, can cause harm, as well as critical or hostile relationships.[234]

This isn't a new idea – concern about spoiling a child storing up mental health difficulties later in life is probably as old as the family. It's an important principle in psychoanalysis that children need to encounter enough frustration of what they want, and they have to encounter it safely enough, in order to be able to develop emotionally.[235] Some have argued that sufficient experience of adequately supported frustration, not getting your own way early and consistently enough, is a necessary precondition to learning to think.[236]

The idea of the 'spoilt child' has been investigated by psychologists since the 1940s. It used to be called the single child syndrome but that's not really fair: there are plenty of people whose experience of siblinghood equipped them with a powerful sense of victimhood to carry into their adult relationships. Anyway, the term seems to have been dropped tactfully as birth rates declined and single childhood became more the norm.

Spoiling doesn't require a wealthy background: it's not about largesse with Christmas presents, it's about you and other people. Any child who doesn't get a fair opportunity to develop a workable accommodation in their mind between themselves and other people as separate and independent is going to come out of it with a distorted set of expectations. Unless and until they manage to get it straightened out, that's likely to lead to a difficult emotional life – of disappointment, frustration, grievance, resentment and self-dissatisfaction – whatever their physical, economic and social advantages.

And there – maybe that's it! That experience of endlessly disappointed expectations and frustration is an experience of things going wrong. Things feel like they go wrong for these people all the time – in their own way, as much as they do for people who can't find work or are victims of bullying or discrimination. That's what *all* these situations have in common – the idea of things being wrong, of things going wrong.

Whenever things go wrong, part of our reaction is about fault. Ideas about inadequacy and unworthiness revive and, with them, rejection and exclusion and feelings of isolation. It's too painful to stay like that, it has to be escaped and the nearest way out is ideas about injustice, grievance and resentment. And that's isolating as well – we're on our own. That's the loop.

And the *experience* of things going wrong has a subjective element: there's what happens to us and there's what happens when it meets our expectations and ideas about the world. Research involving children who had experienced court-documented maltreatment reported that their subjective accounts as adults of how they had been treated were much better associated with mental health issues than the objective evidence. Even for severe cases of maltreatment there was minimal risk of mental health difficulties, if there was no subjective report of maltreatment. But there was a high risk with subjective reports of mistreatment even if that wasn't consistent with the court records.[237] The way people felt they had been treated was apparently a much better predictor of mental health problems than the objective record of how they had been treated.

In a sense, people always 'talk' (think) themselves into trouble, which is why they can talk themselves out of it too (in therapy or without it). The balances are very fine, microscopic differences in how things are seen, what they mean, the experiences and ideas they do or don't connect to. It's about the articles of faith about ourself and the world in which we're most invested. They're mainly implicit – you'd struggle to put them into words for yourself – a culmination of what's happened in childhood and since, the way we've been affected by the people closest to us, the messages they've given us, the messages society has given us.

It's not just a matter of what happens – anything that makes us feel inadequate and inferior involves that loop. It could just be people not getting what they need in order to stay happy enough, not finding enough reassurance to stave off the anxiety and insecurity. And it's obviously true that many people experience social inequality and poverty or childhood abuse and neglect without developing serious mental health issues. You can't predict what will make the difference for different people but, when it happens, it's always about that idea of 'wrong', which everyone is carrying around inside them.

'How does it feel'?

Sometimes things going wrong is just things going wrong; experience of adversity can simply be a very adverse experience. Hyperemesis gravidarum is a condition affecting some women in pregnancy. Sufferers may feel constantly and severely nauseous, they may vomit 50 times or more a day, making it impossible to conduct anything like a normal life, often entirely restricting them to bed for months and causing severe vitamin deficiency (at a point when their bodies are subject to exceptional demands), significant weight loss and potentially lethal levels of dehydration. They often need frequent hospitalisation, isolating them from their families just when they might need them most.

A major life event, which presents enough change and upheaval anyway, becomes an intensely personal physical and emotional trauma. On top of the fear and sadness anyone in that position is likely to feel, it would be quite amazing if ideas of being inadequate – not able to do what you're meant to – wouldn't come into the picture from time to time. And why wouldn't you feel singled out, unfairly treated and resentful from time to time too? In the intensity of what those women are going through for months it would hardly be surprising if those ideas linked up with old ideas about inadequacy, failure and unfairness to become persuasive, dominant parts of their thinking. So, it seems only natural to find that researchers have indeed reported a significantly increased frequency of depression and anxiety in women with hyperemesis gravidarum.[238]

A good deal of research has already been carried out into the effects of Covid 19 on mental health. Unsurprisingly, it's tended to confirm various adverse consequences of the pandemic – infection, bereavement, economic and social consequences of lock-down – having a significant negative impact. One early study in Italy found that more than half of patients hospitalised for Covid 19 scored clinical levels on psychiatric measures one month after treatment.[239]

This research was actually looking at correlations between immune response inflammation and psychiatric disorders and the results weren't entirely consistent with the inflammation hypothesis. For a start, female patients suffered greater levels of depression and anxiety, despite having lower levels of baseline inflammatory markers, but, most interestingly, there was a pronounced inverse correlation between duration of hospitalisation and psychiatric disorder. That is, outpatients and people who spent less time in hospital suffered worse psychological problems from their experience than people who had worse infections (with higher inflammatory markers) and required more care.

The researchers suggested that less healthcare could have increased the social isolation and loneliness of the experience, leading to more psychological problems afterwards. That doesn't actually prove anything, but it doesn't do much to support the idea of inflammation as a very significant contributing element to mental health issues. It does, though, leave intact the idea that it's how we experience adversity that influences the degree of psychological harm we suffer when things go wrong – and that the form that harm actually takes is ideas about ourselves and other people. It's hard to feel so bad about yourself, so inadequate, or so unfairly treated and resentful, or so isolated and alone, if you're receiving highly competent, selfless care for an extended period. In objective terms, the experience is worse – maybe much worse – but in terms of mental health, the outcome seems to be better.

Takotsubo cardiomyopathy is a weakening of the left ventricle of the heart, with similar symptoms to a heart attack, following severe emotional or physical stress. It's been linked to spikes in stress hormones, which are also associated with depression and anxiety, and it's often referred to as 'broken heart syndrome' because of its association with events like bereavement, divorce, natural disasters and serious accidents.[240] The stress (the hormone spike and its immediate physiological consequences) is a physical state and the heart's reaction is a physical process but this physiology doesn't exist in a vacuum. It's ideas that generate that stress – you have to have some kind of love in order to be broken hearted by loss. And those are ideas around the themes we've been talking about – the loss of people and relationships you depended on to feel OK about yourself, the sense of isolation and abandonment when they're gone, the feelings of resentment, against them and other people, and the idea that you screwed up, you're screwing up, there's something wrong with you.

Things going wrong, feeling things are wrong, hurts us psychologically. It summons up the idea that the problem is with us – which doesn't feel good (inferiority and self-loathing). Or with other people – which doesn't suit us any better (grievance and resentment). Or, more usually, because one is so uncomfortable and the other one leads you back to it, leaves us oscillating between the two. Both positions make us feel alone and isolated. PTSD isn't 'just' about flashbacks and nightmares; sufferers very commonly also experience overwhelming feelings of inadequacy, guilt and shame, anger and isolation[241] and those are generally the symptoms that cause the most trouble.

Things going wrong, adversity, can take any form: bereavement, relationship breakdown, illness, injury, redundancy, exam failure, any form of rejection, exclusion, discrimination, getting older, loss of anything we value (including ideas about ourselves), fear, stress – anything that inflames the idea that we're not good enough or impacts or takes away the things we used to keep that idea away. Too extreme an experience of adversity or too constant a diet, can tip people into persistent tormented states of mind. It wouldn't be surprising if that could damage aspects of their physical health too.

A cultural distribution

The idea of wrongness and the experience of things being wrong, and going wrong, attach readily to race, gender, sexual orientation, class, socio-economic status and disability. These are all factors which can be made to carry ideas of difference, outsider status, inferiority or unfairness. And they are also factors which can make it more likely for people to experience disadvantage, inequality of opportunity, prejudice and discrimination in real terms. They can translate into very direct forms of adversity – anxiety caused by financial insecurity, unstable or unhealthy living conditions, over-crowding, a degraded physical environment, exposure to increased risk of crime or violence.

You might expect all this to contribute to a cultural distribution of emotion – different experiences for people sharing particular characteristics making them more likely to experience certain ideas and emotions more often, more persistently or more intensely. And you might expect to find that reflected in statistics on mental health.

The APMS doesn't report directly on sexual orientation, but a number of other sources have produced results suggesting significantly higher rates of common mental disorder for people identifying as LGBT in England[242] and the US.[243] The APMS shows significant differences in the rate of common mental disorders between gender. And we've seen the association with unemployment and socio-economic status. That all makes sense. The APMS doesn't directly address class or disability (though there are the positive associations with chronic physical illness and receipt of benefits and, in particular, disability benefits). The APMS does, however, directly address ethnicity and the evidence is that there is no significant variation in the incidence of common mental disorder across different ethnic groups. That's so surprising it deserves looking at in more detail.

The APMS does include evidence of ethnic minorities being more severely affected in some measures of mental health but they're not particularly useful. Figures for psychosis are higher amongst Black men and men in the Asian group. But psychosis is a very rare condition (affecting 0.7% of the population) which can't tell us much about the mental health of the population as a whole, and the figures for psychosis are already so small it's hard to have much confidence in them once broken down by ethnicity.

The APMS reports higher rates of drug dependency amongst Black men but that isn't a direct measure of mental health and, since it's inferred from regular use of cannabis, there are suggestions it might more reflect a culturally determined lifestyle choice than underlying states of mental health.

The most compelling evidence in the APMS about the mental health of different ethnic groups (the most compelling evidence in the APMS about the mental health of the UK population as a whole), is the data relating to common mental disorders. And that doesn't show any significant variation for different ethnic groups.[244]

Perhaps part of the reason for that is that, if there's a cultural distribution of emotion, there's also a cultural distribution of response and treatment. There are suggestions that mental health problems may be more stigmatized and suppressed in some ethnic groups or may simply be less favoured as an explanation of illness. For example, evidence suggests that, compared to a reference White British population, Bangladeshi, Indian and Pakistani people may be more likely to report somatic symptoms or concerns about physical health and less likely to report symptoms relating to anxiety and phobias.[245] Might that be a reason why those groups don't show higher scores based on questionnaire responses and structured interviews?

Maybe a combination of socio-economic and cultural factors within communities, and the possibility of institutional bias, means that psychological distress experienced in some communities is more likely to show itself in other statistics? For example, the Black population is significantly overrepresented in the criminal justice system.[246] Does that suggest that its more likely for Black people than for White or Asian people that they will end up involved with the police, rather than healthcare services, when they feel excluded, resentful and inadequate? That is a widely held view. It's also argued that racism within the mental health system can make a dramatic difference to ethnic minorities' opportunity to access mental healthcare and their experience within the mental healthcare system.[247]

Certainly, the 2014 APMS showed ethnic minorities accessing treatment for mental health issues at about half the rate of White British people, with the lowest rate for Black adults. Given that the scores for common mental disorders didn't vary significantly between different ethnic groups, that does suggest that people from ethnic minorities who are suffering from mental health issues are less likely to come forward for treatment than White people.

The official figures for detentions under the Mental Health Act (which removes any element of explicit self-reporting) show a very different variation between ethnic groups, with the highest level (289 for every 100,000 people) in the Black ethnic group, the lowest (72 per 100,000 people) in the White ethnic group and levels in between for Asian, Mixed and Other ethnic groups.[248] That seems hard to square with the broadly equivalent rates of common mental disorder found between different ethnic groups in the APMS.

But those statistics for detentions under the Mental Health Act are vanishingly small figures to work with (0.003% of a population). And why do we need to use disparities in accessing treatment or detentions under the Mental Health Act to draw inferences about levels of mental health problems in different communities in this way, when the APMS provides its own direct measure of the incidence of common mental disorder within different ethnic groups? Unless we think there might be a problem with the APMS data in this area?

One of the features of the APMS is that, unusually for surveys of this scale, it uses structured interviews and clinical evaluation of formal psychiatric questionnaires by trained assessors. So, it can claim to be less reliant on self-reporting and therefore, one might expect, less vulnerable to cultural bias within different communities. That may be naïve.

Structured interviews are still a form of questionnaire and these were administered by trained lay assessors. They're not magic windows into people's minds (neither are detailed assessments by professionally qualified clinicians) and they're standardised. The same question could evoke different responses from different individuals for all sorts of reasons – why not different groups too? Maybe there are undetected differences in the way different ethnic groups tend to respond which are masking real differences in the underlying mental health conditions.

And there is research suggesting quite wide-ranging differences between the ways different cultures present their mental states,[249] and, specifically, in relation to self-reporting and responding to questionnaires.[250] In fact, some of this research found these differences applying to the particular questionnaire and clinical interview schedule used in the APMS.[251]

To complicate things further, as the APMS points out, background and experience within ethnic groupings can be very different – for example, the statistics for Black people in the APMS would include recent migrants from Somalia and Black people born in Britain to British parents.

So, there's an obvious question to be asked – does the experience of living as a member of an ethnic minority in the UK contribute to mental health problems? And the answer is we're not in a very good position to say. In the end, it's another illustration of how little we do know and the difficulties involved in finding out.

What is certain is that, one way or another, we are all subject to unremitting social influences and pressures and they have a profound effect. We all have to consult our own mental health as individuals, we all have to try to find a way through.

Maybe the students from wealthy backgrounds suffering twice the national average rates of depression, anxiety and suicidal ideation[252] are going through a different kind of experience of adversity. Maybe they are suffering from a burden of intense expectation about what their life should feel like, about what they should be like. The more elite the background, the more idealised the pitch of ambition for how life should be, for what they should be – not careers necessarily, or not just careers, the kind of people they should be, how they should conduct themselves, how their lives should feel.

When their real experience can't live up to it (because nothing could) they're left with the idea they're falling short, that the problem is with them. Many among the wealthy and high achievers do suffer from an intense pressure for every aspect of their lives to be high enough 'quality' – it causes enough trouble for them, little wonder if it infects their children too.

Maybe a similar intensification of expectation, amplified by social media, has contributed to the increase in mental health problems reported amongst young women (that's an increase which is reflected in the APMS). We don't know.

Messages from family, friends and society colour how we think about ourselves, how we think our lives should be, how we think we should be, what we're entitled to expect. You can be hurt by messages that there's something about you that's inferior, you can be hurt by messages that you should be something you can't be or your life should be something it can't be or by ideas about what other people should be prepared to do for you. It all gets to the same place.

From a clinical perspective, it doesn't do much good to say the kind of experience of adversity – of things going wrong, being wrong – encountered through inflated expectations or aspiration is somehow less valid than the experience of discrimination or social disadvantage. The ideas evoked are the same and the experience can be just as intense and corrosive.

Wrong from the start?

Childhood experience is pretty much universally recognised as a central part of psychological development – the way we are now is shaped by what's gone before. Most people, and most schools of psychology, agree that our childhoods leave us better or less well equipped for the rest of our lives. You might expect that a childhood which left people ill-prepared would be more likely to feed a sense of inadequacy, of something being wrong and result in difficulties in establishing and maintaining supportive and positive relationships (which would have the effect of reinforcing the same ideas around inadequacy). Many argue it's more fundamental; that deprivation of some essential developmental experiences – the experience of being listened to and understood, an opportunity to attach securely enough, just being loved, for example – can create a more profound experiential deficit.

In a series of experiments in the 1950s and 1960s – now regarded very critically but at the time largely uncontroversial – infant rhesus monkeys were removed from their mothers and placed with artificial substitutes. Amongst other things, the research demonstrated that the infants preferred to spend time with an artificial mother made of soft, comforting cloth than a wire one which provided food, and showed extreme anxiety if confronted with alarming situations when their surrogate cloth mother was removed from their cage.[253]

This, together with the severe behavioural difficulties exhibited by many of the monkeys reared by artificial surrogates, was regarded as important evidence in support of developing theories about attachment and it had a significant practical effect on social policy. When you think about it, isn't it remarkable that we know so little about this subject that studies on a different species exposed to the most bizarre conditions miles away (in every sense) from its natural environment could actually influence theories of parenting and the way children were treated in children's homes, nurseries and hospitals? How much should we really take into the outside world from evidence that infant monkeys in a laboratory cage preferred an inert, artificial mother made of cloth to an inert, artificial mother made of wire?

More recently, the devastating conditions found in Romanian orphanages after the collapse of the Ceausescu regime provided an unexpected opportunity to study the developmental effects of quite extreme forms of neglect of children on an institutional scale. There have been dozens of studies, but very few hard and fast conclusions have emerged.

There is consistent evidence that, at the time they were found, high numbers of the children showed delays in cognitive function, motor development and language.[254] There is also evidence – more anecdotal – of disrupted regulation and expression of emotion and impact on patterns of relating.[255] Support has been claimed for the idea that, at least in relation to the more quantifiable, objective, areas of psychological function, the consequences of early neglect can be reversed and that the earlier the intervention the better.[256] But there is also evidence that often social and emotional problems persisted, even after apparently successful adoption, with children brought to the UK, for example, showing strikingly higher rates of contact with mental health services by early adulthood.[257]

There is evidence that some children had suffered from some degree of neurological impairment, with scans showing abnormalities in glucose metabolism in certain structures of the brain,[258] alterations in some regions of the brain and reductions in total brain size.[259] As total brain size isn't generally considered to be a very significant measure, and nobody knows what the precise functions of the affected structures are, or the extent to which alterations in brain development might have been caused, or contributed to, by diet or the physical conditions in the orphanages (or earlier), it's hard to know what any of this adds for now.

But the Romanian orphan studies have become the latest scientific touchstone for an old idea about the primacy of early experience – a one-off, once-in-a-life-time, critical window during which deprivation, or the wrong experience, is likely to lead to long-term or permanent problems with emotional life and mental health (and which, it's claimed, can now be seen in the development of the brain). What's missing in early experience, it's believed, can be necessary conditions for aspects of the human being to be able to emerge or flourish. And if that opportunity has been lost in early life, it can never be fully recovered (though some kind of compensatory approximation might be slowly and painfully achieved over time, often with the support of prolonged therapy).

You can argue about how much support the Romanian orphan studies do offer for that idea but certainly what they don't provide is much evidence of what the key forms of deprivation might be, what's missing – individual aspects of those orphans' experience affect many children in their own homes too – or how it is that they might affect people in the long term or permanently. Perhaps a way of thinking about what it might be that what would happen for early deprivation to cause those kinds of long-term or lifelong effects might involve a buffer against anxiety and experiences of isolation and ideas about inadequacy that's never been there, resulting in an unshakeable experience of something being wrong, for ever. Something to do with attention, attachment and protection that could weigh against the ideas everyone's born with about inadequacy and exclusion and unfairness, and it wasn't there enough?

You would expect that early experience must prepare us, better or less well, to respond to different forms of adversity, that is without being overwhelmed by ideas of inadequacy and exclusion and grievance. Perhaps, part of what happens is that early deprivation leaves people more exposed to these ideas in more situations. We're a long way from knowing.

So, to return to the question: why? What makes people ill? The best statistical evidence available tells us that various factors about adult lives are associated with higher rates of mental illness. They are to do with gender, age, unemployment, benefits receipt, household, lifestyle and physical health. Other evidence, less rigorously prepared in statistical terms, suggests a whole range of other factors are also implicated – including trauma, violence, alcohol or drug abuse and childhood abuse and neglect.

Looking at this range, it doesn't seem sensible to talk about any particular experiences – trauma, bereavement, relationship breakdown, socio-economic disadvantage, discrimination, even early neglect – causing mental illness, in the sense that you could say electricity causes a kettle to boil water. At the same time, there are conspicuous examples of situations which seem to have in common a capacity to feed the ideas – exclusion, inadequacy, grievance, resentment – which seem to cause most trouble to people when they suffer from mental illness. Early experience might undermine our ability to resist those ideas in general or in particular situations but, if you had to say what causes mental illness, it might make more sense to say it's those ideas themselves.

Ordinary human unhappiness

But, the more important impact those ideas have isn't mental illness – it isn't their capacity to push people into states of diagnoseable clinical depression. There are around 7 million people on antidepressants in England[260]– that's serious enough, but the UK adult population is 44 million[261] (which more or less coincides with the one in six adults suffering from a common mental disorder reported by the 2014 APMS[262]). The much greater impact these ideas have is their ability to spoil lives, to get in the way of people enjoying their time, to lend lives a peevish, fretful tone, to make people anxious, rigid and intolerant and take their anxiety out on other people and make them less happy. That gets us all.

When we talk about psychological pain or distress, we're often talking about pressure exerted by difficult ideas we don't want to have (and the unhappiness caused by the things we do to try to avoid them). It's a struggle we're barely aware of to keep at bay ideas about ourselves and others which conflict with what we badly want to think. Sometimes, it's a discomfort that's barely visible, only apparent in moments of irritation – a sudden snapping or lashing out – somebody pressing our buttons. Other times, it makes us wretched – twisting from one untenable position to another. In either case, and anywhere in between, it's a process of denial, trying to escape something.

When we are face to face with something we don't like, when we have to confront it, more often than not, we can come to terms with it. It may make us unhappy, for quite a while, but eventually we can usually get reconciled to the new reality. These hidden processes of denial go on and on and they create an internal tension, a sense that something's wrong and bring a restless, discontented flavour to the way we spend our time.

It's unavoidable: we're always prone to delusion and buying into ideas we like, which set us at odds with the way things really are. We're very good at telling ourselves the versions of things (especially to do with us) that we'd like. We're creative and words are powerful tools: we can construct plausible, often compelling accounts of things which leave out important but less appealing aspects or that fly in the face of something which is true and important. We fool ourselves all the time. It's not a matter of deliberately deceiving ourselves, it's just how the mind works.

But even if we're not aware of the ideas that we're pushing away, this thinking is still happening and affecting us and the reality we're trying to avoid is insisting on having its way. We are restless and discontented by nature: left to our own devices, we get bored, distracted and frustrated – we need change, we just want things different. Quite a lot of the time that pressure for things to be different is coming from ideas about ourselves and not nice ones. Those ideas affect how we feel about what happens to us, the taste left in our mouth by things and how we interact with other people. But most of the time we don't want to know they're there.

That anxiety everybody has about inadequacy is fed by every spiteful teacher, every childhood or teenage humiliation, critical mothers, severe fathers, dysfunctional bosses, competitive colleagues, romantic rejection, the advertising industry, every time some competitive parent gets the better of you in bragging rights and social media. It's endless.

People can feel crushed by it, every encounter haunted by the idea they're not up to it and going to get found out, humiliated – a crisis in every social interaction. In others it sets up an impulse to assert and prevail, which creates a brittle triumphalism, and when it fails (as it sometimes must), feels like a catastrophic confirmation of their worst, secret beliefs. People can become judgemental and harsh, against themselves and others. People can become overdependent on others for reassurance, leading to (secret) impossible demands and expectations. And the intensity of our own emotional states and dependence makes it difficult to see or hear other people, making us unsupportive in relationships.

We all have our quirks, our good days and bad days. At the wrong times, we can all look like basket cases. Subject any of us to enough scrutiny and you'd come up with some fairly odd-looking stuff (at least by the standards of behaviour we like to advertise or own up to publicly). Look at what we watch on TV and in films, the appetite for violence and crime. The other ways we get our kicks: computer games, shock jocks, celeb trashing magazines – all these outlets for hostile impulses.

It is considered perfectly normal for people to set out to get drunk for the sake of it on a routine basis. Look at the tantrums that go on in houses up and down the country (we're talking about the grown-ups here), the compulsive behaviours that don't do us any good (alcohol, porn, biscuits). People get stuck in mistrustful, grudgeful relationships. Or they become too mistrustful, or too rigid and intolerant to sustain close relationships at all.

Friends hold views and behave in ways that you find bizarre, but who's right? What is the right way to live? What's working too hard? What's greed and what's just a sensible, practical interest in money? What's healthy, physical curiosity and desire and what's compulsive, desolate promiscuity? What's a shallow, withdrawn inability to maintain close relationships and what's needy overdependence? Everybody takes up their own position on these things and they can work out well or badly but it's not always easy to tell.

We've all got anxieties, we're all plagued by self-doubt, we all mishandle situations and other people all the time and suffer the consequences. We all live in a state of fairly continuous agitation, we all make compulsive decisions and act against our own interests quite often (anyone who thinks they don't, doesn't know themselves very well). At times we'll all be very unhappy, feel overwhelmed and hopeless.

Nearly half (43%) of adults in the latest APMS self-diagnosed as having had a mental disorder at some point in their lives. At the same time, only one third (36.2%) of the people identified by the survey as suffering from a common mental disorder when the survey was conducted were receiving any form of treatment.[263] If half of us suffer at some point and two thirds of us don't need treatment when we're suffering, what are we suffering from?

According to the APMS, one in six at any point,[264] and according to the NHS, one in four over a year,[265] are affected by a mental disorder. But mostly these people get by: they hold down jobs, they bring up children, they pay rent or mortgages, they go on holiday – maybe they take antidepressants or see therapists, but they lead reasonably productive 'normal' lives.

What's ill?

So, what's ill? And what's well? Who's well? When should we say someone is ill? More than a third of people identified by the

2014 APMS as suffering from a common mental disorder at the time said that they had never had any professional diagnosis.[266] Do we really have a good basis for saying those people are suffering from a disorder just because they exceed a trigger score on a questionnaire?

What makes the difference – what makes some people get a diagnosis or treatment? Usually it's distress, it's unhappiness. How happy do you have to be to be mentally healthy? Some people bear more before going to the doctor. And should we think of everyone who comes for counselling or therapy as ill? It's true that people who come for help seem to want something to change but then who doesn't? Maybe talk is often just talk, a way of working things through or out, rather than a treatment when there's nothing to treat.

What's unhappy and what's ill? Sometimes people's lives may seem short on certain experiences and emotions – laughter, softness maybe – for some it can look like a hard, bitter way of living but maybe it works for them, maybe it feels OK. If a tree falls in the woods and no-one hears it, does it make it sound? If people don't know they're unhappy, are they unhappy? If people end up living isolated, anxious and resentful lives, or tormenting each other in toxic relationships, but they don't feel the need to come for help, and they're not causing enough trouble to other people to require an intervention, is there a problem and whose problem would it be?

But it's also clear that some people suffer a great deal. Sometimes more than they can bear and they kill themselves. Or they develop destructive, compulsive behaviours like eating disorders or alcoholism that cause serious damage to their physical health and degrade the quality of their lives. Or they can't carry on normal functional lives or they harm other people.

What's ill and what to do about it were always going to involve complex interactions with morality, social policy and law and economics but you probably imagined that psychiatry, psychology and psychotherapy would have had more to bring to the situation than we've seen so far. What about neuroscience – that's where a lot of hopes are pinned for the future. Is it going to be able to help on this?

Maybe, one day – it's hard to tell. But definitely not now. The direct access to physiological data (however difficult to translate into anything meaningful) and the unquestionable technological achievement involved, mean most people assume we must be a great deal further ahead than we really are. And, by and large, people involved in neuroscience seem pretty comfortable going along with that impression.

One idea being explored by neuroscientists is the model of a 'sociometer': a sort of fuel gauge of self-esteem, which plays a central role in brain function, underpinning key aspects of our emotional and mental life, needs to be regularly replenished to maintain itself at a certain level and is dependent on social feedback.[267] The evidence mainly comprises scans suggesting that closely related parts of the brain may be implicated in reduced self-esteem through social exclusion, the experience of physical pain[268] and violations of expectations of fairness.[269]

We've been talking a lot about reduced self-esteem through social exclusion and violations of expectations of fairness. Whenever anyone says they've found a part of the brain associated with some behaviour or idea, there's a temptation to think that somehow makes that behaviour or idea more of a 'thing', more embedded in us, more fundamental. But, of course, any thought, any idea we have, must have some sort of physiological corollary in the brain. Locating the physical location of a mental function (and the neuroscience is a long way off being able to claim that for any of the functions of a sociometer with any precision or confidence) wouldn't, of itself, take us very far – we know these things are real.

We were already sure that exclusion and rejection are damaging to us and we've made it against the law to discriminate against people based on factors that we consider particularly harmful. In the UK the current 'protected characteristics' are race, gender, sexual orientation and gender reassignment, disability (including mental health), age, pregnancy and maternity and marriage and civil partnership and religion or belief. That isn't going to protect us from bullying at school or every time we feel like an outsider or ugly or stupid or every time someone makes us feel a little worse about ourselves because we represent something they are frightened of, dislike or mistrust. We're not going to be able to eliminate that but it's capable of causing serious harm.

And we already knew that fairness is an important idea – we know what it feels like when we feel we're treated unfairly and we see how other people react. We didn't need to locate a site in the brain to know that. The problem is fairness is an elastic concept. In 2018, the regulators of the UK insurance industry decided that differential pricing (charging different people with the same risk profile different amounts for the same product, for example because predictive models tell them that someone in one post code is likely to be more affluent or simply because those policyholders never get around to changing insurers) was potentially unfair.[270] Differential pricing was not a new behaviour – it was something consumers and consumer groups had complained about for around two decades. For years it had been considered fair practice – the argument was that people should have some responsibility to take care of themselves and why should customers who took the initiative to shop around subsidise people who were too lazy or naïve? You can see the point and for years that was considered the fairest position – then suddenly that wasn't so clear anymore. In 2021, the position changed again – from the beginning of 2022 it will be against the rules to quote an existing customer differently from any new customer.[271] The people who don't get around to checking the aggregator sites when their policies renew will be protected, the savvy customers aren't going to be able to get such good deal. It's the 'new fair' and it's a complete about turn from the old fair.

There was a long period of time when a lot of people in the UK regarded slavery as a natural, 'fair' arrangement. And in Western Europe and North America, and, at different periods, in other parts of the world too. People who held those views were the product of their time. They took in the ideas around them without noticing, as naturally as they took in the air around them. You can be sure that people in 50 years' time will look back aghast at aspects of our society today which we regard as entirely unremarkable and fair. And what will attract outrage in the future isn't easy to predict from here. Fairness isn't very objective and it isn't an absolute quality – our ideas of fairness change all the time.

How then do we decide what's fair between us and other people in our relationships, in our daily lives? What we should expect from others and be prepared to do ourselves? That's going to be a quite different perspective between different people and probably for the same person at different times in their life. Given the strength of the mechanisms activated when our expectations are overturned, it's something that's likely to make a very significant difference to our emotional life. Get it badly wrong and we're going to spend a lot of time unhappy. Knowing the physical location of relevant functions in the brain wouldn't help us calibrate our own sense of fairness and expectations to keep ourselves healthy.

The sociometer model is a concept borrowed from old-fashioned evolutionary psychology going back to the mid-1990s.[272] Those psychologists, in turn, were adapting ideas which have their roots in the earliest days of psychoanalysis. Sociometer theory 'fits' the neuroscience, in the sense that the neuroscience hasn't contradicted it. It's hard to see how it ever could – it wouldn't matter much to sociometer theory which parts of the brain were implicated in which functions; the model would still hold together. But neuroscience hasn't added anything to sociometer theory either. You could imagine that it might one day – because something like that idea is surely right – and neuroscience might allow us to recognise the neurological basis of depleted self-esteem or a resentful hyper-sensitivity to perceived unfairness, maybe even to intervene more effectively at a physiological level. But, at the moment, the brain scans and sociometer theory are occupying entirely separate worlds, with no bridge to connect them.

In fact, so far, brain scans haven't told us anything that significantly advances our understanding of mental health or mental illness. Even the clearest and most concrete results from neuroscience suffer the same problem as a lot of experimental psychology – of themselves they tell you very little that's of any practical significance. So, as with experimental psychology, people try to link them to ideas – like the sociometer theory – which have been derived independently, and which might be useful and important, but for which there's only the most speculative connection. Often the result is to confuse the picture and devalue the science. You hear a lot about the cutting edge of neuroscience; at the moment, in terms of what it adds to what we know about mental health, there isn't one.

* * *

Perhaps for the time being, whilst we try to do the work which may eventually lead us to a position where we do have reliable, objective methods for defining, investigating and diagnosing mental illness, we just have to adopt a very pragmatic approach. If people are getting by OK, that's 'well'. If they're not, try to help. And who can decide whether we're getting by OK better than us ourselves? Go too far beyond that and you start straying into personal values, morality and social policy. Those may all be areas which can be closely connected with mental health but they're not the same thing (at least for immediate clinical purposes).

Without a workable definition of illness or health, our best proxy seems to be the people who come for help or are sent for it. Those are the situations we need to find a way of responding to. And whilst we're doing that, it seems worth taking more account of the extent to which people's thinking when that happens is dominated by the same set of ideas.

7

WHAT WE TALK ABOUT WHEN WE TALK ABOUT MENTAL HEALTH

There have been dramatic shifts in the way we talk about mental health over the last couple of decades. Conversations about emotional life and states of mind have become more open. In many walks of life there's a greater willingness to acknowledge feelings of insecurity and anxiety (although perhaps still a tendency to see them as theoretical constructs for other people, rather than reconciling ourselves with our own). In many ways, attitudes towards people who require help for mental health problems have become more sympathetic and more understanding. Equalities legislation has protected sufferers from discrimination since 2010. Generally, there seem to have been quite profound and genuine changes in the way many, or most, people have come to view mental health as a subject.

But it would be a mistake to imagine this has translated into the widespread availability of effective support for people who are suffering from mental health issues. With an evidence base as confused as the one we're dealing with, there's no real basis for confidence about which treatments are effective for what – people are being treated largely in a state of well-motivated ignorance. And treatment can be very expensive – how do you justify spending precious resources, from other people's hard-earned income, which could be used for cancer treatments, environmental protection or education, on mental health when the evidence for what works is so poor?

The result has been a lot of prescriptions for antidepressants, because that's been the cheapest form of treatment available and the simplest in terms of demands on healthcare services, and waiting lists of a year or more for psychotherapy on the NHS. Even after a year's wait, it's very likely NHS psychotherapy will be provided by trainees, who aren't getting paid anything at all, or unqualified nursing or paramedic staff. The overwhelming cost-benefits on offer – even against unpaid trainees – mean that providers, the NHS as well as private, are increasingly looking towards online and automated solutions: apps, 'self-directed learning' or automated psychotherapy. These may be effective – there's not much direct evidence at the moment but it's coming fast (and there's no question that people will produce evidence which supports it; there'll be evidence against it, of course, but that will just put it on the same footing as medication and the various forms of traditional therapy). It's possible that in some respects these approaches may even offer some therapeutic advantages over in-person psychotherapy – one can imagine they might be helpful in mitigating feelings of shame and inadequacy, which can become part of therapy, and other troubling aspects of inter-personal relationships which can develop between therapist and client.

But it's an approach being adopted already by people who usually like to make a great deal out of evidence-based credentials, which flies in the face of much of the available evidence about how therapy works. The most consistent conclusion claimed of research on the effectiveness of therapy is that it's the quality of the therapeutic relationship which appears to make most difference.[273] These developments involve largely dismantling the therapeutic relationship or removing it altogether. It looks like another example of picking the evidence you need to support what you want to do (and going out and making it if it isn't already there). And it's often not what people expect when they come for help or what they feel they need.

There may not be any intention to be unkind but, in practice, the experience for sufferers can feel very uncaring and not much help. Less than a third of the children referred to the Child and Adolescent Mental Health Services (CAMHS) in England in 2017 received treatment within a year and 75% of young people are reported to wait so long their conditions get worse or they're unable to access any treatment at all.[274] That's confusing – all these developments in social attitudes, all these fine sentiments in the media and from politicians and healthcare providers, but when you get behind the screen there doesn't seem to be much there.

CAMHS argues that many of these referrals (often from GPs) are inappropriate and should be directed to other sources of support like school counsellors or local community mental health workers. These distinctions are lost on users and their families – they can't get to those sources either. And it's the same story in other areas of mental healthcare, not just for children.

There's a very significant gap between the way we talk about mental health publicly, the expectations that creates and the experience of people who try to access care. People often feel let down and that tends to aggravate ideas of unfairness, exclusion, rejection and lack of worth. Those are ideas that are already occupying people's minds when they come for help.

Crisis?

We've already seen some of the confusion caused by our statistics and the impossible problems we're left with trying to reconcile figures when they are so incomplete and inconsistent or contradictory; here are some more. The APMS tells us that between 1993 and 2014 the incidence of common mental disorder amongst the adult population in England went from 14.1% (1993) to 16.3% (2000) to 16.2% (2007) and 17.5% (2014).[275] Those figures suggest that levels of mental health issues in the UK, or in England anyway, have remained relatively stable over the last couple of decades. They certainly do not suggest that there's been any kind of explosion in mental health issues.

But we saw earlier that the number of antidepressant prescriptions in England nearly doubled between 2008 and 2018.[276] The APMS reflects this too, picking up a pronounced increase in medication-based treatment levels between 2007 and 2014 and increased levels of psychotherapy for respondents with more severe symptoms. The NHS reports that over just 12 months from 2018 to 2019, there was an 11% increase in referrals for psychotherapy in England.[277]

That's strange – our best resourced survey seems to indicate that there hasn't been a significant change in the levels of mental disorder in the general population but treatment levels have shot up. That's suggesting a change in doctors' behaviour, or patients' behaviour, or both, rather than a change in mental health.

It's a similar pattern, but even more marked, if we look at the young as a separate population. It's widely regarded as accepted fact that there is an epidemic of mental illness amongst the young. That's probably one of the things that most people 'know' about mental health. Remember the study mentioned in chapter 1 which suggested children's mental health had got six times worse between 1995 and 2014?[278] As strikingly, referrals to the Child and Adolescent Mental Health Services in England

(CAMHS) were reported to have doubled over just the two years to 2019.[279]

The APMS doesn't cover children – it's the Adult Psychiatric Morbidity Survey. The nearest equivalent for children in England is the Mental Health of Children and Young People in England. The latest version in 2017 [280] found that one in eight children between five to 19 was suffering from at least one mental disorder.[281]

That's significantly lower than the adult population of one in six according to the 2014 APMS (and anything up to one in four in other sources). Rates increased with age, in a relatively smooth progression, so 17-19 years olds were just a little lower than the adult population. Because 17-19 year olds and two-four year olds were only included for the first time in 2017, comparisons with previous surveys are only available for five-15 year olds. They show a relatively modest upward trend from 9.7% in 1999 to 10.1% in 2004 and 11.2% in 2017.

Again, our best source of evidence is suggesting that there hasn't been a dramatic increase in mental health issues amongst children and adolescents. Instead, there's been a fairly steady state over the last 20 years, significantly lower than adult rates, and increasing towards the same kind of rate as children get closer to adulthood. What's going on?

The obvious distinction is that the evidence showing a six-fold increase in mental health problems relied on direct self-reporting by the children or their parents. But the Mental Health of Children and Young People in England report used clinically trained assessments of responses to formal psychiatric questionnaires. The APMS too, which showed no very significant increases in mental health issues over 20 years amongst the adult population, used clinical assessments and established psychiatric questionnaires. But antidepressant prescriptions, referrals for psychotherapy and referrals to CAMHS, which do consistently show such dramatic increases, are the result of people coming forward for help.

In 2018, a detailed review of 36 surveys, involving more than 140,000 participants, to explore mental health and well-being trends amongst children and young people in the UK over 20 years, concluded that, although there had been very significant increases in the reported prevalence of long-standing mental health conditions amongst young people (i.e. how ill people thought themselves), there was no corresponding increase in psychological distress or decrease in well-being as measured by scores on clinical questionnaires.[282]

This was in fact the same research that found the six-fold increase in (self-reported) problems amongst children and that's the aspect of the results that got most widely reported. That's despite the fact that this startling rate of increase only appeared to apply in England (with much lower rates of increase from higher base rates in Scotland and Wales) and what the researchers themselves selected from the results as significant for their conclusion was the dramatic discrepancy between the increase in self-reported problems and the more or less flat rates shown by professional questionnaires and assessments.

Across the population as a whole, and amongst the young too, the same picture seems to emerge – a mismatch between relatively stable levels of the incidence of mental disorders (and psychological distress and well-being) according to clinical evaluation, and very significant increases in the numbers thinking of themselves as unwell and seeking to access treatment.

That's interesting and important because we just decided at the end of the last chapter that, in the absence of any better criteria for what's ill and what's well, our best approach was simply to respond when people come for help. If the way people react to their experience is changing – if similar levels of psychological distress to those we've always experienced are increasingly leading people to seek treatment, we're going to need more treatment.

If we have become more likely to seek treatment for mental health issues, to treat ourselves as ill, have we become more likely to behave in other ways we associate with mental illness? Generally, it seems not, or at least not in ways that are readily measurable in statistics. For example, according to the Office of National Statistics rates of suicide in the UK between 2003 and 2019 have remained broadly level (in fact overall a mild reduction from 12.5 per 100,000 to 11.0 per 100,000[283]). And according to the APMS, hazardous drinking has actually declined quite significantly since 2000. But there is one glaring exception, which is self-harm amongst young women.

The APMS shows an increase in self-reported self-harm by women aged 16-24 from 6.5% in 2000 to 19.7% or 25.7% in 2014 (unhelpfully, there were two different measures – one in five reported self-harm when asked in face-to-face interview and one in four when asked in a written questionnaire, which itself illustrates rather nicely some of the problems with questionnaires and self-reporting). The corresponding figures for young men are dramatically lower and have increased but much more modestly over the same period. In 2000, young women were slightly more likely to report self-harm than men of the same age; by 2014, they were more than twice as likely. And it's not just self-reporting, the number of hospital admissions for self-harm for young women more than doubled in the 10 years to 2017.[284]

APMS figures do show a significant increase (26% in 2014 from 19.2% in 1993) in young women identified with a common mental disorder by clinical assessment, but nowhere near the tripling shown in the APMS for reported self-harm, over a shorter period. So, again, this appears to be more about a change in behaviour than a change in underlying psychological states. And there doesn't seem to be much evidence to support the idea that there hasn't really been a change – the possibility that the increase in reported self-harm might simply be down to better recording and less stigma around self-harm. When asked by questionnaire in the 2014 APMS whether they had ever self-harmed, 25.7% of women aged 16-24 said they had, against 0.6% of women aged 75 or over (with figures of below 5% reported for women down to the age of 45). This appears to be something happening just to this generation of young women.

How and why did we become so much more prepared to think of ourselves as ill and seek help? How did the idea of self-harm become so intimately connected with mental health for young women? And if the ideas we have about mental health can have that kind of power to affect the ways we experience and respond to our own mental states, how else might they be affecting us? It's worth looking carefully at how we think about mental health.

The biological model

One of the biggest changes in recent years has been to try to take some of the stigma associated with mental illness out of the conversation. That makes good sense. We've seen that one of the key ideas affecting people who come for help (perhaps the most corrosive one) is that they're not good enough, unworthy.

For some people, the fact of diagnosis or intervention can be helpful – something has been recognised, an explanation has been provided and something can happen now. But any diagnosis also involves a confirmation of brokenness, of something being wrong. That's going to risk inflaming the underlying feelings of shame and inadequacy.

And a diagnosis, or intervention, is a significant step. Once that line has been crossed, people can't come back. They will always be someone who has suffered from depression, or been diagnosed with a personality disorder, or has received treatment and that will become an important part of how they think about themselves. That's not something to be done lightly, particularly given how unreliable and poorly validated our diagnoses are. And that's partly because, despite all the genuine efforts made to address stigma and prejudice, at some level, everything to do with mental health is still irradiated by ideas of inadequacy and shame.

An important aspect of the more recent approach has been to try to normalise mental health as a condition which can fluctuate, in the same way as physical health. *We all have mental health* means, in the same way as physical health, it's something that could go wrong for all of us. That's a helpful idea.

It's been accompanied by a shift towards a biological model of thinking about mental health. Simply drawing that analogy with physical health might have influenced us to think more about mental health as a physiological condition. At the same time, increasingly sophisticated technology in physical healthcare has allowed more studies on associations between mental health and purely physiological events – neurology, inflammation, gut biome etc – and genetics.

None of those studies has yet done more than establish, often tentative, statistical associations – we haven't found out anything useful or important – but the links are there and this technologically impressive research also tends to reinforce the idea that we're dealing with biological events (which, at some level, we must be).

But it's also likely that the shift towards biological models of explanation for mental health itself owes something to those familiar ideas of failure, inadequacy and self-blame. To the extent we believe mental health is to do with the ideas people have and how they see the world, that means, if they have mental health issues, they're getting something wrong, badly wrong. To the extent mental health is about serotonin levels, or genetics or gut bacteria, it's something physiological that happens to people and there's no need for anyone to feel quite so strongly that they're failing at something. And it wouldn't be surprising if we found it easier to accept that mental health issues are something we ourselves might encounter, if we approached them as 'no fault' - a matter of genetics or physiology beyond anyone's control.

There is no necessary connection between the idea of mental health as a universal phenomenon and biological models. In fact, as we tend to think of mental states as more fluid than physiological ones, it might make more sense to equate the universal potential to experience mental health issues with our thoughts and ideas. But that wouldn't appease the idea that we're implicated in our own troubles in the same way.

And the biological model doesn't just offer a salve to sufferers: the more genetic and biological mental health issues, the more parents, siblings, partners and other people in sufferers' lives can feel absolved. If it's genetic or something any of us could pick up, like the flu, there's nothing anyone could have done, it isn't anyone's fault. That makes it a very appealing model for everyone because otherwise the feelings of contribution, responsibility and blame can be brutal.

But there may be another, less helpful consequence to this shift towards the biological. To the extent mental health issues are something that happen to you, embedded in your physiology or ordained in your genes, there's a limited amount you can do about it. That might help with the punishing cycles of self-blame and self-disgust, but it's also likely to change the way you can think about things getting better.

Taken far enough, the idea of recovery, of getting beyond this situation, recedes altogether – this is how you are, this is *who* you are. If you're affected, mental health issues are just part of your lot, like green eyes or red hair. Even if the biological isn't regarded as absolute, when it's thought of as something mediated by experience, by the time mental health issues arise, the die is cast. Social inequality or childhood neglect may have been the active agent, but now the physiology is set and can't be undone.

On this view, the best sufferers can do is try to manage their symptoms and prevent them impacting their lives too acutely. Medication, therapy, diet, exercise, lifestyle choices, partners, other people – everything can become enlisted in the service of managing their mental states, trying to keep things stable.

More than that, from this angle, mental health issues can become a kind of free pass: a get out of jail card for when things go wrong – *it's not my fault, things got out of control and my depression came back, it's very regrettable but I'm better now.*

All of this only really works if you regard mental health issues as essentially biological and beyond personal responsibility.

This way of seeing things connects to another idea about mental health. If mental health issues are something that happen to people at a physiological level, like, say, Crohn's disease, it becomes easier to see people who are affected as engaged in a life-long struggle to manage their symptoms and live the best life they can in difficult circumstances. There is room for something admirable, courageous about this: the potential for a form of noble suffering. That can be very true, but taken far enough, there's a danger mental health issues can almost become a badge of honour – something that marks you out, almost a matter of distinction.

Layers of motivation again, and not much of it known or deliberate, but you can see an appealing element here for all the celebrities coming forward to talk about their struggles with mental health. Not only are they using their platforms to help address residual ideas of stigma around mental health, but they are revealing themselves as people who have bravely overcome their own personal issues, and to achieve conspicuous success.

And the idea of the individual as long-suffering victim of circumstance or biology connects readily to the idea of sufferers collectively as victims too of social neglect and indifference. People suffering from mental health issues often identify powerfully with the idea of mental illness – it's a very sensitive personal characteristic, it's easy for it to feel defining. They can come to think of themselves as part of a community of sufferers and it's very easy for that to feel like a community which outsiders can't really understand and, ultimately, don't really care about enough.

Caring to bits

We do all find it difficult to understand and care about things that aren't us or, at a pinch, the people closest to us. That's true of the people feeling neglected too, but it's always easy to fall into the trap of expecting more from other people than we would be prepared or able to give ourselves in the same circumstances. If that's what's happening, it's going to tug people back towards ideas of grievance and resentment (and exclusion and self-loathing).

Very often, these feelings of neglect are shared by the people working in mental health. There's a strong sense of being pushed to the margins, ignored and forgotten – stuck away in the newbuild or portacabins at the back of the hospital car park. A large part of the media and political coverage of mental health is invariably calls for more money to be spent. Since 2012 in the UK there's been an objective enshrined in law to establish 'parity of esteem' – equal priority for mental and physical health in the NHS. But enshrined in law doesn't mean legally enforceable as a practical matter. Parity of esteem is an ambition, there are many obstacles and a serious practical one remains how do you responsibly commit resources when the treatment provision is so fragmented and the evidence base for what you're dealing with so incoherent?

When mental health professionals demand more investment in mental health, they don't just mean mental health, they invariably mean their particular form of mental healthcare. When money gets spent somewhere else in mental health, they're generally just as outraged at the waste of opportunity and the use of money in a way they regard as incapable of achieving anything, or anything significant or lasting. Natural enough perhaps, but it's an approach that risks sounding like shrill insistence that there's a scandalous social failure which can only be met adequately by spending public funds in a way that will provide you personally with more secure, better-resourced employment and more income.

When you hear about the urgent need for counselling, or other psychological intervention, after trauma, disasters or conflicts, looked at strictly in terms of scientific evidence, rather than everyone's intuitive response, that isn't clear at all. The research is confused and, we've already seen, some of the best resourced and most thorough studies indicate that therapy offers no,[285] or only marginal, improvement over 'usual care', and antidepressants offer only a modest improvement over a placebo.[286] We're generally very keen to invoke science when it supports what we want to believe, happy to bypass it when it doesn't.

The idea of care is itself very significant. If you're feeling anxious and traumatised, if you're feeling inadequate, excluded, resentful, care, any care, just getting care, can help. The experience of care, on its own can be exactly what people need to get through difficult times – no skilful interventions required, no deep reservoirs of professional experience, just someone being nice to you. But the idea of care has its dangers too – the possibility of developing a dependence on the idea of care, extending beyond a period of crisis into a more persistent mind set – the opposite of recognising other people's separateness and a realistic set of expectations in ordinary life. You can see that happening sometimes too, particularly in more serious, institutionalised cases.

Even ideas like our increased tolerance for vulnerability are not completely straightforward. We are all vulnerable in the sense that we can become upset, we can be caused distress (and more easily than we'd like to think and pretend). A genuine tolerance for that kind of vulnerability would be able to experience it, to accept it as a part of normal experience, without turning it into a mental health issue. Turning that kind of vulnerability – anxiety, insecurity, sadness – into illness would be the opposite of tolerance.

More than that, we've already mentioned a common human impulse, when people are under pressure, to make things worse – perhaps to show others how bad it is, to try to make people care or make them sorry. Hard-pressed parents, people under stress at work – we want to show others what we're going through, we try to get someone to understand. People might stop eating properly – stress can suppress appetite but this is something on top of that. They'll take on more work they know they can't do. They won't get rest, they won't take care of themselves. When it's happening, people seem to seek out the choices that make things more difficult for them. Or they force issues, bring conflicts to a head.

None of its deliberate or calculated but, at the same, we're often aware in a shadowy way that we're doing it. It's perverse but it's not that an unusual aspect of the way we respond to trouble. There's an old idea in mental health that severe mental illness – breakdown – can be a kind of defence.[287] As if there's almost an element of choice involved: we know how to breakdown, we know what it looks like, what it feels like. Breakdown has been described as a return to a state we've already known – a state of disintegration experienced in early childhood.[288] In certain circumstances, when things feel extreme enough, we just allow it to happen. We stop trying to hold things together and just let things go.

Mental states are subjective and so is mental health. Different people respond differently to the same situation. Remember that research suggesting that people's own sense of how they'd been treated in childhood was more important in predicting later mental health issues than the objective record of how they'd been treated in court documentation?[289] A different sense of something being done to you leading to a different level of grievance and resentment and feelings of isolation and worthlessness?

Everyone's heard of the placebo. There is another recognised phenomenon called the nocebo[290] – it's a similar process but the opposite effect. Suggest to someone that they've been treated and they're inclined to feel better; suggest to someone they're ill and they'll feel worse – right down to the made-up symptoms they were told they might experience as a result of taking a sugar pill or receiving non-existent acupuncture (with a retractable needle).[291] The evidence for it is as good as the evidence for the placebo. In the world of physical medicine, doctors regularly tell people coming there's nothing wrong with them. Psychotherapists almost never do.

Are we in danger of medicalising normal human experience? Many people make that argument and not just hard-nosed right-wing commentators or boomers in industry or finance – sociologists, epidemiologists, doctors, psychiatrists, people involved in mental health care too.[292] Are we talking ourselves into an epidemic of attention and treatment? People have gone for help for ever – there's nothing wrong with that, it's a healthy human instinct. It used to be the Church, family, friends – are we now taking our problems to the doctor and the counsellor?

Might it be worse, could we be talking ourselves not just into attention and treatment but into unhappiness and illness? We are talking a lot more than we used to about mental health. Whatever else is going on (even in the purest biological model), these are states of mind. If we can talk ourselves out of them, with therapy, it's likely we can talk ourselves into them too. Or are we just now, for the first time, recognising and responding adequately to distress which has always been there and the quality of our lives will improve as a result? That would have to depend, at least in part, on the quality of our response. Millions on lifelong medication doesn't seem like much of an improvement.

As usual, we're not in a very good position to know. Actually, it's not easy to imagine how we ever would be. But whatever it is, something significant seems to be happening and we're going to need a response – it'd be better if it's a good one.

Normalising mental health issues, and the shift towards biological determinism, may help manage the feelings of inadequacy and shame which are so ingrained in mental illness, but if it also becomes more difficult to see the potential for positive change, could that itself be capable of affecting people's mental health? Might we be not just talking ourselves into trouble but making it harder to talk ourselves out of it too – making it harder for people to use therapy, or any other form of intervention?

We're not helped in thinking about this by the fact that it's not as if the evidence for any of our interventions has ever been that compelling. You can firmly believe in therapy's ability to achieve successful, long-term outcomes for people – to make things better, permanently. You can't point to a body of clear, consistent, compelling evidence though – it doesn't exist. There isn't persuasive evidence against it either – looked at as a whole, the evidence just isn't convincing enough either way. But, even if we can't be very clear what we mean by ill or what makes things better, we're still left with the question of what we might be giving up if we give up the idea of getting better, of being 'well'?

And if this new picture of mental health we've been developing isn't inaccurate and is capable of achieving some very benign effects, it isn't very complete. It's missing some important elements – when we embrace mental health issues, we need to be careful what we're embracing.

Not OK

In July 2019, Jill Higgins went on trial as a result of a motorway crash which killed Daniel Dayalan and seriously injured his wife. The court was told that, following the death of her husband from a brain tumour six months earlier, Mrs Higgins had begun to behave erratically and gone on a number of spending sprees. Two days before the crash she had withdrawn nearly £500 to give to a homeless person and then been unable to pay for her shopping and had to leave it in the shop. After eating in a restaurant, her card was declined, she tried to leave without paying and gave a new tablet computer as payment for the meal. The court was told she then walked from Windsor to Heathrow airport where she tried, but was unable, to take a flight. The police report said that, after her arrest, Mrs Higgins stripped naked in front of officers, rolled around on the ground complaining of abdominal pain because she apparently believed she was giving birth to three phantom babies. Just before the crash, her car was travelling at 127 mph.[293] That can be the reality of serious mental illness. Lots of suffering but nothing necessarily very noble going on.

There are very good reasons to try to address stigma and discrimination around mental health. People affected by mental health issues are often in torment and a sense of unworthiness and exclusion are responsible for much of their distress. They have enough to deal with without adding unnecessarily to that sense of exclusion and isolation or making them victims of discrimination. But there's a danger in trying to pretend that we don't have particular reactions to mental health, or even that they might not have a sound basis. If they're real, those feelings won't go away and we'll just end up saying one thing and doing another (which, you might argue, is what's happening at the moment).

One of the most common reactions to mental illness is fear. We tend to be uncomfortable with mental illness as a subject. It's not a topic the 'well' generally want to talk about. Perhaps that's because we understand so little about it that it feels too mysterious and alarming. Or perhaps it's the exact opposite – perhaps it's because, in our darkest recesses and our deepest anxieties, we sense, a little too close to home, its potential to affect us too. Either way, we're frightened by the topic and we're frightened by the mentally ill too.

Many studies have examined the link between mental illness and violence. As ever, the picture isn't clear or consistent. Leading mental health charities in the UK cite research showing that people suffering from various severe forms of mental illness do not make a statistically significant contribution to societal violence. For example, researchers have estimated that you would have to lock up 35,000 patients with schizophrenia in order to avoid one homicide of a stranger.[294]

That feels like a useful corrective. At the same time, it's a bit like being told you're more likely to be killed by a falling coconut than a shark – it may be true but it's not that much comfort if you're in the water with a shark. Mental health groups also often stress that the mentally ill are much more likely to be victims of violence themselves.[295] Again, that may be true, but it's not really the point people are concerned about. That point is that research does indicate that people living with serious mental health issues do commit violence more often than the general population and significantly more often. Depending on the circumstances, maybe by a factor of three or four; in some circumstances, much higher than that.[296] That's what people are really concerned about – are people who are mentally ill more dangerous to be with? And the answer seems to be yes, statistically they are.

Researchers note that violence in people with serious mental health problems is very often associated with prior experience of being the victims of violence themselves and substance abuse.[297] Therefore, the argument goes, we should regard prior experience of violence and substance abuse as the real predictors of violence, rather than the mental health condition. And it's certainly true that both those factors have a strong association with violence in the general population too. However, since research has indicated that more than half of the people with certain serious mental health conditions have diagnosable alcohol or drug dependency,[298] and substance abuse is also strongly associated with being a victim of violence, the distinction may not be that important in most people's minds. If people with serious mental conditions are statistically more dangerous to be with, you might not care whether it's their substance abuse or their underlying mental illness putting you at risk.

So, it *is* very unlikely that any of us will become the victim of violence at the hands of anyone suffering from a mental illness, but it makes perfectly good sense that the increased potential for violence would colour our attitude to mental illness. It's not particularly helpful to pretend it doesn't. There's a good reason psychiatric units, forensic psychology departments and even outpatient psychotherapy departments in hospitals have panic buttons in consulting rooms and lock-down facilities.

Anyway, that's just rare violent events and severe mental illnesses we've been talking about. Our response to other people's mental health issues isn't just about the risk of being physically attacked. One of the problems with mental illness is that people affected by it are usually very unhappy. When we're unhappy, none of us tend to behave very well. Under intense emotional stress we're likely to become more rigid, blinkered, irritable and self-centred.

All of that is often true of people suffering from mental health issues. That's part of the problem, mental health problems are difficult to be around. Just when they need them most, sufferers risk driving people away, making themselves feel more lonely, isolated, abandoned and resentful and worthless. It's a particularly cruel example of a vicious circle, but the likelihood is they're not suffering nobly at all and other people are paying a price.

Similar to the research showing an association of use of absolute terms with depression,[299] textual analysis of materials produced by people suffering from depression shows an increased use of first-person singular pronouns ('I', 'myself', 'me').[300] That isn't evidence that 'maladaptive Self Focussed Attention', as the researchers call it, is a cause of depression but it's an interesting observation about ways in which people seem to think when they are suffering from depression. And this research avoids a number of the problems (around self-reporting and artificiality) encountered in so many other areas of experimental psychology.

People suffering with mental health issues do have a tendency to be self-absorbed (and not in a way they get to enjoy or want to be – they don't like themselves, remember). They become preoccupied, plagued by intrusive thoughts, trapped in obsessive rumination – it becomes harder to see other people clearly. We saw earlier that sufferers are often acutely aware that they have got caught up in something self-centred. They may feel tremendous guilt for being so unhappy when they feel they can see that, objectively, there is no 'need' to be, that other people have it worse and get by and don't succumb in the same way.

They can hate themselves for being weak, for being selfish, for behaving badly, for feeling sorry for themselves and for the spiteful, resentful thoughts they have towards other people, including the people patiently and tolerantly trying to help them. And, of course, that guilt and self-loathing feed the idea underlying the depression that there's something shamefully wrong about them. But they can't stop it and part of the reason is that the full impact of their behaviour on other people (who will be struggling enough with the conditions of their own lives) tends to be lost on them. That's because they believe that, in some fundamental way, things are different for them. And the biological model supports them in that belief.

So, people's aversion to mental illness – and the stigma inflicted on the mentally ill – probably has as much to do with our own an aversion to unhappiness, and with the anxiety generated by being with friends, family, co-workers who are struggling not to be volatile, moody and self-absorbed, as it does with a fear of random attack by strangers on the streets or the underground. These are difficult things to say about people who are already feeling so bad about themselves but it's an important part of the picture. The unhappiness of people suffering from mental illness is very real. Perhaps the worst form of unhappiness there is. They can be driven to kill themselves because they cannot bear to live in that anguish. They deserve sympathy but nothing is gained by romanticising it.

It's OK not to be OK has emerged as a watch word in mental health. It's the title of a hit song, a popular drama series on TV, it appears in more than a dozen current book titles, in health awareness ribbons and bracelets and the titles and taglines of countless articles, blogs and advice sheets. You can see *It's OK not to be OK* as a rejection of the stigma associated with mental health issues. That's obvious and, of course, it is *OK not to be OK* if that means feeling unhappy, frightened, inadequate, alone or overwhelmed at times. But the phrase is not just a response to a history of social stigma around mental health, it's also a reaction to the burning sense of inferiority and inadequacy which underpins mental health issues and is only likely to be amplified by diagnosis or treatment. It can be a reaction to suffering mental health conditions, it can be tied up with the states of mind that have contributed to them and that's more complicated. Is it OK if the result of mental health issues is living in intense anxiety, tormented by self-loathing and resentment, with extreme difficulty in finding pleasure in anything and pre-occupied with ideas about harming yourself? Is it OK to be caught up in compulsive behaviours which damage your health or prevent you leading the life you'd like? Is it OK to be unable to contain your own emotional life and to keep taking it out on other people?

Your answer may be affected by how you believe these states come about and whether they can be changed. If you take a biological and deterministic view of mental health, your answer is more likely to be *it is OK* – because it has to be.

Like a lot of medical conditions, depression seems to be something that can entrench itself; your chances of getting it are greatly increased if you've had it before. Research suggests at least 50% of those who recover from a first episode of depression suffer from one or more additional episodes in their lifetime, and approximately 80% of those with a history of two episodes experience another recurrence.[301] There's also evidence that the factors predicting recurrence are different from the factors predicting initial onset, suggesting that depression can take on a life of its own within people.[302] It's reported that a third to half of all patients experiencing major depressive disorder relapse within one year of discontinuation of treatment and the greater the number of prior depressive episodes, the higher the probability of a future recurrence.[303] So *being OK* might be important because once you've stopped being *OK*, it may be much easier to go back there and the more often it happens, the easier that gets.

A major problem with *It's OK not to be OK* is that, as a state of belief, it's precarious. It is a reaction to the pain of people feeling that there's something very important that's wrong with them and the fears that brings about exclusion and rejection. *It's OK not to be OK* only exists in reaction to the idea that it isn't *OK*. It can never be bigger than the idea its reacting to and it can never be enough to cancel it out altogether. The feelings of inferiority and shame haven't gone away, people are fighting them all the time, struggling against themselves to be wholly convinced, permanently. And if they've come to identify themselves with mental illness, taken the view that this is just their fate, that's where they're going to be stuck.

Loving yourself

It's OK not to be OK can take on a note of defiant assertion and assertion is an important theme in mental health treatment.

If new skills in assertion manage to make us feel better about ourselves, and that helps to loosen the knot of inadequacy, resentment and isolation, that can be a good thing. And if they allow us to communicate our feelings better to other people, that's almost bound to be a good thing.

But, in all that confusion about what's reasonable to expect from other people, and what other people are entitled to expect from us, it's easy for any of us to feel short-changed. People who come for help often have the idea that they're not very good at sticking up for themselves, that they allow others to take advantage of them. It's rarely true, or rarely true the way it feels – it might not feel like it to us, but most of us do a pretty good job of holding our own. If you look hard enough at couples you know, you'll probably see that, one way or another, things have a habit of equalising themselves.

We've talked about how an urge to assert ourselves over other people, to exercise control, can be quite a destructive but common response to anxiety about inferiority and exclusion. And we've seen how it can be tied to unrealistic expectations and lead to grievance and resentment. If people have already reached the point where they're coming for help, ingraining it as part of their therapy may not always be that helpful. But assertiveness does often occupy a prominent place in therapy and has spun off into a thousand courses in Coaching and Leadership and Business Schools.

Addressing issues with self-esteem seems to be an element of just about every therapy or well-being approach. That makes perfect sense – one of the key themes of this book is how intimately self-loathing, a sense of inadequacy and shame are implicated in mental health issues. The question is how to respond to those ideas in order to help people most. When we feel inadequate, it's easy to imagine that we're at a disadvantage and we're being treated unfairly. What we need, one version of the story goes, is to love ourselves more and, that way, learn to assert ourselves.

Loving ourselves and learning to assert are often associated with the idea of expressing anger – a way to be more authentic. This is another popular theme in therapy – claiming your anger. The idea can take a number of different forms but a common element is about recognition of something that's been done to you. It may involve a refusal to take up old roles, to be what others expect you to be – an opportunity to find a new strength by owning and expressing your feelings, including the ones, like anger, other people don't want you to have. In some circumstances, this can be a useful bridge, a transitional stage of exploring anger in order to understand it and move through it and beyond it – a route for people to learn more about themselves and to integrate aspects of their personality into a more rounded whole. In practice though, that can be tricky to navigate – anger is intoxicating, it's easy for that path through to get lost. Sometimes the path was never there – in this kind of approach, it's not about moving through and getting beyond anger, just expressing it. It's about the primacy of emotion over content or context – these feelings matter because they are the feelings you have.

At its worst, that looks like a toddler stuck in a tantrum – the prospect of useful, and perhaps painful, discoveries about yourself and other people gets lost. Nothing much can change – if people were very unhappy, they're likely to stay very unhappy, just better at telling everybody about it. There's a fine line between authenticity and self-centredness – it's easy to confuse the two.

Self-love and assertiveness as themes for therapy or wellbeing fit neatly with the idea of mental health issues as belonging to the put upon – victims who've had something done to them. That isn't necessarily always the case – or not in the way that people often mean by it. Even if, in some sense, problems are always the result of something done to us, that may not be the most helpful idea to give people. Victimhood is a damaging state of mind – it neatly encapsulates inadequacy, resentment and isolation. People can get hooked on the energy of assertion over others. The result can be a brittle, precarious sense of self-esteem which is dependent on assertion over others and idealised versions of the self. It's unlikely to help if it just feeds the same unrealistic expectations, resentment and sense of isolation that's brought them for help in the first place.

Victims of depression will be victims in real life (we all are in different forms and degree). Alongside the crumbling, precarious sense of self-worth, there's a deep resentment for being made to feel like that and often a desire for revenge for what's happened to them – it's something like hatred. If we can't tolerate being made to feel weak and inadequate, fury and attack are the result, in the mind if not the act. When assertion becomes extreme and compulsive enough – becomes the thing people depend on to avoid catastrophic feelings of lack of selfworth – you end up with teenagers stabbed on the bus for disrespecting each other.

One leading theory of violence and criminality (there are many) is as a misguided attempt to assert an excluded self on others, on society, to equalise a perceived grievance and unfairness.[304] Something really quite similar can be happening with the assertiveness themes you encounter in the well-being industry – the same core ideas, the same underlying mechanisms, just a matter of degree and different expression. It may be less destructive and dangerous for other people but it's not necessarily much healthier in psychological terms for the individual.

Those *Be Awesome* tee shirts can smack a little of desperation. People who do actually feel OK about themselves generally don't need to say it so often or quite so stridently. All those injunctions to self and overt celebrations tend to indicate the opposite. People who really do feel strong don't have to talk about being strong all the time. We only need those kinds of instructions to ourselves if those aren't the ways we feel – they're reactions to feeling something else.

Love yourself is generally a reaction to the idea that we're not loveable, that there's something wrong – it really wouldn't be necessary to say it otherwise. And the likelihood is, the more urgent the expression of how much we love ourselves, or should, the more powerful the secret conviction it's responding to. That conviction is not only that we're not loveable, but we might not be very pleasant at all. And that idea feeds off the knowledge that inside we're spending a lot of time feeling some pretty unpleasant things – envy, grievance, resentment, a desire to punish people, something pretty close to hatred.

Those feelings come from disappointment and somewhere behind that disappointment, ideas about what to expect from others and life which haven't turned out. If that's because they're unrealistic, based on an insufficient sense of other people's separateness and independence, surrounding ourselves with hearts and wall plaques saying *Love* isn't going to change the reality of how we're spending a lot of time feeling. If part of the issue is not getting other people, the idea that our problems are due to caring too much for others, being too giving for our own good, may not be helpful.

What you need is more for yourself – offer this to people and they're likely to lap it up. We all want that version of ourselves – *I just give too much and don't keep enough back for me.* It's very rarely true – we can kid ourselves with all sorts of rationalisations about selflessness, but most of what we do is mainly about us. Not our partners, not our children – us. To the extent we even try, most of the time we can't see them clearly enough to know what the people around us would really want or need. So, we end up imposing our own needs and expectations on them anyway. But, usually, we don't even try that hard – what we like to think of as done for others is fairly thoroughly corrupted by our own motivations and agenda. Of course, other people are probably doing the same to us – and they might well do worse – but we risk storing up trouble for ourselves if we try to take refuge in the delusion that we're just too giving and need to do a better job of taking care of ourselves.

Often the 'learning' these messages will offer – the assertion – is about strength: about being strong enough to do it on our own terms, not needing other people, imposing our way, getting what we need and being ready to go it alone. Standing on your own feet is a kind of strength, but there have been other versions of strong to going it alone. Strong enough to support other people, to care enough for someone else and take their feelings and needs into account, strong enough to be able to try genuinely to imagine someone else's perspective and compromise your own way, strong enough to put up with things in other people which you can't change but which cause you pain, to suffer what you have to in order to be with the people you need. There is a danger that the kind of strength being advocated here becomes the strength to live with resentment, discontent, self-loathing, isolation, depression, anything rather than take other people adequately into account.

And isn't loving yourself a curious idea? Isn't that something we should be doing to other people? It's true we need to find ways to manage the insistent idea that we're not good enough, but isn't it a more realistic understanding of ourselves, a reconciliation to ourselves as we are but with a healthy desire to do better, that we should be after – not self-infatuation? Particularly as that attempt at self-infatuation is doomed. Which is just as well – we feel guilt and shame for the damaging and destructive things we do; it feels wrong, it feels like something bad inside us. What we do with that is another matter, and it doesn't always find a good outlet, but if we didn't feel that, we really would be hideous people. When you're feeling filled with insecurity and resentment towards the people you depend upon, it's an awful experience – it's idle to pretend that you can love that, or that you should. People can't make themselves love themselves; it doesn't work.

Here's an extract from an article about comedian Sofie Hagen who may be making a similar point in a different context:

> 'Hagen's book also acts as a guide for women who are overweight or obese to find happiness and learn to accept that their body is – if not beautiful – then, at least, just fine. This last message is somewhat at odds with the current body positivity movement, which urges everyone to love their body, whatever their shape or size. Hagen recalls speaking on a panel with a prominent figure from the movement. Every time the panellist would say "love yourself", the crowd would whoop and cheer, and Hagen would respond: "Yes, but how?"

> Her question only spawned more slogans, more cheers – and no answers. "Loving your body can feel impossible," says Hagen, "and just another thing to fail at. You fail at dieting, and then you fail at loving your body. And even if you love your body, you might not love it all the time…....It's like my ears. I feel very neutral about my ears. I don't have bad or good things to say; they're just ears. And if I could feel like that about my whole body, that would be amazing"'.[305]

The idea of loving yourself is often accompanied by an aspirational faith in an idealised life. The idea that life is, or should be, 'beautiful' is interesting, maybe in some sense true and potentially useful – it might help us to notice and appreciate aspects of our lives we could otherwise miss. But it's not the whole reality of anyone's life. Science (useful, relevant science which gives us consistent, objective information about important things we want to know) tells us we're highly evolved primates, who didn't feature for the first thirteen-and-a-half billion years of an entropic universe. Most life forms seem to cling on to a narrow evolutionary niche by their fingernails. Most people feel they're clinging on in a similar way a fair amount of the time. Pretending life is (or could, or should, be) like a shampoo ad is likely to be a mistake.

There's a danger with these ideas – they set up unrealistic expectations and a forced experience of life. Underlying them is a performance, a 'better you' version of yourself and a 'better than you' triumphalism over other people. That tends to entail a fretful, precarious wrestle with the world which doesn't do anyone any favours. If you've bought into these ideas too enthusiastically, if you've got carried away with how your life ought to feel, you are going to be more likely to think something's wrong. It is, but the problem isn't the way you feel, it's the way you think you should.

Aspects of everyone's lives are often going to involve anxiety, humiliation, hurt, anger, resentment, spitefulness, selfishness, shame and guilt (and the discovery of that isn't beautiful either, it's what it is). Which isn't to say that people can't also have dignity, courage, affection, insight, wisdom and connections with each other which are full of enjoyment and a good amount of security and happiness.

To believe too firmly that life should be beautiful, in the way we try to sell it to ourselves, is going to impoverish our real experience. And the word 'sell' is used advisedly since we use that ideal, the idea of a beautiful life, to sell ourselves homes, holidays, cars, white goods, music festivals, extreme sports, toothpaste, insurance and everything else you see marketed by beautiful people who seem to be having a much better time than you are.

The problem isn't helped by celebrities who won't stay off our screens telling us how beautiful life is – and perhaps how bravely they struggled in the past (at a point when they were pretending to us everything was wonderful too). 'Life is beautiful' too often involves trying to persuade yourself of something and avoid facing up to the fact that it's not like you expect it to be (what you've bought into) – more unrealistic expectations cueing more underlying sense of failure, self-dissatisfaction, discontent, exclusion, grievance and resentment.

Of course, there are ideas behind the theme of loving yourself which are intended to be more nuanced and realistic – around forgiving yourself, forming a kinder, healthier relationship with yourself, less vulnerable to self-persecution – rather than unqualified self-indulgence. But too often in practice, it translates into hyper-sensitivity, defensiveness, over-assertion and aspirational idealistic expectations which can never be met. People get stuck in frenetic cycles oscillating between the self-love they keep trying to claim and the self-disgust they're trying to ward off.

Treating Mental Health

The same ideas around inadequacy which bring people for help can find their way into treatment too.

Most obviously, in relation to what we claim to know. If you're an expert, being an expert is going to be an important part of what *you* depend upon in order to feel OK about yourself and that means knowing stuff – not knowing does not feel good if you're supposed to be an expert. And the rest of the population too would like to think there are people out there who know about this stuff. It's a very important, emotive subject, it affects us all, the people we care about and all the people around us.

So, people take it on trust that there are similar levels of knowledge and expertise around mental health as there are for engineering, computer science, geography or physical medicine. There aren't, but the result is a powerful and pervasive tendency for everyone to try to persuade ourselves that we know more about mental health than we do. It is astonishing how little we know about mental health. Most of the time when people say they 'know' something, they don't; not by the standards of knowledge we ordinarily apply in other fields.

One of the most widely quoted statistics about mental health is that half of all mental health problems are established by the age of 14[306] – it's something that's generally taken as fact.[307] The main research tool underlying this finding is asking adults about their childhood memories. You probably thought something more sophisticated was going on. No, these findings are based are retrospective accounts, by people who may be in quite disturbed states of mind, relying on memories going back decades. A striking feature of the Grant Study at Harvard University, which followed a group of Harvard graduates with continued physical and psychological examination for the rest of their lives, was how often and seriously people in later life misremembered what had happened to them earlier. Later accounts by participants of what had happened earlier in life routinely and significantly contradicted the records taken at the time – it's a remarkable demonstration, from a unique piece of research, about how much gets misremembered or imagined when we look back.[308] And the recollections underpinning that statistic about the onset of mental health issues in childhood generally don't even relate to facts, they rely upon highly subjective judgements, particularly in relation to less severe conditions like depression and anxiety – how sad or anxious did *you* feel as a child? What's more, high levels of confusion, obsessive ideas, ritualistic behaviour, even auditory hallucinations, are widely regarded as features of normal development in childhood and adolescence, which makes it even harder to distinguish the symptoms of early-onset mental illness. And by definition, statistics gathered this way won't capture mental health problems which have gone unidentified and untreated.[309] Those guys – one third of people suffering from a common mental disorder according to the 2014 APMS[310] – never get asked when it started.

So, all in all, it's a really terrible way of deciding that half of all mental health issues start by a particular age. Yes science – as in an attempt to apply scientific methodology – has told us something here. But in this context, applied in this way, the scientific method just doesn't work well enough, it's much too fallible to talk about 'knowing' anything. It's as if the researchers have got lost in their own methods – there doesn't seem to be much in the way of a sanity check going on: lifting their heads up to ask how much sense what they're doing makes, what it would add or how it relates to other research. It's a kind of desperate recklessness. Mental health experts want to know, they want to feel competence and a sense of purpose (we all do), they want to be able to make a contribution, but wanting to know can easily turn into acting like we know. That's uncomfortable and it often comes to rely upon its own vehemence – if you say very emphatically that something is very clear and very important, it reinforces the impression (to you too) that you must know what you're doing. Not knowing isn't a popular stance – there's a lot of pressure to feel and sound as if we do know. It's not deliberate but most things that matter aren't.

'One in four' sufferers, 50% of mental health problems established by the age of 14, a mental health crisis amongst the general population, or the young, the effectiveness of different treatments – none of it stands up to scrutiny as established fact. Putting any of these things forward as unqualified assertion, or with selective evidence taken in isolation, saying 'we know', is seriously misleading – but it happens all the time. If you made claims that way about a company's shares on the stock market, you'd risk going to prison. And the stock market isn't a world you'd normally want to think of as setting higher standards of transparency than science.

Other effects can be more subtle. There are power imbalances when you go to see a doctor – you're suffering, frightened, maybe desperate, and they have the expert knowledge you're depending on to make things better. It's similar with a therapist.

When people are in the position of providing care, they take up the role of care-giver – the focus is on somebody else's needs and they become the one who's OK, the well person. That can be an arduous role but there's also a potential pay-off – for a while we escape our own problems. There may be professional anxieties involved but taking up the professional role, being the competent person, can be a welcome distraction from the everyday feelings of anxiety and inadequacy that trouble everyone.

There is a potential for therapy to be experienced (and delivered) as a highly critical, debilitating examination of everything the client is doing 'wrong'. Behind this is an ideal being held out – a heightened, perfected state you can (and ought to) be living in, embodied in the form of your therapist or the idea of a therapist. It is a delicate balance because, on one hand, if a therapist isn't somewhat resolved, people might be entitled to ask what do they have to offer? And, on the other, if there weren't problems with your life, why would you be there?

But this natural tendency can be magnified by the clinical style and ideas adopted in therapy, some schools more than others. Therapists are usually expected to assume a highly thoughtful, blank, non-reactive stance, with no or minimum self-disclosure. Generally, it'd be frowned upon for the therapist to provide any indication that they might have, or have had, similar experiences or anxieties to the ones the client's bringing. In those circumstances, it's all too easy to portray what's being talked about as deficiencies, inadequacies, aberrations, abnormalities rather than what they more usually are, which is painful manifestations of universal human experiences.

As well as promoting an idea, which is a very important misconception, that it would be possible (or even desirable) to live without a number of completely natural anxieties which are inescapable and integral aspects of the human condition, the therapist is working with the illusion that they, personally, are free of them. Even though they may be quick to acknowledge to themselves, or in private with colleagues, that this isn't really true for them (and maybe can't be for anyone), the idea, which they adopt as a therapeutic stance, still has a life in their heads in the room and in the heads of the clients they're seeing. Who's getting what out of this? If, as is always the case, low self-esteem and feelings of inadequacy are involved, it touches right on the issues that brought the client there.

Many people have written about the way mental health and well-being have been commercialised, industrialised even. Recent examples include *The Happiness Industry – How the Government and Big Business Sold Us Well-Being* by William Davies or *McMindfulness – How Mindfulness Became the New Capitalist Spirituality* by Ronald Purser. The point here is how much of it is built around selling idealised, impossible states of mind – serenity and competence that the sellers don't really feel and no-one could. This tendency was called out by one of Freud's closest colleagues in the early days after the invention of psychotherapy [311] and that didn't go down well. It was part of the critique of the anti-psychiatry movement of the 1970s and it's raised regularly by individual practitioners who are often well regarded and respected within the therapeutic community [312] but it's never really been taken seriously by the mainstream. It's the talking cure's Achilles Heel, equivalent to psychology's drive for formulation and psychiatry's diagnostic classification and they all come from the same misgivings – about what's really known, about what your field of expertise is really worth. Perhaps psychiatry's quaint willingness to expose the serious limitations and problems with its diagnostic system in its own literature is the result of an increased sense of security from having a medical qualification and all the infrastructure of a hospital behind you, but psychotherapy has never shown a willingness to examine itself as robustly.

This temptation to present yourself as existing in a kind of rarefied state is perhaps at its most obvious where mental health moves into well-being and lifestyle. Again, it's not deliberate enough to be fraudulent – it's not even cynical. It's just the way the mechanism works: people want to feel better (everyone's trying to manage the idea that they're not good enough) so they imagine an idealised state of mind in which they might. The more they come to rely on that fantasy to feel better about themselves, the more they need to inhabit it. Practising it publicly, teaching it, selling it, are good ways of feeling that they're inhabiting it more completely. Other people buy into the same idea and feel worse about themselves too. The 'super sorted' guru or sage is the same as the *Be Amazing* tee shirt wearer or the compulsive Instagram poster or the celebrity peddling a 'beautiful' story about how they've come through all their errors to a new understanding (again). They don't feel nearly as good inside as they're pretending most of the time. Nobody has it all sorted the way motivational speakers and inspirational influencers would have you believe – it really wouldn't be necessary to put on that show if they weren't reacting against something.

But this tendency isn't confined to the more spiritual and aspirational aspects of well-being practice, many of the concepts used in psychotherapy involve pretensions of super-human standards of insight and rationality. Many of the concepts used on clients are demeaning and so vague they're impossible to challenge – therapists talk about their clients not being able to experience joy or describe clients as not 'fully alive' (quite a common theme in the literature and a really amazing statement to make about another human being). One of the most influential books on psychotherapy was called *On becoming a Person*. In different circumstances, a therapist might say all this involved a quite serious attack on other people, a demonstration of superiority.

The reality is there is no such thing as 'secure attachment': only different styles and degrees of insecurity – and no wonder when you look at how anxious, inconsistent and fallible the people we're meant to attach to. I have never met anyone who couldn't be made to fit the diagnosis of Borderline Personality Disorder on close enough scrutiny. At that level these aren't diagnoses, they're just names to call people and unpleasant ones. Particularly unpleasant because if an expert labels you this way, there's really no way to defend yourself – the concepts are so vague and universal. People assume there must be a body of real knowledge behind them which makes them capable of the kind of concrete meaning we normally attach to terms in science and medicine and capable of being applied reliably. There isn't.

One of the reasons many people dislike and mistrust psychology and therapy is their superiority, their air of stood-back scrutiny and secret knowledge (sometimes in danger of straying into opaque, shamanistic cult membership). All too often accompanied by an air of smugness – the sorted ones, who know the way and set up an impossible standard of rationality and reason their own lives and conduct come nowhere near.

As if there was a formula, a way to be. The idea of a therapeutic mission – overcoming ourselves to live a perfected life in a balance of wisdom and fulfilment – is another form of idealism.

We're always straining after a version of ourselves that we'd like to be. It's a bad habit which can keep us pretending to ourselves and others, too unaware of what we really think and feel. And if we can't connect enough to ourselves – if too much is built on things that aren't real feelings, or ignored real feelings, if too many reactions are based on what we'd like to think, rather than how we actually think or feel about something – it's that much harder to be connected to other people.

Part of the pressure that keeps us locked into these false versions of ourselves comes from the idea that we're getting it wrong. Making people think there's some standard of elevated thought and behaviour (that there is a way), that others are achieving and they can't, perpetuates that idea. The idea of being 'sorted' in that way is idealised pap – just another response to the feeling that something is wrong. It can do real harm.

* * *

Confusion defines our approach to mental health. We confuse mental health issues with normal human experience – and we can't tell when we're doing it. We sanitise mental health issues – or at least the more decorous ones. We look away from the fact that people with mental health issues are living with thoughts and ideas which cause them and other people a great deal of trouble and unhappiness. We hashtag and sloganize mental health, turning it into a cause and sufferers into victims (we don't seem to feel the need to do that in the same way with cancer). And the support we actually put in place, the resources and treatments, come nowhere near the expectations we've created in the minds of the sufferers or the people trying to help them.

At every turn, in the way we think and talk about mental health, and treat it, you can trace the same core ideas around inadequacy. We are drawn to ways of thinking about mental health that prioritise helping sufferers try to evade feelings of inadequacy and shame, even when that risks keeping them stuck in illness or feeding feelings of grievance, resentment and isolation that might make them iller. Mental health professionals try to take refuge for themselves in ideas of superiority, imposing impossible theoretical mental states and standards of behaviour, even though that makes them and the people they're treating feel worse. And all the time we're selling ourselves a happiness or wellness industry (selling ourselves everything really) based on idealised pictures of how it's possible to be, how we ought to be, which make everyone feel worse about themselves and feed the ideas that dominate people's minds when they come for help.

8

OTHER PEOPLE

So, what's to be done? Well, *an* answer is that we've been addressing something which *is* useful and important all along.

Before we start, it's worth looking at happiness. Happiness has very little to do with intelligence or intellectual life, at least directly. It's the feelings people have inside them which are their happiness or unhappiness. That's what happiness and unhappiness consist of.

The most powerful, far-reaching and persistent feelings we have are around our ideas about ourselves and other people. Those are ideas we can't get away from. Intellectual pursuits, absorption in a task, beauty, nature can offer their own forms of happiness but most of what we feel is to do with us. So that's going to determine most of our happiness or unhappiness. Achievements, wealth, possessions are really only relevant for how they affect our ideas about ourselves.

And how we feel about ourselves is very largely dependent on how we think about other people. There are a number of reasons for that. One is simply the strength of feeling other people arouse in us.

Grievance and resentment sour us. That affects everything and makes it harder, or impossible, to enjoy anything whilst it's going on. When people are in these states, they might not think of themselves as being unhappy – there's an energy to the situation and grim exhilaration and triumph to be had in exacting retribution. But these are unpleasant states to be in – agitated and restless; deep down, it feels like something's wrong.

Spend too much time like that and we start to dislike ourselves for it. This is quite an intense form of unhappiness, which can go on for a long time or become persistent.

It's similar with acute anxiety – a shrivelling up inside which stops people being able to have other feelings, to respond to things properly. The difference is that people who are feeling intensely anxious, know immediately that they are unhappy – people who are stuck in grievance and resentment may take longer to realise it. In practice, the two states go together very closely – anxiety breeds resentment and our own resentment and aggression makes us anxious.

On the other hand, when we feel well disposed towards other people – particularly the ones we're closest to – we feel good about ourselves: settled, secure, open-minded and responsive. We enjoy being ourselves and there's a powerful sense of care towards others, a generosity of spirit. Here's an example of this kind of state of mind from W.B. Yeats:

> I sat, a solitary man
> In a crowded London shop,
> An open book and empty cup
> On the marble table-top.
> While on the shop and street I gazed
> My body of a sudden blazed;
> And twenty minutes more or less
> It seemed so great my happiness
> That I was blessed and could bless.[313]

Here's something similar in a stray piece of journalism about the songs of the summer: *There is a moment on every dancefloor in which you sneak a glimpse of your friends dancing, lost to the music, and feel a great surge of love towards them.*[314]

Those are opposite ends of a continuum but there is always a flavour to everything that happens to us and everything we do – more or less well disposed, more or less benign or hostile – to do with how we are feeling towards other people. It touches everything.

If this isn't an area science hasn't been able to get at directly, for what it's worth, the critical importance of relationships to happiness and mental health is something experimental psychologists seem to have been happy to recognise. The conclusion drawn by the long-term director of Harvard's famous Grant Study – which has tracked the physical and psychological health of 268 (male, white) graduates over their lifetimes[315] – is that what the results show is that the *only thing* which *really matters* in life is relationships with other people.[316] That's a view endorsed by the inventor of the well-known Dunbar's number (a proposed cognitive limit to the number of stable social relationships we're capable of maintaining) who came to the conclusion that the number and quality of relationships has the greatest impact on well-being and risk of death than anything except giving up smoking.[317] These aren't scientific results, they're more personal conclusions about the nature of things drawn by people who have spent a lifetime involved in science.[318] In terms of scientific evidence, they're no more valid than the conclusions of someone who has spent a lifetime in clinical work but perhaps, in real terms, they're no less valid either.

Another reason why the way we feel about ourselves gets mixed up with how we think about other people, is that the way we see ourselves is powerfully influenced by how we imagine other people see us or would like them to. If we think other people feel positive towards us, it makes us feel good about ourselves; if we think other people feel negative towards us, we feel worse about ourselves. We prize the aspects of ourselves we imagine others might admire and we despise the things we think they would look down on. So pretty much the whole time we're thinking about ourselves, we're thinking about how we think other people see us.

And, at the same time, we're also constantly comparing and measuring ourselves against other people. It's not a choice to compare ourselves to other people – we can't make ourselves not do it; it's going on constantly, automatically, whether we're aware of it or not. But when we think about other people, we do something quite strange.

Our experience of our own states of mind, particularly unpleasant, distressing states of mind, is so close up, so intense, that we find it hard to imagine things could be the same for others. And it's the belief that things are different for other people that gives the ideas that cause us most trouble much of their power.

We may struggle to see them as separate and independent when it comes to what we expect them to do for us, but when we compare ourselves to other people, we tend to invest them with a solidity, an authenticity, an emotional cohesion and rationality that we don't feel in ourselves or feel only intermittently and precariously.

We may be able to laugh at them and aspects of their lives (it's likely we do – a bit of superficial triumphalism, even if it's affectionate, is a necessary consolation) but being able to look down on people a bit, maybe even sneer at them a little, doesn't get rid of the subterranean idea that, in some profound respect, they're better than us – free of the things we dislike most about ourselves.

This affects everyone – it's universal. One of the biggest and most damaging misconceptions is that other people are free from the things that trouble us most about ourselves. As a result, those things feel uniquely and shamefully personal to us. When things are going fine, we lose sight of these aspects of ourselves and it doesn't matter much that they feel unique to us. When things are going against us, these ideas about ourselves come to the forefront of our minds and that misconception becomes much more important.

Young children's obsession with 'naughty' and 'bad', the hyper-sensitivity about appearance and social insecurity in our teens, the relationships we damage because we couldn't quite trust anyone to love us, the sense in later life of defeat, that life hasn't been how it should have been – all of this feels intensely personal. What gets missed at each point is how much everyone else is affected in the same way.

And if, at some level, we do 'know' that, a lot of the time we don't really possess it. We don't live by it – it's a theoretical idea, without much weight in our more emotional life. The result is that it's easy to feel excluded from a community who (we're sure) are united in feeling more competent and confident than we do or, at least, not afflicted by the same deficiencies as us.

When this idea is in focus, our achievements and abilities are discounted, they pale beside the deeper feelings of inadequacy and inferiority. Those are just accomplishments; this dissatisfaction goes much deeper – it's about our whole worth as a person.

Trying to be OK

In reality, like you, most people aren't that happy, most of the time. Or, a better way to put it might be to say there's quite a lot they're unhappy about. We all lead our lives in parallel streams, trying to be happier than we wholly are or, rather, trying to keep away the ideas that make us unhappy. We try to behave as happy and confident and self-assured as we'd like to feel – it's reassuring and it helps us get on with our lives. It's not exactly pretending, even to ourselves, it's aspirational and unconscious – we act the way we want to be. And, largely, it works pretty well, most of the time.

Most of the time, people don't have much idea how they feel – they're just getting on with things, not really one thing or another. Most of the time, it wouldn't make sense to ask whether they're happy or not. If you did, people would probably look a bit confused, shrug and say they were fine. And that would be right, most of the time.

But it's not the whole picture – there's a channel of anxiety and insecurity and need and (often) resentment which we try to keep away, in a drain running alongside the rest of our lives. All the time we're taking care of business, occupying ourselves with work, game shows, football, shoes, love or humour, painful, difficult ideas and thoughts are flitting round the back of our minds – a kind of shadow life behind the main stage.

Even when we manage to put them entirely out of view, they're always touching us and influencing the way we think and behave – still reaching into our daily lives and often in ways that cause us trouble. When things aren't going well, when we experience adversity, they take more space front and centre – we become more aware of them and they can overwhelm us.

These ideas are quite different to the more deliberate thinking we do in our more rational lives – they can't be reasoned with in the same way. They're pre-cognitive, we don't really think them; they're just there, pre-formed. We are born with them in the same way as we are born with the muscles in our backs.

When people, including psychologists, discuss themes like self-esteem, not feeling good enough, unfairness, grievance, rejection, resentment, abandonment, loneliness, what invariably gets missed is their ferocity. That's what hurts people who come for help – the ferocity of these ideas – intrusive, compulsive patterns of thought which rob them of their peace of mind and their ability to enjoy anything and which they can't get away from.

So, a lot of people who come to therapy come because something has broken through and they can't put it back. They don't come because they've become unhappy, they come because they've seen something about a form of unhappiness which was always there – and it shocks them. It's hard to go on as they were – impossible to unsee it entirely – the idea that they're not as happy as they thought they were, as they've been trying to be, as they think they ought to be. They weren't deliberately faking anything before, they were just trying to be OK. And what else are we supposed to do?

We're not nearly as rational as we'd like to think. No-one lives their lives like a game of chess – we can't predict ourselves, let alone other people. So, we have to try things out – we have to try to make them work and part of trying to make them work is living them as if they do work. Homes, jobs, marriages, we try to make our lives work by living them as if they do work.

But the potential for people's determination to present themselves to themselves in line with their desires and expectations to lead us into trouble is obvious, particularly when it gets too far from the reality of how we do feel.

And, even though we're doing the same thing ourselves, we're constantly taken in by it in other people. That's what makes us susceptible to the idea that it's different for us – other people really are that composed and contented, other people really are free from the same secret misgivings about themselves.

You can see the performative element reaching its peak on social media and in the public personae of celebrities. Actually, given they've become dependent on something as extreme as performing in public in order to try to feel OK about themselves, there's a good chance celebrities are more insecure and unpredictable than you are and that their lives feel more chaotic and precarious than yours. From time to time, you see this when the performance slips and things fall to pieces – another divorce, another bout in rehab. Till they re-emerge on the chat-show circuit, even more self-assured and resolved than they were, perhaps now with added wry self-acknowledgement.

This wouldn't matter except part of the way this parade works is that for anyone to get to relieve their feelings of inadequacy this way, in order to finish the job, they have to push those feelings of self-dissatisfaction into others. In order to feel better about yourself, other people have to end up feeling a little worse about themselves. People don't, usually, know that's what they're doing and people don't, usually, know it's being done to them, but that's the transaction. Psychotherapists recognise this mechanism, and make much of it in some forms of therapy, but seem oddly reluctant to accept they may be implicated in a similar process themselves. So, it's not nice, but there's a sort of honest revenge in celebrity-magazine photos of cellulite or gleeful reporting that behind Nigella's showboat lifestyle, there were bags of cocaine on the fridge, allegations of hundreds of thousands of pounds of credit card theft by household staff and photos of her husband with his hands round her throat.[319]

Because the point is, it is everybody. Not just your close friends, a few people who make their living writing about this stuff and a community of people suffering from mental health issues. There is no breed apart who have it all taped, are on top of it all, or are immune to the things you find most troublesome about yourself. We love that idea – that it is possible to figure it all out, to be a total winner and that some people are.

Hedge-fund managers are the most glamorous, revered and reviled figures in finance. They tend to operate by taking contrarian positions, betting against the market, and they're often activist, intervening in corporate situations to shake things up – it's all about being smarter than everybody else – and the returns can be stratospheric. One of the earliest hedge-funds was Long Term Capital Management, founded in the mid-1990s by perhaps the most successful bond trader of his generation. With more than a billion dollars of initial capital – an astonishing amount to raise for a new fund in those days – and two Nobel-prize-winning economists on its board, LTCM had a mystique of complete intellectual invulnerability. This was different, the paradigm had shifted – these were the smartest guys on the planet and they *had* figured it all out. And that wasn't just impressionable journalists, seasoned grown-up finance professionals believed the same things. You couldn't put your money with LTCM, being allowed to invest with them was like getting into one of the most exclusive clubs in the world – a licence to print money. And everybody involved made a lot of money, for a while.

In the fourth year LTCM failed, spectacularly. The losses were so calamitous there was concern for the global financial system and the Federal Reserve had to step in. It doesn't matter why the fund failed, how unpredictable the circumstances were, whether the rescue was the right option or how it could have all been different – people can argue about that for ever. It doesn't matter that the scale of failure means that some kind of heroic glamour still attaches to the people behind it. The point is – it failed. The smartest guys in the room (and that's what they were trying hard to be because that's the way they'd found to feel better about themselves) weren't as smart as everyone wanted to think they were. They weren't in the dotcom bubble either. Or in 17th century tulip mania. They never are. The idea that some other people can work everything out is a part of how we view ourselves and how we judge ourselves and it's never right.

We do something similar with the major decisions in our lives. Most important choices involve a trade-off and at times aspects of those trade-offs are going to feel uncomfortable – at times maybe very uncomfortable. That discomfort gains force from the idea that it ought to have been possible to get this absolutely 'right' – no downsides, no uncertainty, no regrets, unequivocally the correct choice. And that idea depends on the belief that there are people who do.

Looked at logically, how could that ever be right on most of the big issues facing us – choice of partner, career, what job to take, whether to have a family, whether and how to try to balance family and career? There is no perfect solution – taking one path means giving up another and there can't be a scenario in which you don't occasionally feel a sense of loss, missing out or sacrifice. That's the conventional formula but it doesn't put it nearly strongly enough – there can be few parents who haven't at times felt like weeping with frustration at what they've taken on and what they've given up. And there probably aren't many people without children who haven't occasionally been affected by a numbing sense of their lives being narrower and emptier than they might have been.

Often, there isn't even a sensible basis for trying to judge whether we made the 'right' choice. Move to a new city or country for a job and after six months the decision might look one way, after two years a different way and something else again a decade later. When do you decide whether it was the 'right' call? And all the time, any number of things outside your control, that could never have been predicted, will intervene – the credit crunch, coronavirus or just the people you meet.

But when it feels like our choices are pinching us, we don't just accept that it's the inevitable price of having to make decisions whose consequences are so ramified and contingent on future events and circumstances we can't influence. It's all too easy to convince ourselves we screwed up and beat ourselves up for it. And then veer away from that, because it's very painful, into furious self-justification. And then swing back again into self-blame. And so on.

Or, we try to inure ourself against the discomfort involved in the idea that we could have missed out, or lost something, or made a mistake by simply refusing to have it – refusing to entertain that idea. Which comes to the same thing as beating ourselves up about it – it's just too uncomfortable an idea to be able to live with in peace. And, anyway, it's too late – it doesn't work. If that's how we're reacting, the idea is already there and affecting us (and those around us).

Or, the fear of making a mistake, of not getting it right, can become paralysing. It can trigger levels of anxiety which make it impossible or traumatic for people to make decisions or they sabotage their own choices by not really giving them a chance to succeed, turning away at the first obstacle, not following through, not really trying.

Rationally we should probably accept that it doesn't really make much sense to think of these decisions as 'right' – they're too big for that. The best we can probably do is try to have as good a process as we can making our choices – and then focus on trying to make the best of the consequences, make the best of the hand we're dealt. That's not generally how we approach things and, in part, that's because we have an idea that somewhere there are people who are always nailing it and we should be able to as well.

There isn't really much reason to be envious of anyone – anyone at all. You might envy some aspects of their life (intellect or beauty, wit, achievement, wealth) but in every essential respect, in terms of the things that cause you most trouble – the precarious self-esteem, the sense of isolation, the vulnerability to resentments – the conditions of their life aren't any different to yours. You might want something they've got, but it's no better inside their head.

This can seem like a ridiculous thing to say because we are so primed to set people up, to think it must be different and better for them. It finds perhaps its most extreme expression in the Star syndrome – a kind of communal fantasy in which people become transformed into separate beings in another dimension where things can't be the same. Of course, they are – here's Paul Anka, the writer of *My Way*, on Frank Sinatra:

> Shit happens to everybody every day, whether you're Frank Sinatra or Joe Blow….Of course he had regrets – that's why we sat around and drank every night. You could hear it come out in him, from Ava Gardner, to whoever … .[320]

Rich, handsome, supremely talented, maybe the biggest Star in the world for a time. But, married four times and reportedly engaged twice more (so that's at least five serious break ups) and biographies report a history of mood swings and violence, drink problems, obsessive cleanliness and hygiene issues and a life conducted in fear under the shadow of organised crime figures he felt compelled to fraternise with. Generous, on occasion courageous, but also capable of mean-minded, spiteful threats and acts against people with less wealth and power. Poor confused, unhappy, lonely, regretful, drunk, Frank. You wouldn't really want to be him. The Stars alive today, and protected by defamation lawyers, aren't living in a separate dimension either.

Good luck, good choices, achievement, success, privilege, all matter. Things going well really helps – it's the opposite of adversity. But things can feel like they're going wrong if the things going right come at too high a cost. All those lawyers with mental health issues – things *are* going wrong: they're making themselves do too much they don't want to; it's too hard, too much anxiety. And things going right can only protect us so far against things going wrong in other aspects of life.

People can say one thing and do another. People can think one thing and feel something else at the same time. People can think two opposing things at once. And just because they can see something is happening, just because they can talk about something, maybe even laugh at it, doesn't mean it isn't hurting them. You can say you're OK and feel OK for a long time and still be living with something that could become unbearable.

In 2019, aged 49, Dr Jeremy Richman killed himself. By all accounts, Jeremy Richman was a very impressive man. He was an eminent neuroscientist, working on research into antidepressants, and a faculty lecturer in the Psychiatry Department at Yale. After his six-year-old daughter was murdered in a school shooting, he and his wife established the Avielle Foundation, a charity to fund research into the brain and violent behaviour and foster community engagement to apply the insights from that research.

Dr Richman was an inspirational speaker. You can find his talks online and they reveal remarkable depths of thoughtfulness and compassion – extraordinary responses to the most terrible of circumstances. As his wife said after he died, he 'had every tool in the toolbox at his disposal' and, at least from the outside, the impression was of someone doing OK – active, energetic, purposeful, positive, with a firm grip on life as worth living and a great deal to live for. Here's a flavour of him:

> When I point out the environmental factors that predict violence, people cross them off and say "I'm fine" but the fact is that if you are not actively engaged in protective factors for brain health – building community, developing empathy, engaging in challenge – then you are moving downstream, and that is a fact of life.[321]

Jeremy Richman was a very capable man, with more intellectual and emotional resource than most of us, and family support, and somebody murdered his child and he gave the appearance of being OK. It's so easy to be taken in by what people say, by their determination to persuade themselves of something. It's just as hard to spot when we're doing it ourselves. And a lot of the time, we don't have much choice – what else was Jeremy Richman supposed to do but try to be OK?

The point isn't what might have caused this man to kill himself, why that day he succumbed and felt he couldn't go on. The point is that people try hard to be one way, that they can persuade themselves they're one way, they can sound like that and think that's how they are themselves but it's not true or it's not the whole of the truth. We take ourselves in, we take others in and we get taken in by others. One result is that when we stop feeling

OK, we all feel worse about ourselves – we are all more affected by the idea that there's something wrong with us, because we imagine things are somehow different for other people.

Getting to peer behind the curtain and the enriched sense of other people's predicaments that brings – how their own personal anxieties and over-sensitivities, all the things they don't like about themselves, are standard issue – has been helping psychologists and psychotherapists get by for ever. When you can see the same thing going on for others, you realise, in the most important sense, that nothing in particular is wrong in your life.

When it becomes apparent how often other people feel low, overwhelmed and lonely. That, however good a job they're doing at pretending they know what they're doing, they don't. That all of them, every single one, without exception, has an internal life which feels just as rickety and unstable as yours. How much of the time they behave compulsively, without any real control over what they're doing. How much of what they say and do is designed to make them look good – self-serving, a bit fake, in just the same way you catch yourself doing and despise yourself for. When that's the case, there's really no need to feel so bad about yourself.

This is about the things no-one usually tells you. They don't get spelt out in novels or autobiographies or films. The internal monologue is really very similar for everyone – the same pre-occupations and ruminations, distracting us from what's actually happening around us. Everyone's states of mind are just as fleeting and powered by the same undercurrents of anxiety and doubts about self-worth.

The idea of everyone struggling in this way might seem a gloomy view. It needn't, it's liberating – if this is how we're meant to be, it has to be OK. Also, it's the truth and, in the end, most of the time, we're probably better off working on the basis of the truth. And it's not like we're saying people are never happy or that everyone is extravagantly unhappy, we're just recognising that people are restless, insecure – and some of the key ideas driving our discontent are to do with it being different for other people.

The answer might seem to be to tell each other the truth, but we can't do that because a lot of the time we're trying not to know about this stuff ourselves. If we're going to find out how it is for other people, by and large, we're going to have to work it out for ourselves.

Turning the gaze outward

So, the focus needs to shift. Rather than inward (where therapy usually directs you), the gaze needs to turn outwards – towards other people (which is, of course, how psychologists and psychotherapists spend their time). We need to look more closely and kindly at other people and take more seriously the idea that things might be the same for them. That requires a degree of concentration, it doesn't come naturally.

Waiting rooms, train journeys and bus stops can provide a useful opportunity. Smart phones have spoiled things a bit, but there are still places where you can often see other people when they're not distracted in a task or animated by company. Look at the way their faces subside into a kind of wistful vacancy – you can see them go entirely inside themselves and most of the time it doesn't look very comfortable. You can be pretty sure they're asking themselves the same kind of anxious questions as you – 'what did she mean when she said that?' or replaying the same kind of spiteful fantasies of getting their own back, making other people pay. Get better at it and, when you look around, you can see the same kind of thing in the blank faces walking towards you on the pavement.

Here are some practical tips for seeing other people. It's not a matter of conjuring tricks to try to read minds, it's about applying a different approach to other people – paying a different kind of attention than you normally would, paying more attention, and looking for signs of what you should expect to find there, which are the same things you find in yourself.

The first is, of course, you can't, not really. Other people are separate and, ultimately, they're unknowable, even the ones you need and depend upon most. Seeing other people is guesswork – that's important, everything is tentative, it's easy to be wrong and you can never really know when you're right. But we rely on guesswork all the time, in all sorts of vital aspects of our lives, more than we generally acknowledge – obvious enough with things like economic forecasting, but also there in metallurgical grades, mechanical engineering and medical diagnoses. There's nothing wrong with guesswork in the right context but we need to take our guesswork seriously. Some guesses are more educated than others and the quality of our guesses makes a huge difference to our lives.

Another is to pay as much attention to what happens as to what people say. We're all extremely good at fooling ourselves about what we really feel about things and what we really want. We can say (and believe) all sorts of things when our real feelings and ideas are very different – it's too easy to think we think the things we think we ought to think. What keeps happening to people can offer a much more reliable guide than what they say – the girl who describes herself as loving and caring but has fallen out with her family and keeps falling out with everyone else, or the guy who says he's independent and likes to be on his own but never doesn't have a girlfriend.

One illustration of the unreliability of words is how often the things people say are a reaction to having had exactly the opposite idea. When someone volunteers, apropos of not very much, that they have no regrets about some decision they made, the chances are they do and maybe quite powerful ones. They've only said it as a reaction to a sudden misgiving they didn't want to have – the purpose of the statement was to dismiss an idea before it could bother them. It's usually (largely) an unconscious mechanism – they probably had no or little awareness of the qualm they experienced and they moved on with their equanimity more or less intact. But it was there and it affected them and it will affect them again. It made them say the opposite to what they meant and we all do it. When someone says they don't blame you for something, it generally means they blame you but they might be trying hard not to.

Another tell-tale is the faults people pick out in others. Things they tell you about yourself, can be an important clue to what's going on for them. If you find yourself being accused of being very angry, and you really didn't think you were, there's a good possibility you weren't, but they were. Quite often, the things we accuse other people of are the traits we inflict on them ourselves. The reason they suggest themselves so readily as an explanation when we're unhappy with other people is because we're acutely sensitive to them as things we're unhappy about with ourselves.

This principle applies particularly to parents. As a rule, whatever we complain about most about our parents, we do that too. And not as a small peripheral thing we can think we've beaten because we can see it and laugh at it, but as a core part of our behaviour. The reason we detest that trait so much in our parents is precisely because we sense that it's in us too. We try to convince ourselves that we must have it under control because we know it's there and we can laugh at it (in our parents), but it's a major fallacy that because we can see and laugh at something, we're beyond it. Whatever people find most infuriating about their parents is likely to be a default setting that makes its own important contribution to the tone of their own relationships and is always there for other people to have to deal with.

Jokes are revealing. 'It's only a joke!'. Sure, but why *that* joke? Humour has had a bit of a bad press in this book so far, but that's not the full picture – you can do a lot with humour. It *can* be a screen for aggression – that kind of slippery 'only joking' way out. It *can* often be evasive, a way of avoiding real feeling – another kind of denial. Or it can be part of a healthy coping mechanism. We have a lot of ideas in our heads – this book is really about coming to terms with the worst, so we can engage with the best. Making light of something can be a healthy aspect of encountering something difficult – a tolerant acceptance, perhaps sometimes the most interesting and wisest way of responding to some of the things that cause us trouble. Maybe a degree of entertaining self-deprecation, or deliberately exaggerated grandiosity, to detoxify those ideas around inadequacy? Or a sense of absurdity to provide perspective on some of the painful things that happen to us. You can't always tell what's being done with humour but it's always telling you something – there's a reason that joke selected itself, it wouldn't have come out of the mouth (even as a joke) if it wasn't in the head.

The last tip is to look out for excess. It's been mentioned before: whenever someone's reaction or behaviour seems too much, more than the situation calls for – too emphatic, too loud, too excited, trying too hard, too angry, drinking too much – it's to do with anxiety. And in some form or other, that anxiety will invariably relate back to ideas about self-worth, inadequacy and exclusion. You see it in work meetings, the things that don't need saying, that have no purpose other than someone just needing to register their presence in a group – and you see it in social settings too. It's so commonplace it doesn't really tell us very much about an individual situation but it does help reveal something about the underlying levels of discomfort we're all living with all the time.

The ramifications of being able to see other people more clearly are endless.

It usually involves a jolt of recognition and empathy – there's care and warmth in it. So much of our effort and achievement has superiority and dominance at its heart – as compensation for the idea that we're not good enough: this is an antidote. Getting a more realistic picture of other people helps to dispel the idea that we're uniquely flawed. That allows us to soften on some of the attributes we don't like in ourselves (which is a more genuine and lasting acceptance of yourself than you're likely to find in any lifestyle programme of self-love) and in others. People become more tolerant and forgiving, of themselves and others.

Ironically, given it involves a realisation that no-one else knows what they're doing either, it helps with trust. Trust is hard won and will always have its limits, but it's likely to be more difficult to the extent we harbour secret feelings of inadequacy and vulnerability – somehow weaker than other people, and at risk of having things done to us. That gets easier the clearer the idea becomes that other people are just as confused and bewildered in their lives as we are. We might still not follow their advice, but now it's more a matter of judgement than mistrust.

And whilst other people may not have much idea what they're doing, if we're honest and accept our own capacity to mislead and confuse ourselves (which gets easier when we can see that's standard), we'll see that sometimes someone else's perspective is just what's needed, precisely because it is another perspective. There are plenty of times and situations where the last person we should trust entirely is ourself.

Dialling down the idea that we're working under some kind of personal handicap, also helps with over-dependence. If we can see that, however it might look from the outside, they are in fact up against the same things that trouble us most about ourselves, we understand better that there is a natural limit to what other people can do for us. That feels better, we accept the natural limitations of the situation more readily and our dependence becomes more proportionate. It's easier to forgive people when they let us down – it can help us decide better what matters and what doesn't, what's forgivable and what isn't. Insecure attachment and avoidant attachment have their roots in insecurity, a sense of not deserving to be loved, a buried anxiety about being found out and rejected. In fact, all attachment is linked to insecurity, those ideas are an integral part of us.

Correcting the sense of ourselves as uniquely weak and vulnerable, by seeing other people's predicaments more clearly, helps us govern our own behaviour too. Many of the poor choices people make in life are the result of compulsive reactions to feelings of inadequacy and self-dissatisfaction. If we can take on board more firmly that other people share the things that bother us most about ourselves, our ideas about our own inadequacy lose some of their force and so do these compulsions. There's more potential for the choices we make to be freer, better.

And when we can see more clearly through some of the presentation other people have prepared for themselves and the world, it takes away some of the pressure on us to perform the same old version of ourselves. We can stop trying to impress or please so much. That's a very good thing because pretending never feels entirely comfortable. It's always a strain to maintain something you're trying to be and it can feel downright dishonest.

We're very sensitive to feeling fake – imposter syndrome is probably a universal experience. Inauthentic feels shifty and shameful. And we're frightened of being found out – we can't settle and be at peace with ourselves and it erodes our trust in situations and other people. This isn't necessarily about saying things that aren't true (though that can happen), rather paying a little more attention than we'd like to admit to the effect what we do and say has on other people. We're never going to not care how we imagine other people see us, but the idea that there's something peculiarly wrong can make us overdependent on validation by other people. If that idea relaxes, it gives us the opportunity to try out other ways of being, to be more ourselves.

But the most important effect is that seeing other people more clearly, seeing them more as they are, necessarily involves coming to see them more as separate and independent from us. That helps to make our expectations of them more realistic. And, ultimately, most of our happiness and emotional well-being is going to depend upon our capacity to come to terms with reality.

Coming to terms

Disappointed expectations can be a problem with the world or a problem with people's expectations. If it's a problem with the world (an illness, an injury, an abusive relationship, a neglectful childhood) hopefully their luck will change. If expectations are realistic enough and the world starts to behave more like it normally does, things ought to get better. Unfortunately, there is never any guarantee that luck will change and things don't always improve – every median has outliers. Some people, like Jeremy Richman, encounter experiences no-one should have in their expectations. Some things you can't come to terms with.

If it's a problem with expectations, people might (more or less laboriously and painfully) learn more about how the world works, gain more realistic expectations and come out of it. Or they might get stuck. When our expectations are badly off, we're going to live more frustrated, disappointed lives, we're going to be unhappy more of the time and we're more likely to become ill.

Right at the heart of things is our expectations about other people. Other people are separate from us – they see things differently, they need different things and they have different agendas. No-one gets this right all the time. It's impossible – the need and dependence, and the expectations that flow from them, are too strong. They're meant to be, that's what ties us together.

This is where trust comes in – trust is important because of the inevitability of disappointment. Can we suspend the normal rules in our most intimate relationships and protect them with a sense of trust to help us overcome disappointment and suspicion when our expectations aren't met – *it's OK because it's only you*? How far should we?

It's not just expectations of other people. The more realistic our picture of how things actually are for others, the better we can resist idealised fantasies about how our life ought to be. That's going to help avoid feeling like a failure without having to resort to something unfair having happened to us or someone else being to blame.

There is a question of balance here. People need a healthy sense of potential for their lives – there's no reason to settle for being less happy than we could or should be, and expectations need to be set accordingly. But when it goes badly wrong, we're tugged towards the ideas that are uppermost in the minds of people when they come for help. The pursuit of idealised lifestyles and extreme states of happiness tends to leave people swinging wildly on their emotions, trying to sustain the illusion, trying to keep the show on the road, trying to pretend they're not feeling something else.

No-one can tell us where to draw the line – everyone has to try to find it themselves. What's for certain is that we don't get the same sense of beaming fulfilment from engaging with our bank online as the perfect looking people in the ads, or derive the same real joy from a cup of coffee. Just because people 'know' these images aren't real, doesn't mean they don't get in (that's why they're everywhere). And one of the things they do, apart from making us want to buy life insurance so we can have a future filled with *that* kind of peace of mind (and an empty white sand beach), is contribute to setting our ideas of how it is possible to feel, how other people feel.

At some level, without really registering it, the contrast with our own experience makes us feel that little bit dissatisfied with our own lives. It's easy to laugh at and belittle but it's very hard to keep out and it's able to have that effect because of those ideas of inferiority and inadequacy, pre-set inside us all and ready to go. Taking a closer look at real people helps reset the balance. You can see that really no one else is getting a free ride. That's important – how can you enjoy the good things you have if you always feel things should be better?

Perhaps in order to avoid becoming very unhappy, we have to be able to bear the idea of being unhappy from time to time? Maybe we should think of mental health as the capacity to be unhappy without getting caught up in a loop of disappointment, self-dissatisfaction, grievance and isolation? Looked at with any degree of objectivity, our expectations of happiness often don't make much sense. Life *is* hard – even assuming things go well, there is plenty to cause us trouble. That is, cause us real, intense unhappiness, at times.

We will age and lose beauty and vigour – physical discomfort and debility will become more and more of a feature of our lives. Those aren't little things and it's a punishing myth to imagine that you should be able to navigate them entirely gracefully, without powerful feelings of loss. Even that's too much the formulaic language of therapy – nobody goes through these things without occasionally overwhelming feelings of despair and hopelessness.

All forms of work inevitably involve degrees of humiliation, compromise, pretence and pressure (so do most other kinds of relationship) – as well as the very positive benefits it brings. The world is a crowded, competitive place and competition for resources means the economic system calibrates itself ruthlessly to squeeze the maximum out of everyone – plumbers have to do the best they can to get the money they need and it's the same for professional footballers or Goldman Sachs partners. One way or another, everyone's performing at their limits.

We can't have it all and we can't make perfect choices – it's inevitable that there will be times when it feels hard to live with some of the consequences of the decisions we have made. And not just mild, picturesque regret – most people live under some kind of shadow of loss and many go through periods of anguish and bitter self-recrimination (and the things they do to avoid feeling that). Things outside our control happen all the time; we make mistakes all the time. And as a species we just seem to have something a little restless and fretful inside us.

For all these reasons, no one gets to stay that contented for very long. That doesn't mean there's something wrong with your life or with you.

Psychotherapy often seems to try to make a virtue out of unhappiness and to look for the positive side of negative emotions. People make things change, the story goes, as a result of being dissatisfied or frustrated – that's how things get better. That's not always entirely convincing, at least in a clinical context. The kind of unhappiness that brings people for help is generally pretty horrible, it spoils lives – the sufferers' and other people's – much better to avoid that if you can. And, unfortunately, being unhappy in that way isn't always a great state to be in in order to learn about the world or to make our best decisions. Not being able to tolerate being unhappy probably does involve some kind of limit on your ability to learn about the world. But, just because you're very unhappy, doesn't mean you're going to find a solution and become less unhappy.

There are perfectly respectable arguments against the examined life for its own the sake. It's not as if there appear to be obvious answers beckoning us – and we have an unbroken record of our efforts going back two and a half thousand years now. Whilst our lives feel contented enough to us, perhaps we'd do better to leave well enough alone. We are the people we try to be – those versions of us are valid. We want to live in the daylight and that's where we want to meet other people too. It's a mistake to live too much in the shadow world.

But the reality is that some volume of disquiet, anxiety and discontent are almost permanent companions for all of us. Everybody has these ideas around inadequacy, grievance and resentment and isolation running alongside the rest of their lives. So, it seems better to be ready to recognise that when you have to, or not be in headlong flight from it – because that often seems to lead to reckless or destructive choices which cause trouble to us and others, making ourselves and them more unhappy. If we can recognise that they are there, that we do live with these ideas, we can reduce the chances of them taking over and controlling how we feel and behave.

Better, too, to recognise this about others, to be aware of their predicaments. Because the greatest unhappiness seems to come from the idea that it's just you, and that's founded on misconceptions about what it's realistic to be and how (other) people are. The point isn't to try to rehabilitate these feelings or to try to make a virtue out of them. Often, they are unproductive or destructive. The point is if everyone has them, they don't say much about us, they're not the important thing. That leaves us freer to think about other ideas we have about ourselves, other things we feel, the other more positive aspects of our lives and what we want to do with them and how we treat other people.

And the most important place to recognise this, to get

this right, is where it's needed most, in our most intimate relationships – which is also where it's hardest to do.

Close up with other people

The people we care about and need most will disappoint us. For any relationship of intimacy to work, you need to have legitimate expectations which get met regularly enough, but these people can't possibly deliver everything we want from them. No one could meet the (secret) inconsistent, shifting expectations we foist upon them. Degrees of resentment must creep into our closest relationships, at times, over time. These are the people for whom we have compromised, to whom we have provided care, with whom we have put up, to whom we have most exposed ourselves, whose stories we have humoured and to whom we have most got used.

Shedding illusions might reconcile us to a more realistic picture of the world (or it might not), but it will inevitably involve feelings of disappointment and loss. Everyone has a temper, everyone has resentment, grudges are held – subdued, a long way back and greyed out, maybe, but still there, in the mix. There's also need (desire), gratitude, affection, generosity but when these sharper feelings strike, in the moment, they will feel intense, disturbing and upsetting.

Your secret, shameful experiences – your hidden resentments and grievances, your occasional fantasies of leaving the people you love when you're hurt, your sideswipes about their family, the sports they like, the values they hold, which are really about them, your pointed praise of qualities in other people you feel they lack – all the little dishonest, unpleasant devices you occasionally stoop to, can be extremely difficult to live with. For you, that is, the people they're aimed at probably aren't aware of them most of the time.

It's a serious point – if we find the experience of those ideas and feelings in ourselves traumatising, the situations and relationships that evoke them become traumatising. It's traumatic because those ideas connect directly with the idea that there's something wrong – with our lives, with us. If those are key situations or relationships, there's a real danger of an inability to tolerate aspects of ourself, and our own emotional life, driving the major events of our life, rather than any sense of what we really care about, what's important to us and what's in our interests. People do often make major decisions or (because that may be lending the process a rationality it doesn't deserve) take major steps in life because they can't cope with the experience of their own emotional life.

It's similar to what we saw with anxiety disorders and OCD – the problem has more to do with the way we respond to our own feelings and ideas than the situation that generates them. If we don't realise that these kinds of impulse are, in fact, an inescapable and occasional part of everyone's life, if we believe that they are specific to us or our situation, our response to them will be stronger, more extreme. The more we can keep in mind that these kinds of reaction are normal and inevitable – everyone has that – the more it might be possible not to bite down hard on them, to try to see them in perspective and work out what's important. They *could* be telling us something very important about our situation – this way we get a better chance of finding out.

The more time we spend in extreme reaction to the ideas we find in ourselves, the more unpleasant and toxic our lives will feel and the more we're likely to cycle in and out of feelings of inadequacy, guilt and shame on one hand, and resentful justification on the other, and the more time we'll spend feeling isolated. We'll also be likely to feel more of a sense of loss of personal agency, of things being done to us. Things *are* always being done to us, but it's a state of mind as well as a state of fact.

It's the same spiral we've seen before – the system comes under strain from the tension and instability. We'll become more anxious, we might become withdrawn or defensive, hyper-sensitive, irritable, maybe even downright vicious. In these circumstances, therapies that put too much emphasis on authenticity and self-assertion can feed the trauma people's own reactions are causing them – the sense of things being wrong and the sense of things being done to them. There may be an issue with lack of assertion in the sense of feeling too insecure or worthless to be able to express what they want or need effectively (though there are plenty of people around who feel they can't assert whilst the rest of the world thinks they're pretty good at it), but it's very rarely to do with thinking about other people too much (though there are plenty of people who will tell you that's their problem). In fact, thinking more clearly about other people – to get a more realistic sense of other people's predicaments and difficulties and overcome the feeling of operating under a handicap – is a very effective way to manage lack of self-worth and gain a genuine sense of capacity to assert. You can't feel so wrong or so hard done by or so weak and insecure, unless you think it's somehow different for others.

If any of this sounds easy or simple, it isn't meant to. Dealing with other people close up is an endlessly shifting task and always impossible to get completely right. Thinking about other people in this way involves trying to decipher what might be going on for them (or even just trying to maintain an open mind), in the middle of all their changeableness and inconsistency, whilst trying to ride the currents of our own emotional life. And it follows from what we've been saying that quite a lot of the time these other people are going to be behaving in irrational, difficult, foolish ways (much like us).

The effort of trying to satisfy the needs and meet the wants of someone who isn't you, who sees things differently and expects different things, takes its toll. You can't see what they think (most of the time, neither can they) but their state of mind is the biggest influence on your happiness. At the very least, you inevitably lose some freedom of choice, maybe a great deal, and some peace and quiet too, maybe even the possibility of being on your own at all. Most close relationships – marriage, parent and child – spend a certain amount of time being conducted towards the edge of the individuals' tolerance.

For some, the price might be too high and they actively choose not to do it, to be alone. A different kind of unhappiness maybe – more self-determined, free from the old cues for acute feelings of abandonment, grievance and resentment, and everything that comes with them. Something is always likely to feel missing – it may suit them better. But, by and large, we don't do well on our own. Most of us need to find ways to get on with people close up. Getting it right enough is like a trick of the mind, between two people, a habit you can get into and don't want to get out of. There is a limit to what we can put up with to be with the people we want to be with, what's true enough to yourself and what's too much. Perhaps it never gets entirely settled.

Statistics paint a bleak picture of how often relationships break down. According to the Office of National Statistics, as of 2017 around 42% of marriages ended in divorce in the

UK.[322] And the rate of relationship breakdown is much higher for unmarried couples. When serious relationships breakdown – however much we try to present it differently to ourselves and others, however strong and genuine the feelings of relief and escape might be – it does us a form of harm. These people have a life in our heads and, when they go, it's like having a part of our brains torn out. And, when they go, they can often take with them some part of our capacity to trust and love. Often, the end of a relationship entrenches a sense of grievance and resentment. At the same time, relationships that don't end can become saturated with past disappointments and bitterness and resentments. That can look frankly toxic, it doesn't seem easy or good to live like that either.

The most painful aspects of things that go wrong are usually about other people – neglect, abuse, infidelity, relationship breakdown, bereavement. It's often true even with what seem like entirely personal misfortunes – one of the most difficult aspect of illness is the demands it makes on others and how we feel they support us or let us down. No-one is going to think exactly like us but we've seen that the idea that they should, particularly the people we're closest to, is baked in. Every time we get reminded sharply enough that the people we depend on most feel differently, that different things are important to them, it's discomforting – and 'discomforting' (whether we recognise it or not at the time) means a rehearsal of abandonment.

Because we sense this, we spend quite a lot of time (when relations are good) finding the common ground to emphasize and avoiding the differences – maybe even suppressing ourselves and what we really feel a little in order to do that. When relationships get weaker, we may actively seek out the differences, exulting in the gaps and may feel that we're reclaiming some parts of ourselves which had been taken away from us.

Really, it's our fault – the more realistic approach to any relationship would be to recognise that other people occupy a quite different world, with themselves at its centre (in the same way you are of yours), and that subtly different laws of nature apply there – 'up' isn't 'up' in precisely the same way, very little works exactly the same. That's easy to say (and well-being guides and therapy tell you this is what to do), but it's impossible to do all the time. The unconscious processes we've talked about are too ingrained, the mesh of mutual dependence is too strong. We will always fall back into the same old patterns of thinking and the gurus who claim it *is* possible (especially the super-sorted ones who give you the impression they're doing it) are doing you a disservice and handing you a stick to beat yourself with.

At the same time, the more realistic a sense we can have of separateness, the more we can tolerate the idea that these people we depend upon do, in fact, have their own completely independent perspectives and agendas, the less frightened we will be when that becomes apparent and the less dramatic our reaction. It's also likely to mean we can better appreciate the efforts they make towards us, and feel less need to bend ourselves around a fantasy of oneness or exert pressure on them to do the same.

So, a degree of loneliness, not feeling understood and not getting what we want, are going to be part of every relationship. As ever, those feelings are much more emotional and painful than that sounds. We're so used to using these words, talking around these things, that we lose sight of just how existential, how desolate they feel when they strike. They can be lived with better through patience, tolerance, resignation, humour and an ability to feel disappointed and sad. It's hardness, grievance, resentment and self-loathing that bring people for help, that cause real trouble.

To be capable of keeping relationships lasting and positive, we have to be able to bear disappointment enough. Loving well means taking enough responsibility for your own disappointment. To love other people properly we have to have enough sense of them as separate from us – if we can't, disappointment and resentment will bury the rest of what we feel.

The people we depend upon most not seeing things the same as us, thinking things that are important to us don't matter, thinking things that aren't important to us do, not understanding when we're upset, saying the wrong thing, being mean and spiteful (and knowing they're doing it), losing people because they die or leave us, losing our youth, our beauty, our health, all these things will be part of living a successful life, as good a life as it is possible to have. If we can shed the delusion that it ought to be, or could be, different, maybe we never need to be so unhappy again.

And, whatever the situation, something that always has the capacity to cause trouble is the idea that things are different for me and it's better and easier for others. It's a self-lacerating ignorance of how it is for other people – if we don't like ourselves enough, part of the reason is going to be because we've got the wrong understanding of other people. If you don't like yourself, take a good look at the people around you. If you can see, working away in other people, the same ideas that trouble you about yourself, if your sense of there being something uniquely wrong with you releases its grip enough, you become less acutely sensitive to the idea of being wrong.

Remorse

And that's very important because the only real consolation for the way things are, the way we are, is that we can do better. And our chances of doing better are going to improve if we are able to recognise that we've got it wrong. Maybe to be the person you'd like to be, you have to be able to take seriously enough the possibility that you have been a shitty one. People who don't have enough sense of their own capacity for harm are more likely to cause it.

We are all moral, in our own terms – that constant potential for ideas of inadequacy and wrongness to resurface keeps us needing to think well of ourselves. The worst things we do, we do because we won't allow ourselves to see what we're up to. It's hard to recognise how much pretence, fear, aggression or malice can be involved in what we do – because we can't allow ourselves to accept our capacity to be motivated like that. So, we do it again and again. But, even if we can't acknowledge it, the fear and malice are still there and making us feel bad about ourselves. It's a well-being cliché – *to find self-esteem, do estimable things.* The flip side is true too – doing shitty things makes us feel shitty.

The truth is you've been involved in most of the things that have caused you trouble and you have done things that have hurt other people, maybe even spoiled their lives a bit, because we all do. That's not OK – why try to love yourself for that? Doing our best isn't always enough, if it falls way short of what's required. And, anyway, much of what you've done to cause harm to others won't have been doing your best, it will often have been thoughtless and sometimes it will have been tainted by malice. You should feel bad about yourself and you will. And you are going to do new things that justify you feeling bad about yourself. More than that, sometimes people get hurt even though we're sure we're doing the right thing. We might be – sometimes you can't avoid hurting people or causing them trouble. Saying it isn't our fault isn't the point – things are worse for someone and we're implicated.

All the ways we fail people – can't give them what they want from us, can't prevent them having to be unhappy in a particular way. People can't chase this stuff away with assertiveness training, authenticity, self-love or unconditional acceptance of the self – they end up shuttling between self-righteousness and self-justification and their own sense of inadequacy, shame and guilt. Trying to keep these ideas away at any cost is a huge effort involving stress, anxiety, distortion, internal conflict, over-reactions – excess all over – but if it feels too catastrophic to be in the wrong, there may not be much choice.

It's not a matter of trying to avoid hurting other people and recognising when we've caused harm because that will make the world a nicer, kinder place (though it probably would). This is entirely self-serving – it will make your world a better place. Recognising that we've got it wrong and trying to make good makes all the difference to how we feel.

Whatever else we may be feeling at the time, when we've caused harm, or wanted to, it prompts ideas of guilt and shame and a sense of inadequacy. If those ideas can't be lived with at all, they have to be avoided and that's usually through blame, grievance, resentful self-justification. Those are hostile, aggressive states of mind and they're amplified because they're being co-opted into doing a job of keeping other ideas away. Aggression (including our own) always causes us anxiety. At the same time, we're being dragged down by the spiteful thoughts inside us, the peevishness and grievance – even if we're barely aware of it, we *are* feeling worse about ourselves. And none of this works – the original guilt and shame and sense of wrongness are still there; we haven't dealt with them, we've just tried to drown them out.

Denial and conflict like this involve a cycle of difficult emotions, none of which can be tolerated for long. The pressure to twist away from what we're trying not to feel at any point will affect the way we behave and the choices we make. They are likely to be more impulsive and less rational and that may involve a greater potential for them to be against our best interests and to hurt others and damage relationships. That's important too – mistakes matter, mistakes can make lives worse, mistakes can create the adversity that make us feel unfairly treated, excluded, resentful and isolated. And, since they're our mistakes, they redouble the cues to feel inadequate and all the things we'll do to try to avoid that feeling. It's when things are going wrong enough that the trouble starts and that doesn't have to be very wrong at all.

Everybody gets in these states of mind from time to time. Mostly, they lift on their own and we become more open to other ways of seeing the situation. Those are probably ways of seeing things which are fairer to other people, which involve more sense of their perspective and the possibility we've caused trouble – we've been in the wrong, or in the wrong too. That does presuppose, though, enough capacity to take seriously the possibility of being in the wrong and being able to live with it.

If we're not capable enough of seeing and understanding some of the damage we've done, these states of mind can't lift. It's just self-righteousness and victimhood, fretfulness and self-assertion and the secret conviction that there's something inadequate and unworthy about us, going on and on. We don't like ourselves and we can't get away from it because we can't get away from ourselves. That could be restricted to something, or things, we've done, to a particular situation, a shadow from the past, or it could be more generalised. It's part of the experience of depression. That isn't to say that depressed people are depressed because they can't take enough responsibility for their own behaviour and mental states, but suffering from a sense of inadequacy which doesn't let us accept enough of our own capacity for causing harm is a good route to depression.

An essential element of happiness and mental health is a sufficient degree of integration – the mind being enough at peace with itself, not fighting to not think ideas or not remember things it can't tolerate. High up on that list are the things we've done and feel ashamed of. Reaching some kind of accommodation with the harm we've caused allows us to feel OK about ourselves and move on. Remorse is painful but it has a bitter-sweet quality, there's care and concern in it and it doesn't close us down, it's not the end of the road – there's the possibility of making good. People can be troubled by all sorts of painful ideas and emotions – loss, grief, remorse itself – but it's the cycles people get stuck in that really cause problems. Feelings always change but denial-fuelled loops can go on for ever.

Part of what's needed to keep our feet on the ground is realism, which includes a sense of compassion from a proper awareness of people's fragility – how vulnerable they are and we are. It can be hard when you feel barely competent, barely in control yourself, to realise how much others are dependent on you for their emotional security, to feel OK about themselves. It's hard to live up to the responsibility that entails and the harm you can cause. It's harder when you don't realise everyone else feels like you.

Our best prospect of behaving better, being someone we can actually enjoy being, treating other people fairly, having relationships and a set of expectations that keep us away from the ideas which dominate people when they come for help, is to have a sufficiently realistic view of ourselves to know what we're capable of, how mean, petty and spiteful we can be, what it looks like and how it happens and what it means and what it doesn't.

You are likely to be a little grabbier and more frightened than you'd generally want to admit. Your motivations for doing things may often be more self-centred and less noble than you usually like to think. Quite a lot of what you want to think of as done with others in mind is actually done because it suits you. Quite a lot more of the things you do than you'd like to recognise are done with an eye on the effect they might have on other people. You're not above manipulating and controlling your loved ones' behaviour (why not, you depend upon them?) and most often it doesn't really occur to you to wonder what they really need in a situation.

Worse, your first reaction would probably be to say of course you try to avoid hurting other people but, if you are honest enough with yourself, you will probably find that you are actually quite prone to irritation and taking sneaky little pot shots to punish people. That, quite a lot of the time, there can be some quite malicious ideas around and it's quite easy for them to leak out. You might find, in fact, you don't try to avoid hurting other people nearly as much as you imagine.

Often people are very ready to say they're 'upset' but less prepared, at least in personal relationships, to say they're angry.

Or, they're quick to display anger but reluctant to acknowledge hurt, even to themselves. Anger is invariably part of what 'upset' consists of. In fact, anger (however hidden and internalised it may be) is the flipside to a great deal of what we feel – anger is the companion piece to anxiety and we're anxious most of the time. When we're hurt, anxious or frightened, grievance and anger are always there and (at least) the idea of retaliation rarely far away.

Grievance and resentment have a tormenting, edgy energy which sticks to situations – tormenting ideas and feelings generally stick. The anger that sticks to things can cover up the hurt. When it happens enough, it's easy for people to forget about the need that led to the hurt in the first place. Losing sight of your need is a good way to act against your own interests – it's a good way for people to make mistakes.

Authenticity isn't just a matter of not pretending things to other people, it's also a matter of not pretending (so far as possible) to yourself. It's about trying to recognise and acknowledge what we really think and feel, so we can understand what matters to us and not spend so much time reacting against ideas we're trying not to have.

It is going to help you to be able to take all these possibilities about yourself seriously if you've worked out that's how other people are too, because it means there's nothing really wrong or that shameful here. And if you can take these possibilities seriously, you can do better – overcome these impulses more often, be more authentic, less selfish and kinder, which feels much better.

Of course, generally, at the time, what we're doing feels like the right thing. We think we're seeing things the right way and we're justified in behaving the way we're behaving – obviously enough, otherwise (mostly) we wouldn't do it. Later, we might have second thoughts and, if we're lucky, an opportunity to do something about it, to make good. Sometimes that only comes too late – it's always easier to see our mistakes in the past, particularly once we've convinced ourselves we've become a different person.

We may be able to see that we were in the grip of some idea that was making us see things a particular way. We may even be able to trace that idea to something that's happened to us, some experience in our past. That's really what damage is – being left with ideas which make us see things in unrealistic ways that cause us and other people trouble. Part of the form damage takes is not being able to see it – otherwise we'd behave differently. Damage invariably comes from hurt and involves ideas about inadequacy, rejection and isolation. Those ideas are usually at the heart of the experience that's caused the damage, but, also, the things that happen to people to cause damage often carry their own sense of shame and inadequacy. And the idea of being damaged is itself about there being something wrong with you. Mitigating that idea is mitigating the damage.

Probably, we can never entirely take on board the trouble we cause and the things we get wrong. Probably, that's just as well. And there are always likely to be ideas of justification or extenuation around. That seems right too – things are complicated, circumstances do need to be taken into account, things need balance. We don't have to sink into despair for getting things wrong. It's probably enough that we can take seriously the possibility that we might have got things wrong and that we can engage with the idea that, one way or another, we caused trouble to someone else.

That's likely to be enough to let in remorse. Remorse is not the same thing as shame or guilt (though they may be around in some degree too). With remorse you tend to find compassion, appreciation, gratitude, affection and, most of all, a desire to make good, an impulse of reparation. Shame and guilt look in at yourself, remorse looks out at other people. Shame and guilt are too intense to sustain by themselves, they tend to be accompanied by grievance and self-justification – remorse is more settled and lasts.

A healthy, proportionate sense of remorse and a desire to make good for the harm we inevitably cause is a tremendously powerful quality for mental health. If we're trying to make good, it means we're sufficiently free from self-loathing to be able to accept our own capacity to cause harm and to take responsibility for the harmful consequences of our actions – it is the sign that, at least for that moment, we have come to terms with ourselves as we are. And it means we're thinking about other people as separate from us, we're able to imagine how they've been affected – it involves care, it involves connection and grievance and resentment have been left behind. It means we're a long way from the ideas and feelings that bring people for help.

About the best experience we can have is when we feel right about the people closest to us – filled with affection, appreciation and gratitude. It's the opposite of souring – it's like carrying a jewel around in your head. It's never going to be a permanent state of affairs – it comes and it goes; other ideas intrude. But it's easier to spend more time feeling like that if we have a realistic sense of what's important to us, including what we need from other people, a strong enough sense of their separateness and independence from us and enough sense of our own capacity to cause trouble.

Appreciation and gratitude are the result of recognition and acceptance of our own vulnerability and dependence and other people's separateness and a readiness to coax or negotiate what we need from them, rather than assume it or demand it. Our vulnerability derives in large part from the idea of our own inadequacy and being able to manage that vulnerability is partly about coming to terms with our own sense of inadequacy.

Other people are separate and independent – it's not clear what other people owe us, if they owe us anything. And all we have is other people, whatever else we have. If we want to know what it's like not to have other people, it is that feeling when we wake up in the middle of the night, just us and the dark, and feel completely alone and at sea. We need to appreciate them and it helps to have a proper sense of how things are for them and what they have to put up with from us.

There is very little we can do to change the way we are (though that happens throughout life by itself). What we can do is come to terms enough with ourselves as we are. That enables us to behave differently – to be less anxious and insecure, less compulsive, less aggressive, more generous, more balanced, more thoughtful. We can live more deliberately, be more of ourselves. Having enough capacity for remorse is a very important part of that and perhaps enough of that capacity for remorse is something we should feel entitled to expect from the people we let into our lives as well.

***

The biggest obstacle to remorse is our own sense of inadequacy. It's that the acknowledgment of having got it wrong, or caused harm, will inflame the idea that we're not good enough more than we can manage.

The thing we hate about ourselves most is the idea that we're not good enough. We hate having that idea inside us. It's made us feel weak and cowardly and ashamed from our earliest days – something wrong from the start, something contemptible, which has been undermining us and spoiling things for as long as we can remember. So, it gets pushed down as far as we can, where it can direct things and control us without us knowing.

That is the starting point for so much of what causes us trouble. We hate having that idea inside us and we hate ourselves for having it. When we realise that everyone else has that idea too, that self-hatred can fall away.

Mistakes are not consequence free, and they can be disastrous. The more that's gone wrong in a life, the more adversity, the more the evidence that there is something wrong with you and with your life. And the more opportunity for disappointment, grievance, resentment and feelings of exclusion.

The good news is, however bad things are, whatever's happened in a life, it always seems to be possible for people to go back to that starting point and to re-examine themselves, other people and their lives with this new perspective. It is never too late to realise that it's not you – other people are also living with the same idea that there's something wrong with them, all of them, and other people are trying to feel OK about themselves. Therefore, that doesn't matter very much about you. The idea that we're not good enough can't hurt us so much when we realise everyone else has it too.

All the things we learn, all the trivial things we want our children to know, we're never taught that. All the things we've achieved, all the things we can do and we don't know this basic thing about ourselves.

9

THE REST

Remember when you were a child, you used to wonder what was wrong with grown-ups – your parents and their friends? Why they cared so much about the things they seemed to care about, did such stupid things, drank too much, got so sentimental or irritable, how so much of what they did seemed off-key, too try-hard, how they seemed to have no sense of style and cool? Now kids wonder the same thing about you.

The answer, or a large part of it, is loss. Your parents had time to lose things and it hurt them. Now you have too. Lost your parents maybe, siblings, friends, every break-up takes its toll. If nothing else, loss of ideas about yourself and other people, lost illusions, lost potential, lost choices and options as paths are taken. The loss of things you used to believe in – ideas you took strength from. What doesn't kill you makes you stronger? Maybe, but not always and some of these are wounds, they disfigure, leave scar tissue.

The brain has to try to adjust to all this and it's not seamless. Most of the processing is unconscious, constantly shifting assumptions, beliefs and expectations. But it can't entirely keep us intact. Parts of the old truths and realities stay embedded, memories are there to confuse. It's messy, no wonder grown-ups lose their touch.

You're going to take knocks – some of them very hard. You won't get things you want – grades, college place, job, promotion, house, car, holiday, all the things people are trying to sell you. We'll tell ourselves we don't care about those things, or some of them anyway – it's not true, we always care. We're never immune to not getting what we want (because it makes us feel worse about ourselves, it connects with the idea we're not good enough, it is a kind of adversity). And at some level, we'd all like more money. Even the most high-minded of us know there are things we want and can't get, if only peace of mind.

Loneliness is a constant issue. We all feel it and it gets into our relationships. The people you need most don't see things the same way you do, don't get you the way you want. It always jars – you'll bury it and recover, but there's a little dent in how you feel, a bruise and sometimes it'll be very painful. Even if you manage to behave well (which isn't always going to be the case), other people won't and they'll hurt you. You'll lose other people, they'll die or relationships will end. Even if it feels like an unqualified good thing to be out, you felt differently once and it's a loss of the way you used to feel.

Ageing brings its own set of issues. Your body will let you down – it will cause you increasing discomfort and pain (and living with pain tends to make us unhappy), you will lose strength, become unable to do things you used to do. It gets harder to find a sense of excitement and adventure. That's not surprising, you're not encountering things for the first time very often, you've seen it before, or something like it. But more than that, a kind of cellular metal fatigue seems to set in, for most of us at least – the skin on your hands gets a little less elastic, maybe something similar happens to the cells in the brain. Things get a little more stolid, harder to find the same kinds of pleasure you used to. All of this is a natural development, a different outlook at different stages of life. And, if you're young, this might sound OK – it's not, entirely, or it certainly won't always feel like that.

We tend to become more anxious as we get older – about threat and about our abilities now, which can restrict our options and activities, and more anxious about further decline. Age increases our chances of bereavement, separation from family, loss of cohort and loneliness. It also involves loss of established roles – no longer a worker, no longer an active parent, it's easy to feel passed by, excluded, irrelevant. Just getting older, spending more time alive, provides opportunities for unhappiness as the limitations of our worldview get found out and we encounter new disappointments.

Disappointment tugs us towards negativity – ideas of inadequacy and failure, grievance, resentment, isolation. Whatever the disappointment – just loss, getting older, things which can't be our fault or anyone else's – that's the way part of the mind goes. It's a question of how strong those ideas are in people and what other ideas are around.

And, for what it's worth, the APMS suggests that, at least in terms of common mental disorders, things get better with age – people over the age of 65 experience common mental disorders at roughly half the rate of those in working age and the rate drops again for those over 75.[323] That's a striking statistic. Maybe, as we get older, many of us become more accepting of ourselves and others. Maybe there's simply been more time to absorb the lesson that other people are dealing with the same issues we are, that our experience is not so unworthy and for our expectations, about others and about life, to become more realistic and to gain a greater sense of security, of who we are, and become less apologetic about the self as a result. What a nice idea.

But – here we go again – there's also evidence to support a very different picture. The Mental Health Foundation's *Fundamental Facts* 2016 (which is the latest version) quotes several studies reporting much higher rates of depression amongst the elderly than the general population.[324] One, using self-reporting and a different questionnaire and scale to the APMS, claimed rates of depression for the over-65s in England as high as 28% for women and 22% for men[325] (the 2014 APMS found rates of only 10.2% for people over 65 across the whole range of common mental disorders).

What are we supposed to do with that? Is this similar to the mis-match we saw earlier – evidence of strikingly higher rates of problems when the information is gathered entirely through self-reporting rather than through clinical assessment (even though that's ultimately reliant on self-reporting too)? The APMS remains the most thorough, independent research available, but it only covers private homes; it doesn't tell us about a lot of people in institutional care and care homes, which you would expect to include a good number of the elderly.

Evidence of higher usage of antidepressants amongst the over-65s (one in five against one in six of the population as a whole)[326] might at first blush appear to offer something to help clear up the confusion – except that, we've seen antidepressants are also used to treat a range of physiological conditions (that's how powerful and indiscriminate their effect is). That range of physiological conditions includes a number which would be expected to affect older people more and the figures might also reflect an age-related bias in medical practice (an increased tendency to prescribe medication to the elderly).

One recent study claimed that antidepressant usage amongst the over-65s had doubled in two decades, but there had been no increase in the underlying levels of depression.[327] In fact, it reported the majority of respondents using antidepressants didn't have depression at the time (although the authors also suggested that the doubling of antidepressant usage with no corresponding reduction in rates of depression might indicate that antidepressants were not providing a very effective response to late-life depression).

And a noticeable feature of these studies is the dramatically different figures they each reported for both for levels of depression and antidepressant usage. So, do people, statistically, get happier or unhappier as they get older? We don't know that either.

Even in the short term, it's not that easy for us to be happy and stay happy. We want things we can't have. And we want them more when we can't have them or if they're difficult to get. We want mutually exclusive things, which we can't have together. What we want changes so we don't want it anymore. We're very capable of getting it wrong and the things we want don't make us happy. And most of our happiness depends upon interactions with other people who are just as inconsistent and wayward as we are.

Nothing here is meant to represent a solving formula. You could do everything suggested in this book just right (except you can't, because you can't) and there would still be plenty in life to cause you trouble and make you unhappy. In fact, the ideas in this book can involve their own burden. Whilst the idea we're worse than others can be a source of torment, the hope other people might be 'better' than us can be a comfort. The world can lose something of its lustre when you realise other people are just as frightened, confused, venal and self-centred as you.

Maybe we even have a need to believe other people are stronger than us or that things can be better than they are. Maybe the delusion that people are the way we want them to be and will behave the way we want them to, is important in helping create strong attractions and bonds. Maybe in order to fall in love we have to believe that somebody is better than us. And then it's a matter of discovering the ways they aren't and trying to love them anyway?

There's a thin line between shedding illusions and losing faith. And some people *are* singled out. Other people's problems may not be much consolation when theirs seem ordinary and yours are catastrophic and eclipse the sense of promise in the world. What happens to people if they find it impossible to sustain enough belief in other people or the potential in life? Belief in the potential for things – hope – is important. If you can't believe in it, maybe you can't experience it, maybe it can't happen? Maybe it can happen, despite you, but it's harder, less likely. There's a danger of self-fulfilling scepticism here which could become hopelessness.

Nothing in this book promises happiness, but some of the ideas in it may help to manage a particular form of unhappiness which seems to be very prevalent and maybe becoming worse. And using these ideas is itself the art of the possible – there's nothing to get entirely right and somehow make yourself immune from anything. A better balance here, a better balance there, is likely to make us able to deal better with blows, to manage our side of relationships and to be less afflicted by the ideas that bring people for help.

That still leaves plenty to contend with. And it leaves plenty of scope too to explore yourself, your childhood or your cognitive distortions or adopt any number of other approaches to help manage your mental health. Any of that may be helpful, perhaps very helpful, but there isn't a panacea. Whenever people find a new way of thinking about something which feels like a breakthrough, which seems to offer some kind of solution, it's never enough, it doesn't hold. You'll quickly find yourself fixated on a new source of frustration and dissatisfaction – there's always more. Certainly, though, things can be better or worse, very much worse.

Nothing here is a radical counter-proposal to what's going on in the treatment of mental health. In fact, there aren't any new ideas here at all. The idea of depression having its roots in self-hatred goes back to the origins of psychoanalysis.[328] There are dozens of different theories of depression but many of them revolve around adversity,[329] feelings of inadequacy,[330] social exclusion[331] and unrealistic expectations.[332] Feelings of inadequacy are one side of the Cognitive Triad, which underpins CBT's treatment of depression, 'Conditions of Worth' is a key element in person-centred therapy and the punishing super ego is at the heart of psychodynamic ideas around mental health. There's a sense of an endless reformulation of the same kinds of ideas, viewed from slightly different perspectives without the researchers or clinicians seeming to notice how much they're all agreeing with each other. And how important that might be.

What is different here is the idea that we don't invest enough in looking at other people and their experience as a means of addressing 'negative self-image' rather than, for example, painstakingly trying to unpick faulty negative thinking and self-schema or trying to uncover the childhood foundations of a mistaken belief in one's inadequacy.

If one of the weaknesses of therapy is that we don't know how it works, one of its strengths may be that there appear to be any number of different ways it can help.

Integration of the personality, reconciliation to feelings like vulnerability and anger which had to be suppressed. When you say you're angry about something you're also saying you're frightened or hurt. Generally, it helps to know that – it's a more realistic, accurate picture of affairs, so more likely to lead to good decisions (and mental health problems tend to form around things going wrong) but also you make more sense to yourself and that feels better.

Equally, when you're feeling frightened or hurt, you're likely to be feeling resentful and harbouring shadowy ideas about retaliation. Seeing what you're caught up in when you're in it helps. If you're feeling resentful and you can see that's what's happening, you feel less resentful, it subsides. You don't even necessarily have to be able to see these things. A more integrated emotional life means more potential to move fluidly between mental states. A natural process that makes you less likely to get stuck. Other perspectives can present themselves, it becomes easier to see things to appreciate, to be grateful for. And you'll be less likely to lash out.

Patterns of behaviour, stock responses, the past repeating itself, the pre-formed versions of ourselves we offer up – options we switch in and out of like optometrists' lenses – and get stuck in. Therapy can be an opportunity to offer up something else, to experience things differently, to re-calibrate how they affect us, what's important, what matters to us. This doesn't necessarily have to be something that gets talked about or deliberately thought about, it can be something which just happens in the course of the therapy without anyone remarking on it. But, at the same time, the idea of things having an explanation is itself something that can be helpful – issues can feel less awful, less unworthy just because they can be talked about.

As a minimum, there's the self-attention and care involved in the experience – care is an important idea. If you're feeling worthless, resentful and isolated, someone just being nice to you is good, and this comes with a layer of validation, from a stranger, an expert, which you can't get from friends. The relief of talking about things bottled up, secrets you couldn't tell anyone else, the release of shame. Being listened to, understood, accepted, those are experiences you'd expect to make people feel less inadequate and less isolated, more connected. Just spending time like this can be a valuable experience in itself: a different way of feeling about yourself, a new flavour to life.

Naming something, spelling it out, often allows people to move on, think about it in a different way and leave something behind. That's really where Freud started – all people needed was to be able to say something. For what it's worth, one of the most consistent indications from the research on the effectiveness of therapy is that users who experience the most beneficial results report a good quality relationship with the therapist.[333] In fact, the quality of the therapeutic relationship is frequently cited as the single most important factor for success.[334] No healing hands, no magical therapeutic skills or dazzling interpretation, perhaps people just need to experience a healthy positive relationship and a setting which enables them to say something they couldn't before.

One of the most valuable benefits of therapy, when it can take place, is the experience of really opening up to another person, revealing your most honest intimate ideas, placing yourself, to that extent at least, into their hands – and being entirely receptive to what they say. That doesn't mean slavishly thinking they're right or doing what they say, but it's a level of trust and openness to another person which is hard to do.

Something similar happens in a 'good' argument. If you've been fair and tried to see the truth in what they've said, it means you have refreshed your sense of them as a separate person with a different perspective from you. Perhaps you've been able to take on board the way something has been for them, how they have been affected by it, how it's different to you but valid. And if you've been brave and honest about showing your own feelings, it means they've had a chance to do the same with you. The result is you've made contact with the real person rather than the figment in your head (which had maybe turned aggressive and malicious) and you feel closer and more connected (and probably a sense of remorse too and a desire to make up and put things right). Harder perhaps in some ways in our closest relationships with everyday stresses and tensions and baggage but something that, maybe once visited in therapy, can be got back to with other people, becomes more available, more natural. Perhaps therapy can be an opportunity to find another way to be in a relationship, to fall out and stay together, to get what you need from people.

On top of that, there's the possibility of gaining some insight into yourself from the process. Most experiences with therapy involve some degree of self-questioning – allowing the most punishing and persecutory ideas and emotions to subside for a while can usher in more open-minded thought processes, to re-evaluate old issues and the opportunity to learn from taking risks with locked down defences and rigid thinking less in the way. Better insight into the self can lead to better decisions and choices but it demands a degree of self-reflection and it involves flirting with ideas of error, failure, inadequacy. That can be arduous, it needs to be done with care to be most effective. The greater the infiltration of ideas around superiority between therapist and client, the harder that becomes to do well.

Beyond all this, maybe even the possibility of some kind of

wisdom from someone else – someone who has had training and spends their time thinking and talking about the issues which bring people for help. And the potential for a warm positive human relationship working on our capacity for affection and gratitude, perhaps. Maybe even some kind of re-parenting that allows development which has been blocked or diverted to re-engage.

All or any of that can be, and is, claimed for therapy.

Therapy often involves ideas around inadequacy and self-worth, even if they're not explicitly drawn out and acknowledged. What's different here is the emphasis on the extent to which those ideas derive their power from not realising that other people have that too. And the deliberate decision to shift some of the focus away from self-scrutiny for people who are already suffering from acute self-consciousness – remember the research suggesting an association between maladaptive Self Focussed Attention and depression.[335]

It's easier to open yourself up to whatever therapy has to offer, if new possibilities don't so much risk making you feel hideous about yourself. Aspects of ourselves that seem shameful and repellent become easier to accept – can be integrated – if we can see them (and that impulse to find things about ourselves repellent) in other people. You can spend a lifetime trying to understand yourself, your family history, your patterns but if you still believe there's something uniquely wrong and inferior about you, there's a limit to what can be achieved. If there's a chance to re-engage with the world with this idea subdued, the mind has a better chance to rebalance itself.

Freud's original idea was that all mental health problems derive from repression of a sexual impulse – bring the secret out and the internal conflict is resolved. That's a very specific proposition and his was a very specific technique – free association, several times a week, maybe for several years, to allow something deeply hidden, causing conflict, guilt and shame to be expressed and work its way through. Perhaps now we're seeing that it's the guilt and shame causing the harm, not the sex of itself. Sexuality was presumably even more fertile territory than it is now for guilt and shame in middle- and upper-class Western society in the early 20th century, but other forms of guilt and shame are available. The core idea attached to guilt and shame, however they arise, remains *there's something wrong about me, other people are better*. And that's how other people feel too.

There are other differences here. The idea of remorse is probably most important to followers of Melanie Klein – a disciple of Freud who has arguably superseded him in terms of influence on the clinical application of psychoanalysis, at least in the UK. A rationale behind Kleinian technique is that, through an intense process of the therapist surviving the client's aggression and hostility, several times a week over a number of years, the client comes to experience the therapist as a separate person in a way they hadn't been able to before. And, what's more, a person to whom they have caused harm, or tried to, allowing a sense of remorse and a desire to make reparation, enabling a new more developed model for relationships with other people.

The way these ideas are expressed, people tend to find them strange and perplexing, hard to engage with. And, anyway, in the psychoanalytic tradition they're to be kept hidden from the client – an arcane, secret body of knowledge, only for initiates. So arcane, in fact, they're often not made explicit in the literature and get argued about incessantly by practitioners. These forms of therapy tend to rely on highly subjective, intrusive interpretation – communications are often deliberately opaque and sometimes intentionally provocative. Practitioners argue that explanation is not how lasting change at a deep psychological level is achieved – change, real lasting change, they say, happens through experience, things being gone through. But there isn't much evidence to support that contention, outside highly subjective accounts in psychotherapeutic literature, and it's perfectly fair to ask what there is to prevent those accounts from being unduly self-serving.

In any therapy, the possibility of unconscious manipulation of the process by the therapist can never be excluded. In this kind of therapy, which now can hardly ever get carried out in the kind of intense, long-term model for which it was designed, the obscurity of what's going on and the deliberately provocative approach, involve their own dangers. It can be all too easy for the target themes to get confused or lost – progress can often feel interminably slow and halting. Things can get bogged down in dependence and aggression with a client caught up in endless second guessing of themselves, or worse, and somebody has to pay for all this.

Tolerance of separateness and a capacity for remorse are key therapeutic values in this tradition and those are straightforward enough ideas. How much of this reluctance to find a form of language that will make sense to people and just tell them what you think is going on – the way doctors do – might be down to this being something that's working for the therapists? We all need to find ways to feel OK about ourselves and, at some level, most therapists probably do get to feel that, at least in some respects, they're a little better than their clients. That's natural and it's probably usually harmless enough in most situations but these guys are doing it in a fight. Whatever more benign motivations and objectives are around, and whatever else is going on, there is a risk of therapists getting to exercise their own aggression and salve their own feelings of inadequacy in a setting they control and for which they write the rules. Given the importance of the ideas of inadequacy affecting the people who come for help, that might not be good.

Mental health treatment isn't confined to psychotherapy. People in mental health tend to fall into one of two vehemently opposed camps on medication or a grudging, fudged middle ground. There's very little in the way of constructive, informed discussion. In part, that's probably a result of the fragmented nature of mental health care and the different vested interests that creates – drugs are prescribed by doctors, who don't have the training (or time) to practice psychotherapy, and psychotherapists don't have the training (or legal power) to prescribe drugs. It's two tribes with different education, skills and approaches who often don't even come across each other at all. But it's also a result of the incoherent nature of the evidence base – there's something you can cherry pick to back up any view you want.

It is a very good thing that we have medications which can help people when they are experiencing the worst kinds of breakdown because we don't have very much else – it's very hard to reach them, those experiences can go on for a long time and they are about the worst thing that can happen to anyone.

As things stand, it's difficult to argue too that medication doesn't have a valuable role in the treatment of common mental health issues like anxiety and depression. Not everybody responds to therapy or gets better over time and common, mild problems can become more extreme over time if people are left suffering. And that role isn't necessarily restricted to just the short term – for some people medication seems to have the potential to offer long-term management of symptoms and the opportunity to lead less unstable, disturbed lives. But medication doesn't, of itself, offer much in the way of things getting better, in the sense of a cure. The side effects can be serious and over long periods of time they can have a very adverse effect on quality of life. There are concerns that some psychiatric medications might affect physical health and, if people want to give them up, that can be very difficult to do. All of that may still be better than the alternative for some people but to believe that's the best we can do, you probably have to stick pretty closely to a fairly pure version of the biological model – you have to see depression and other mental illnesses treated with medication as a disease, like diabetes, which needs to be constantly managed with medication to keep someone healthy. And plenty of people do.

And psychotherapy and medication aren't the only ways people respond to mental health issues. We could say that, one way or another, our whole lives are organised around our mental health. In this sense, they probably always have been – there is only the world and the way we see it: *The mind is its own place and, in itself, can make a heaven of hell, a hell of heaven.*[336] But, increasingly, managing their mental health is an explicit part of the choices people make in how they spend their time and money. If there appear to be a limitless number of ways people can fall into mental health problems, there seem to be a limitless number of ways to take care of mental health too. And surely one of the consequences of being prepared to admit how little we know about mental health ought to be an openness to different ways of thinking about managing it?

The idea of trying to manage our mental health – recognising there is something to take care of and paying attention – is itself probably a good start. But it's not that straightforward: one of the problems people struggle with is anxiety about their own state of minds, over-thinking things, scrutinising themselves too much. Paying attention isn't enough in itself, it depends how we're looking at things – there is a potential to worry too much about our feelings, to bring punishing unrealistic expectations to our own experience and talk ourselves into trouble.

Seeing other people more clearly helps – the realisation of how much trouble there is for other people to deal with and a more realistic idea of how happy we ought to expect to feel, as a backdrop against which to assess our own experience. And if we can manage our own ideas of inadequacy better, we can free up valuable emotional and mental space to work on something else very important for our mental health – how to make the best use we can out of our time. Because, surely, it's not enough to avoid becoming very unhappy? Everyone wants more from their lives than that.

Most of us have to go after being happy, have to make some effort. It doesn't just happen often enough on its own, we need to make some good choices. And it's not simple to work out how to enjoy ourselves, to find out what makes us happy. It helps if we can work out when we are actually having a good time. We can definitely mess things up by trying the wrong things too hard – all those big nights out that get spoiled with too much booze or anything when an honest appraisal the next day would tell us we didn't really enjoy ourselves at all. That means not being too distracted by ideas of inadequacy, and comparison with others or idealised lifestyles, into trying to like or want particular things in order to feel better about ourselves. We may like the idea of being someone who enjoys clubbing, but if the reality is we don't, and we keep doing it, it's going to confuse things. It can be surprisingly difficult to work these things out but a little easier if your expectations and your assessments of other people are more realistic.

And whatever it is we do actually like and enjoy is going to change over time – a 23 year old enjoys different things to a 43 year old, to a 63 year old. It's not always easy to keep up with yourself. The process is likely to be helped if we're not having to spend too much time and energy overcoming an idea that things aren't sexy, fun, young or wild enough or that we're messing up because we're sure things are calmer, more peaceful and fulfilling for other people.

Mindfulness has attracted a great deal of attention in recent years. It's a difficult term to pin down – it gets used by so many different people in different ways in different contexts. In almost any form, it seems to be something which can be useful to people and it's been incorporated as an explicit element in some forms of therapy.[337] Some of the 'joy in coffee' lifestyle aspects can seem a little effortful – like an overwritten passage in a novel – not natural, unsustainable. And, more seriously, all that overstatement and pitching things too high, can lead to everyone feeling they're not managing to get as much as they should out of this experience and feeling worse about themselves.

But stepping back and noticing what's going on, around us and in our thoughts and feelings, is invariably helpful. Noticing brings things to our attention, there's an opportunity to experience them more consciously and to appreciate them more, or in a different way – to live a more inhabited life. There's a long-established school of thought that lack of connection with physical experience can be associated with unhealthy states of mind,[338] mindful experience of physical states can offer a useful counterweight.

Mindfulness can be a helpful device to escape from rumination, to break repetitive thought patterns or to find some relief from compulsive, intrusive ideas. It's particularly valuable when we feel overwhelmed by anxiety or other unpleasant emotion – and it's particularly valuable because that's a disturbing, frightening experience and can be dangerous. The moment you can watch yourself, see what's going on and think about it, it hasn't got the whole of you anymore – that part of you that's able to observe yourself is outside the experience. Getting a pen and paper and writing down what's going on, when you're in the middle of it, can be a useful practical step in concentrating the effort and breaking the spell.

In fact, a piece of paper can be a very useful tool for mental health. Some find it helpful to try to direct their own thoughts – messages to themselves, or formulas, to correct or balance what they see as unhelpful or distorted thought processes. That's really a key element of CBT. Gratitude Journals, for people to write down things to celebrate in their lives, have emerged from Positive Psychology and CBT onto the High Street. This makes good sense – there are elements of noticing, an opportunity to escape from intrusive ideas but, more than that, much of what you find to be grateful for will be the actions of other people. In order to be able to appreciate their generosity or thoughtfulness, there's been an act of imagination by you about how it is for them, a recognition of separateness. It's the opposite of resentment – the simple idea of being in someone's debt can be good for us.

Journals or diaries can also offer people a way of examining themselves and reconciling to what they find. We all tend to use ourselves as laboratories to try to understand the world and other people. It's a less structured and self-directed version of something that happens in therapy. The first deliberate attempt at psychoanalysis was probably Freud's analysis of himself conducted with a notebook.

For those that can, exercise often seems to have a positive effect on mental states. Research has claimed that people who exercised experienced significantly fewer days in a month affected by poor mental health than people who didn't exercise.[339] As ever, there are important caveats which could entirely undermine the results. The researchers had to attempt to match the two groups for physiological and sociodemographic characteristics and mental health history (none of which was ever going to be precise), there would have been any number of other variables which couldn't be controlled for and you'd have to hope were smoothed out in the numbers – though it was a very large sample size, which helps – and the results relied on highly subjective self-reporting. Interestingly, it appeared there was a healthy range – exercise above certain levels was actually associated with worse mental health. That might also make sense – pursue anything to extremes and you risk it taking on obsessive, punishing qualities: perfectionism and ideas around not being good enough. Remember that potential association between mental health issues and elite sports?[340]

But, research aside, and whatever the potential causes – endorphins, escaping rumination, connection with physical experience or a sense of purpose, competence and progress to counter feelings of inadequacy and worthlessness – many people suffering from mental health issues report that exercise has helped them.

Exercise is going to be a good way of avoiding a number of important physical problems too and we live in our bodies. If it's good for physical health, ultimately it should be good for mental health; if it's bad for physical health, it's likely to end up bad for mental health too. Feeling physically ill has a powerful effect on mood and the kind of ideas people are likely to have. Exercise can lend a sense of structure and routine into a life and those are also qualities which people have reported finding helpful in managing anxiety. There may be something there about performance and ritual, repetition and a sense of control.

There's been a great deal of research into potential connections between sleep and mental health.[341] All of it compromised by the kind of problems we've been talking about throughout this book and none of it able to conclude whether difficulties with sleep are more likely to be a consequence of mental health problems or a cause – but everyone senses its importance. In fact, sleep disruption may be the single most commonly targeted area across different psychiatric questionnaires and remember its prominence in the diagnostic classifications for depression in ICD-10 and DSM-5.

Some people seem to be able to get by with much less sleep than others, but that doesn't mean that it's not affecting the way their minds work and how they experience the world. Aside from the physiological effects on health, and impact on cognitive ability, feeling overtired is stressful and stress activates the idea that something's going wrong – we're not doing well enough or we're not being treated fairly. And sleeplessness itself may be the result of anxiety.

Being able to get by without sleep may feel like an advantage in terms of getting things done; it can be a necessary requirement for success in some fields, but it's also likely to be affecting the ideas people are living with and how they feel about the people around them. That's capable of reducing the quality of people's lives, and perhaps quite dramatically, in ways they don't realise.

Many of the techniques people use to try to improve sleep patterns include elements of mindfulness. Exercise, too, is often regarded as helpful to healthy sleeping patterns. And sleeping well is likely to help people to exercise and to regulate impulse – and manage potentially addictive behaviours – to lead a healthier lifestyle.

As well as a depressive – and so having a powerful effect, eventually, on lowering mood – alcohol is a toxin. We're unlikely to feel good about ourselves (or much else), if we spend the day half-poisoned because of the night before. That's also likely to have an effect on the kind of ideas that occur to us and how we experience things, particularly if it's something that happens regularly over a period of time. Added to that, we're likely to have ideas of weakness, shame and inadequacy around our inability to control our behaviour. And if we're drinking too much it's very likely we're not behaving very well – more guilt and shame to contend with – and we'll be damaging relationships. There's a good chance it'll be the ones closest and most important to us. All of that translates directly into people's mental health.

There is a good case to be made for diet as a tool for managing mental health too. That research suggesting a link between gut biome and depression[342] – maybe an ineffective digestive system makes people more likely to feel depressed, perhaps by making us feel generally unhealthy, or maybe depression has an adverse effect on our digestive system or perhaps influences diet. Studies have claimed evidence for direct links between diet and mental health,[343] even to the extent of associating particular mental health conditions with particular dietary issues (fruit and vegetable intake and depression and added sugars intake and anxiety).[344]

The same for links between inflammation and depression[345] – maybe the physical discomfort from inflammation (joint ache, back ache, head ache, muscle pain) promotes depression or maybe, as some research seems to suggest,[346] the persistent stress associated with depression inhibits cortisol from carrying out its functions on the regulation of inflammation and it's depression driving the link with inflammation. Either way, it's very likely that yoga, stretching, massage could all be helpful.

Actually, anything that makes us quieter, calmer and helps us, for a time, to dial down the agitation and anxiety that are always running inside us is probably worthwhile for that reason alone. We've seen that the core ideas which dominate people when they come for help are connected with each other – feed one and the others are activated too. If we feel less anxious, we're likely to feel a little better about ourselves and less isolated from other people. Meditation, relaxation techniques, going to your quiet place – it's all good, it's likely to help.

Finally, a lot of people report that access to nature helps their mood and mental health. That makes a lot of sense too. That's the environment we evolved in and for – why wouldn't being deprived of it be bad for us? It's been speculated that we have a biophilic instinct – an innate drive to connect with nature and natural processes.[347] Or maybe it's the scale and indifference of nature, or empathy for other life forms – witnessing another way of being alive – that gives us a sense of distance from our anxieties and perspective. Maybe it's simply distraction – another way to escape the same circular patterns of thought and introspection. Maybe it's just doing something. Nobody knows how it might work, but most mental health organisations are happy to promote contact with the natural world as a positive step for managing mental health.[348]

We may be convinced it's right but we haven't found convincing scientific evidence to support that yet. Even with the best data available, the effects are slight and the results are confused and severely compromised by often unavoidable limitations in the way research can be carried out[349] – how to define greenspace, how to measure different kinds of access to different kinds of nature and the old problem of measuring well-being reliably.

Similar to exercise, recent research has suggested that you can over-egg it: time spent in nature as a result of 'green prescriptions', or family or social pressure, was found to be less beneficial than self-directed time spent in nature.[350] It seems to be a theme – make too much out of anything (exercise, sleep apps and aides, mindfulness, even just the idea of mental health) and you introduce pressure, performance, the idea of not getting enough out of it, not doing well enough, not being good enough. And the same research found that people suffering from depression were accessing nature just as often as people who didn't have any mental disorders and people suffering from anxiety were actually accessing nature more often. If that's right, it might suggest that green spaces may be able to ease the symptoms of depression and anxiety but they won't help people to avoid mental health problems or help them to recover.

Anecdotally, talking to people, there seems to be a persuasive case that, approached in the right way, any and all these things people are doing can be quite effective ways for them to manage their mental health. And even if that only means managing the symptoms of mental health issues, that's valuable – distress and mental health are often inseparable. But don't expect any of it to be supported by a body of consistent, compelling evidence anytime soon.

***

It's reported that the NHS budgeted £12.2 billion to treat mental health in 2018/19.[351] But that's just the psychiatric diagnoses the NHS recognises. Nobody knows how much is being spent in the private sector in treating the same kind of mental health issues. And nobody knows how much is being spent addressing other issues which might also be regarded as mental health related in the form of counselling, coaching or alternative therapies. Though, it has been estimated that, in total, poor mental health costs the UK economy between £74 billion and £99 billion a year.[352] Yet, despite all this money being spent on it and all this cost, it's really very difficult to find definitive statements you can make about mental health.

There is evidence that people who suffer from diagnosed mental health conditions can recover – the NHS claimed a recovery rate of 49.3% for people receiving therapy in 2016/17 [353]. But it isn't possible to know how much of that recovery was due to treatment and what might have happened over time anyway. There isn't much visibility on the extent to which recovery persists either – mental states fluctuate, how many of these people would still be recording sub-clinical scores on assessment forms a year later? In fact, since diagnosis and recovery depend upon people's evaluations of their own highly subjective states of mind, how confident should we be talking about either? Somebody records a score of 12 on PHQ-9 in January and 9 in March – 10 is the cut-off for a clinical condition; something has been measured but can we really say they were depressed before and now they're not? Can it really be that simple?

We all have mental health. Yes, we all have states of mind and they can involve terrible levels of suffering or they can confuse or mislead us or cause trouble to others. Some people come (or are sent) for help. Others who may be experiencing similar states of mind don't come. Often people who come for help stop coming and often it's because they say they don't need help anymore. But, also, quite often people continue to receive help for a very long time or for life. We don't have any reliable method to classify different kinds of condition that bring people for help on the basis of physiology. And there are a number of obvious and significant problems with the classification system we have developed. How much more is there we can really say at this point?

Well, one thing we might add is that when people come for help, they seem to be dominated by the same set of core ideas. Those ideas are about inadequacy, resentment and isolation, they are inter-connected and they are a feature of everyone's mental life.

Whatever you may, or may not, be doing to manage your mental health, this is going to help – everyone has that idea that they're not good enough in them and everyone is trying to feel OK about themselves.

People are more fragile than you think, including you. Try not to make other people feel worse about themselves. Try not to let other people do it to you.

ACKNOWLEDGMENTS

I owe a debt of thanks to many people for their help in producing this book, including friends who have been unwitting sounding boards as I worked ideas through, but I am very grateful to Sandy Henderson for his careful reading and thoughtful comments during the writing. Whatever else this book is, it's better for his attention. Thank you too to the clients who've spoken to me so honestly and intelligently about what's caused them trouble. This book is really all about taking responsibility for your own unhappiness. It's a very impressive thing to watch people doing.

Not everyone wants to kick the tyres hard all the time and not everyone wants to be around it. Akko, thank you for putting up with it, and me, and for the sense you bring and delight.

Jonathan Coppin is a psychotherapist in London.

NOTES

1 https://www.who.int/news-room/detail/30-03-2017--depression-let-s-talk-says-who-as-depression-tops-list-of-causes-of-ill-health
2 https://www.england.nhs.uk/mental-health
3 https://www.hopkinsmedicine.org/health/wellness-and-prevention/mental-health-disorder-statistics and Prevalence, Severity and Co-morbidity of 12 month DSM-IV disorders in the *National Comorbidity Survey Replication* –Kessler R, Tat Chiu W et al: *Arch Gen Psychiatry* 2005 (62).
4 http://www.euro.who.int/en/health-topics/noncommunicable-diseases/mental-health/news/news/2012/10/depression-in-europe/depression-in-europe-facts-and-figures
5 *The World Health Report 2001: Mental Health: New Understanding, New Hope*
6 Global, regional, and national incidence, prevalence, and years lived with disability for 301 acute and chronic diseases and injuries in 188 countries, 1990-2013: A systematic analysis for the *Global Burden of Disease Study 2013*: Vos T, Barber R et al (2013) *The Lancet* 386 (9995)
7 https://www.who.int/news-room/detail/30-03-2017--depression-let-s-talk-says-who-as-depression-tops-list-of-causes-of-ill-health
8 NHS prescribed record number of antidepressants last year BMJ 2019; 364 https://doi.org/10.1136/bmj.I1508
9 Office for National Statistics – *Overview of the UK Population: November 2018*
10 https://www.bbc.co.uk/news/health-47740396
11 https://www.independent.co.uk/news/education/education-news/teenagers-mental-health-problems-emotional-well-being-action-children-a8589261.html

12 https://www.theguardian.com/society/2018/sep/11/mental-health-issues-in-young-people-up-sixfold-in-england-since-1995

13 https://www.theguardian.com/society/2018/jul/12/sharp-rise-in-under-19s-being-treated-by-nhs-mental-health-services

14 https://www.thetimes.co.uk/article/freshers-declaring-mental-illness-up-73-in-4-years-00sw2bdb2

15 *No Health Without Mental Health: A Cross-Government Mental Health Outcomes Strategy for People of All Ages.* Department of Health, 2 February 2011

16 *The Five Year Forward View for Mental Health* – A report from the independent Mental Health Taskforce to the NHS in England, February 2016

17 https://fullfact.org/health/misquoted-and-misunderstood-have-one-four-people-really-had-mental-health-problem

18 *Adult Psychiatric Morbidity in England, 2007* – Results of a household survey: McManus S, Meltzer H, et al (2009) The NHS Information Centre for health and social care

19 For what it's worth, the *National Comorbidity Survey Replication*, using different collection methods and different diagnostic criteria, estimated lifetime prevalence of mental health disorder of about 1 in 2 in the US. Lifetime prevalence and age-of-onset distribution of DSM-IV disorders in the *National Comorbidity Survey Replication* – Kessler R, Berglund P et al: Arch Gen Psychiatry 2005 Jun; 62(6)

20 *Mental health and wellbeing in England: Adult Psychiatric Morbidity Survey 2014.* McManus S, Bebbington P et al (eds) (2016) Leeds: NHS Digital

21 See, for example, Mental health and well-being trends among children and young people in the UK, 1995–2014: Analysis of repeated cross-sectional national health surveys:

Pitchforth J, Fahy K, et al *Psychological Medicine*. doi:10.1017/S0033291718001757

22 *The World Health Report 2001* – Mental Health: New Understanding, New Hope

23 https://fullfact.org/health/misquoted-and-misunderstood-have-one-four-people-really-had-mental-health-problem and *Mental Illness in the Community – The pathway to psychiatric care,* Goldberg D and Huxley P, 1980, Tavistock Publications Limited

24 Confusion isn't restricted to the UK: many sources in the US refer to a headline one-in-four figure relating to adults with diagnoseable mental disorders, derived from the *National Comorbidity Survey*, and others refer to a one in five figure, derived from the 2019 *National Survey on Drug Use and Health*. Both sets of data relate to the previous 12 months but used different forms of structured interview and the NCS-R includes substance abuse disorders, whereas the NSDUH excludes them

25 https://www.telegraph.co.uk/news/2020/11/05/covid-graphs-wrong-death-toll-will-not-surpass-first-wave

26 https://www.nbcnews.com/health/health-news/who-changes-covid-19-mask-guidance-wear-one-if-you-n1226116

27 https://www.theguardian.com/commentisfree/2020/jun/05/lancet-had-to-do-one-of-the-biggest-retractions-in-modern-history-how-could-this-happen

28 https://www.theguardian.com/society/2021/mar/01/pfizer-oxford-covid-jab-prevents-hospitalisation-older-people

29 https://news.sky.com/story/covid-19-how-common-have-blood-clots-been-after-the-astrazeneca-jab-and-should-we-be-worried-12246472

30 https://www.hopkinsmedicine.org/health/wellness-and-prevention/mental-health-disorder-statistics

31 http://www.euro.who.int/en/health-topics/noncommunicable-diseases/mental-health/news/news/2012/10/depression-in-europe/depression-in-europe-facts-and-figures

32 Mental health and well-being trends among children and young people in the UK, 1995–2014: Analysis of repeated cross-sectional national health surveys: Pitchforth J, Fahy K, et al *Psychological Medicine* 2019 (49) doi:10.1017/S0033291718001757

33 https://www.independent.co.uk/news/education/education-news/teenagers-mental-health-problems-emotional-well-being-action-children-a8589261.html

34 Mental Health of Children and Young People in England, 2017, NHS Digital 2018 https://digital.nhs.uk/data-and-information/publications/statistical/mental-health-of-children-and-young-people-in-england/2017/2017

35 *Mental health and wellbeing in England: Adult Psychiatric Morbidity Survey 2014* McManus S, Bebbington P et al (eds) (2016) Leeds: NHS Digital

36 Health Survey for England – 2005, Health of Older People: Volume 4, Mental health and well being: NHS Digital - https://digital.nhs.uk/data-and-information/publications/statistical/health-survey-for-england/health-survey-for-england-2005-health-of-older-people

37 https://www.mentalhealth.org.uk/statistics/mental-health-statistics-older-people

38 https://www.theguardian.com/society/2018/aug/10/four-million-people-in-england-are-long-term-users-of-antidepressants

39 https://www.nhs.uk/news/mental-health/nearly-quarter-14-year-old-girls-uk-self-harming-charity-reports and https://news.sky.com/story/nearly-a-quarter-of-girls-aged-14-self-harm-11484532

40 https://digital.nhs.uk/data-and-information/publications/statistical/hospital-episode-statistics-for-admitted-patient-care-outpatient-and-accident-and-emergency-data/provisional-monthly-hospital-episode-statistics-for-admitted-patient-care-outpatients-and-accident-and-emergency-data-april-2012-to-august-2012

41 https://digital.nhs.uk/data-and-information/find-data-and-publications/supplementary-information/2019-supplementary-information-files/admissions-for-mental-health-and-self-harm

42 ibid

43 ibid

44 ibid

45 https://www.ons.gov.uk/peoplepopulationandcommunity/populationandmigration/populationestimates/bulletins/annualmidyearpopulationestimates/mid2019estimates#ageing

46 https://www.nhs.uk/conditions/antidepressants/uses

47 https://bnf.nice.org.uk/treatment-summary/antidepressant-drugs.html

48 https://inews.co.uk/news/health/gp-appointments-15-minutes-standard-length-royal-college-501676

49 *Everybody Lies – What the Internet Can Tell Us About Who We Really Are* Stephens-Davidowitz S, 2017, Bloomsbury Publishing

50 Cultural differences in survey responding: Issues and insights in the study of response biases, Kemmelmeier M, *Int J Psychol.* 2016 Dec; 51(6)

51 How Reliable is the DSM-5? Mad in America, Cooper R, *Science Psychiatry and Social Justice* 2014 https://www.madinamerica.com/2014/09/how-reliable-is-the-dsm-5

52 *The Psychopath Test - A Journey Through the Madness Industry*, Ronson J, 2012, Picador

53 *The Great Pretender – The Undercover Mission that Changed our Understanding of Madness*: Cahalan S, 2019, Canongate
54 The Reliability of Psychiatric Diagnoses Revisited, Aboraya A, Rankin E et al: *Psychiatry* (Edgmont) 2006 Jan; 3(1)
55 The Breivik Case and what psychiatrists can learn from it, Melle I, *World Psychiatry*, 2013 Feb; 12(1): 16-21
56 See for example, *Mad, Bad and Sad – A History of Women and the Mind Doctors from 1800 to the Present* Appignanesi L, 2008, Virago, *Lost Connections – Why You're Depressed and How to Find Hope* Hari J, 2018, Bloomsbury, *Manufacturing Depression – The Secret History of a Modern Disease* Greenberg G, 2010 Simon and Schuster, *Bad Science* Goldacre B, 2008, Fourth Estate, *Bad Pharma: How Drug Companies Mislead Doctors and Harm Patients* Goldacre B, 2012, Fourth Estate
57 *The Happy Brain* Burnett D, 2018, Guardian Faber, *Bad Pharma: How Drug Companies Mislead Doctors and Harm Patients* Goldacre B, 2012, Fourth Estate
58 How Reliable is the DSM-5? Mad in America, Cooper R, *Science Psychiatry and Social Justice* 2014 https://www.madinamerica.com/2014/09/how-reliable-is-the-dsm-5
59 Psychiatric diagnosis 'scientifically meaningless' https://www.sciencedaily.com/releases/2019/07/190708131152.htm
60 Psychiatric classifications: validity and utility, Jablensky A, *World Psychiatry* 2016 Feb 15(1)
61 See for example, Inter-Rater Reliability in Psychiatric Diagnosis, Matszak J and Piasecki M, *Psychiatric Times* vol 29, No 10 October 6, 2012
62 The Reliability of Psychiatric Diagnoses Point – Our Psychiatric Diagnoses are Still Unreliable, Aboraya A, *Psychiatry* (Edgmont). 2007 Jan; 4(1), Diagnostic Issues and Controversies in DSM-5: Return of the False Positives

Problem, Wakefield J, *Annual Review of Clinical Psychology*, 2016, Reliability in Psychiatric Diagnoses with the DSM: Old Wine in New Barrels, Anheule S, Desmet M et al *Psychotherapy and Psychosomatics* 2014; 83 https://doi.org/10.1159/000358809

63 Revisiting the Marshmallow Test: A Conceptual Replication Investigating Links Between Early Delay of Gratification and Later Outcomes, Watts T, Duncan G et al *Psychological Science* May 25, 2018

64 https://www.nytimes.com/2010/02/03/health/research/03lancet.html%20 and https://medicalxpress.com/news/2019-03-anti-vaccination-activists-scientific-breakthroughs-beneficial.html

65 How important are the common factors in Psychotherapy? An update, Wampold B, *World Psychiatry* 2015 Oct; 14(3)

66 Where are the commonalities among the therapeutic common factors? Grencavage L and Norcross J (1990) *Professional Psychology: Research and Practice* Vol 21 (5)

67 Neuroimaging Abnormalities in the Subgenual Prefrontal Cortex: Implications for the Pathophysiology of Familial Mood Disorders, Drevets W, Onguer D et al *Molecular Psychiatry* 1998, May 3(3)

68 Functional neuroimaging studies of the effects of psychotherapy, Beauregard M, *Dialogues in Clinical Neuroscience* 2014 Mar 16(1)

69 https://www.nhs.uk/conditions/dementia/diagnosis-tests

70 Early brain development in infants at high risk of autism spectrum disorder, Hazlett H, Honbin G et al: *Nature* Vol 542 (2017) https://www.nature.com/articles/nature21369.edpf, and Investigating functional brain network integrity using a traditional and novel categorical scheme for neurodevelopmental disorders , Dajani D, Burrows C et al *Neuroimage Clinical* 2019;21

71 Structural neuroimaging correlates of social deficit are similar in autism spectrum disorder and attention deficit hyperactivity disorder: analysis from the POND Network, Baribeau D, Dupuis A et al *Translational Psychiatry* 9, 72 (2019), and Update on Atypicalities of Central Nervous System in Autism Spectrum Disorder, Shuid A, Jayusman P et al *Brain Science* 10(5) May 2020

72 *The Gendered Brain – the new neuroscience that shatters the myth of the female brain,* Rippon G, 2019, The Bodley Head

73 Puzzlingly High Correlations in fMRI Studies of Emotion, Personality and Social Cognition, Vul E, Harris C et al *Perspectives on Psychological Science* 4:3 (2009)

74 https://thepsychologist.bps.org.uk/volume-28/april-2015/what-has-neuroscience-ever-done-us

75 Mood Is Indirectly Related to Serotonin, Norepinephrine and Dopamine Levels in Humans: A Meta-Analysis of Monoamine Depletion Studies, Ruhe H, Mason N et al *Molecular Psychiatry* 2007 Apr 12 (4)

76 Comparative efficacy and acceptability of 21 antidepressant drugs for the acute treatment of adults with major depressive disorder: a systematic review and network meta-analysis, Cipriani A, Furukawa T et al *The Lancet* 2018, vol 391, issue 10128

77 https://www.nhs.uk/news/medication/big-new-study-confirms-antidepressants-work-better-placebo

78 Initial Severity and Antidepressant Benefits: A Meta-Analysis of Data Submitted to the Food and Drug Administration, Kirsch I, Deacon B et al *PLoS Medicine* 2008 Feb; 5(2)

79 The Placebo effect in psychiatric practice, Bernstein M, Brown W *Curr Psychiatry* 2017 Nov; 16 (11)

80 https://www.verywellmind.com/long-term-effects-of-antidepressants-4158064

81 https://nypost.com/2017/09/14/study-finds-antidepressants-increase-risk-of-death
82 https://www.verywellmind.com/long-term-effects-of-antidepressants-4158064
83 Effectiveness of Psychological Treatments for Depressive Disorders in Primary Care: Systematic Review and Meta-Analysis, Linde K, Sugterman K et al *Annals of Family Medicine* January, February 2015 vol 13 no 1
84 Does psychotherapy work? An umbrella review of meta-analyses of randomized controlled trials, Dragioti E, Karanthos V et al *Acta Psychiatrica Scandinavia* 2017 vol 136, issue 3
85 https://www.ncbi.nlm.nih.gov/pubmed/21901675
86 Acupuncture and Counselling for Depression in Primary Care: A Randomised Controlled Trial, MacPherson H, Richmond S et al (2013) *PLOS Medicine* 10(9): e1001518
87 The comparative effectiveness and efficiency of cognitive behavioural therapy and generic counselling in the treatment of depression: evidence from the 2nd UK National Audit of psychological therapies, Phybis J, Saxon D et al (2017) *BMC Psychiatry* 17:25
88 Epidemiology of atrial fibrillation: European perspective, Zonio-Berisso M, Lercari F et al *Clinical Epidemiology* 2014; 6
89 Epidemiology of atrial fibrillation. The rising prevalence, Padanilam B and Prystowsky E in Atrial Fibrillation: From Bench to Bedside Totowa, NJ:2008
90 Worldwide Epidemeology of Atrial Fibrillation: A Global Burden of Disease 2010 Study, Chugh S, Havmoeller R et al *Circulation* 2014 Feb 25; 129(8)
91 Controversies about atrial fibrillation mechanisms: aiming for order in chaos and whether it matters, Nattel S and Dobrev D *Circulation Research* 120(9) 2017

92   Cellular and Molecular Mechanisms of Atrial
     Arrhythmogenesis in Patients with Paroxysmal Atrial
     Fibrillation, Voigt N, Heijiman J et al *Circulation* 2014 Jan 14;
     129(2)

93   Very Long Term Results of Atrial Fibrillation Confirm That
     This Therapy Is Really Effective, Tutuianu C, Szilagy J et al *J
     Atr Fibrillation* 2015 Aug-Sep; 8(2)

94   "Sobering" Long Term Outcomes Following Ablation of Atrial
     Fibrillation, https://www.medscape.com/viewarticle/735306

95   Flecainide: Current status and perspectives in arrhythmia
     management, Andrikopoulos G, Pastromas S et al *World J
     Cardiol* Feb 26, 2015; 7(2)

96   Mortality and morbidity in patients receiving encainide,
     flecainide, or placebo. The Cardiac Arrhythmia Suppression
     Trial, Echt D, Liebson P et al *N Engl J Med* 1991; 324

97   Twenty-five years in the making: flecainide is safe and effective
     for the management of atrial fibrillation, Aliot E, Capucci A et
     al *EP Europace* 2011 Feb; 13(2)

98   Short- and long-term efficacy and safety of flecainide acetate
     for supraventricular arrythmias, Hohnloser S and Zabel M
     *American Journal of Cardiology 1992:*70

99   Usefulness of flecainide for prevention of paroxysmal atrial
     fibrillation and flutter: Danish-Norwegian Flecainide
     Multicenter Study Group, Pieterson A and Hellemann H
     American Journal of Cardiology 1991 Apr1; 67(8)

100 Prevalence of iatrogenic admissions to the Departments of
     Medicine/Cardiology/Pulmonology in a 1,250 bed general
     hospital, Atiqi R , van Bommel E et al *International Journal
     of Clinical Pharmacology and Therapeutics* 2010 Aug 48 (8) doi:
     10.5414/cpp48517

101 Scaling-up treatment of depression and anxiety: a global return

on investment analysis, Chisholm D, Sweeny K et al *The Lancet Psychiatry* April 12, 2016

102 https://www.theguardian.com/society/2019/apr/22/exercise-helped-with-my-anxiety-but-i-became-obsessed-therapy-was-the-answer

103 https://www.theguardian.com/society/2018/may/22/patrick-melrose-captures-heroin-addiction-perfectly-it-brought-my-memories-flooding-back

104 https://metro.co.uk/2018/03/23/10-men-open-up-about-the-first-time-they-had-a-breakdown-due-to-mental-illness-7408250

105 https://www.metro.news/scene-will-young-is-leaving-behind-his-gay-shame-and-tricky-pop-past/1594834

106 https://www.stylist.co.uk/people/jameela-jamil-letter-to-inner-bully-self-esteem-acceptance-self-love/289600

107 Living with Tourette's, Hale L *Therapy Today* November 2018 Vol 29, Issue 9

108 *Beginning Again: An Autobiography of the Years 1911 to 1918* Leonard Woolf, 1975, Harcourt Brace Jovanovich

109 https://www.telegraph.co.uk/family/life/meet-petersons-controversial-family-plagued-health

110 https://metro.co.uk/2020/01/21/social-media-daughters-death-fighting-accountability-12090011

111 Changing the course of comorbid eating disorders and depression: what is the role of public health intervention in targeting shared risk factors? Becker C, Plasencia M et al *Journal of Eating Disorders* 2014 2:15, and What we do, do not, and need to know about comorbid depression and personality disorders, Van H and Kool M *The Lancet Psychiatry* vol 5, issue 10 October 2018

112 https://www.theguardian.com/global/2019/sep/22/how-to-survive-a-twitter-storm-tanya-gold-fat-shaming

113 https://www.theguardian.com/society/2018/feb/12/eating-disorders-nhs-reports-surge-in-hospital-admissions

114 The Impact of Acute Stress on the Neural Processing of Food Cues in Bulimia Nervosa: Replication in Two Samples, Collins B, Breithaupt L et al *Journal of Abnormal Psychology* 2017, Vol 126, No. 5

115 https://www.nhs.uk/conditions/personality-disorder

116 Personality disorders and depression, Fava M, Farabaugh A et al *Psychol Med* 2002 Aug; 32(6)

117 https://www.nhs.uk/conditions/antidepressants/uses

118 Genome-wide association analyses identify 44 risk variants and refine the genetic architecture of major depression, Wray B, Ripke S et al *Nature Genetics* 50, (2018)

119 Dynamic facial expressions of emotion transmit an evolving hierarchy of signals over time, Jack R, Garrod O et al (2014) *Curr. Biol* vol 24, issue 2

120 Expression and the nature of emotion, Ekman P (1984) in *Approaches to Emotion*, eds Scherer K and Ekman P, Hillsdale, NJ: Erlbaum

121 Basic Emotions, Ekman P (1999) in *Handbook of Cognition and Emotion* Dalgleish T and Power M (eds.), Sussex, UK: John Wiley & Sons

122 *The Emotions: Facts, Theories, and a New Model,* Plutchik R (1962) New York, NY: Random House

123 Self-report captures 27 distinct categories of emotion bridged by continuous gradients, Cowen A and Keltner D *Proc Natl Acad Sci USA* 2017; 114(38) doi:10.1073/pnas.1702247114

124 The circumplex model of affect: An integrative approach to affective neuroscience, cognitive development, and psychopathology, Posner J, Russell J et al *Development and Psychopathology* 2005; 17(3)

125 Exploring Comorbidity Within Mental Disorders Among a Danish National Population, Plana-Ripoll O, Bocker Pederson C et al *JAMA Psychiatry* 2019 76(3)

126 Differences between unipolar mania and bipolar -1 disorder: evidence from nine epidemiological studies, Angst J, Rossler W et al *Bipolar Disorders* November 2018, Vol 21, Issue 5,

127 https://www.independent.co.uk/life-style/health-and-families/features/the-psychiatric-disorders-that-might-have-made-anders-breivik-into-a-mass-murderer-a7402126.html

128 Self-esteem in a broad-spectrum approach for mental health promotion, Mann M, Hosman C et al *Health Education Research* vol 19, issue 4, August 2004

129 https://www.mind.org.uk/information-support/types-of-mental-health-problems/self-esteem/about-self-esteem

130 Understanding the Link Between Low Self-Esteem and Depression, Orth U and Robins R *Current Directions in Psychological Science* 2013; 22 (6) https://doi.org/10.1177/0963721413492763

131 Self-esteem and depression revisited: Implicit positive self-esteem in depressed patients? De Raedt R and De Houwer J *Behaviour Research and Therapy* vol 44 issue, 7 July 2006

132 The Relationship between Self-Esteem and Depression when Controlling for Neuroticism, Mu W, Luo J et al *Collabra: Psychology* (2019) 5 (1) https://doi.org/10.1525/collabra.204

133 Once again, there are studies which claim to show the opposite – an association of low self-esteem in childhood and adolescence with depression in later life: for example, Psychosocial risks for major depression in late adolescence: a longitudinal community study, Reinherz H, Giaconna R et al *Journal of American Academy for Child and Adolescent Psychiatry* 32 (1993)

134 Review: Low self-esteem and internalizing disorders in young people – a systematic review, Keane L and Loades M (2016) *Child and Adolescent Mental Health* vol 22 issue 1

135 *The Gendered Brain – the new neuroscience that shatters the myth of the female brain,* Rippon G, 2019, The Bodley Head

136 https://www.metro.news/lewis-hamilton-puts-brakes-on-personal-doubts/1057709

137 *Lost Connections – Why You're Depressed and How to Find Hope* Hari J, 2018, Bloomsbury

138 www.apa.org/pi/wpo/sexualisation.html

139 https://www.diabetes.co.uk/news/2020/dec/more-than-73-of-american-adults-overweight-or-obese.html#:~:text=The%20latest%20data%20from%20American,BMI)%20of%2025%20to%2029.9.

140 Increases in Depressive Symptoms, Suicide-Related Outcomes, and Suicide Rates Among U.S. Adolescents After 2010 and Links to Increased New Media Screen Time, Twenge J, Joiner T et al *Clinical Psychological Science* 2017 vol 6, issue 1 doi/10.1177/2167702617723376

141 *The Coddling of the American Mind – How Good Intentions and Bad Ideas are Setting Up a Generation for Failure* Lukianoff G and Haidt J, 2018, Penguin Random House

142 https://www.theguardian.com/society/2018/nov/22/why-do-more-young-people-have-mental-health-problems?

143 Mortality, severe morbidity, and injury in children living with single parents in Sweden: a population-based study, Ringback Weitoff G, Hjern A et al *The Lancet*, vol 361, issue 9354, January 25, 2003, Single Mother Parenting and Adolescent Psychopathology, Daryanani I, Hamilton J et al *Journal of Abnormal Child Psychology* 44 (2016) and Only Children Were Associated with Anxiety and Depressive Symptoms among

College Students in China, Cheng S, Jia C et al *International Journal of Environmental Research and Public Health* 2020, 17

144 Mental health in young mothers, single mothers and their children, Agnafors S, Bladh M et al *BMC Psychiatry* 19, 112 (2019), Quantitative Review of the Only Child Literature. Research Evidence and Theory Development, Falbo T and Polit D *Psychological Bulletin* 100(2) September 1986

145 Increases in Depressive Symptoms, Suicide-Related Outcomes, and Suicide Rates Among U.S. Adolescents After 2010 and Links to Increased New Media Screen Time, Twenge J, Joiner T et al *Clinical Psychological Science* 2017 vol 6, issue 1 doi/10.1177/2167702617723376

146 https://www.washingtonpost.com/news/wonk/wp/2015/12/01/researchers-have-discovered-a-surprising-reason-we-smile-in-photos

147 Psychological Effects of the Western Film: A Study in Television Viewing, Emery F *Human Relations* vol 12, issue 3, 1959 https://doi.org/10.1177%2F001872675901200301

148 https://www.theguardian.com/sport/2019/mar/15/she-had-changed-did-a-concussion-push-kelly-catlin-to-a-breaking-point

149 https://www.insider.com/michael-phelps-mental-health-scarier-than-ever-during-pandemic-2021-1#:~:text=Michael%20Phelps%20told%20Insider%20his%20mental%20health%20has,taking%20a%20deep%20breath%20from%20time%20to%20time.%22
https://www.independent.co.uk/voices/serena-williams-post-natal-depression-beyonce-rumi-instagram-mental-health-a8483286.html
https://furyjoshua.com/news/tyson-fury-mental-health-awareness-week-2021/

https://www.express.co.uk/life-style/health/1409387/freddie-flintoff-health-latest-depression-symptoms
https://www.express.co.uk/life-style/health/1356198/Victoria-Pendleton-health-latest-depression-symptoms
https://metro.co.uk/2019/09/25/frank-bruno-opens-male-mental-health-recalls-medication-made-cuckoo-10806483/
https://www.dailymail.co.uk/sport/rugbyunion/article-6951431/Jonny-Wilkinson-opens-mental-health-World-Cup-win.html
https://www.the-sun.com/sport/2414647/mike-tyson-bruno-sky-documentary-tears/
https://www.mirror.co.uk/news/uk-news/gazza-backs-mental-health-campaign-10234599
https://www.dailymail.co.uk/sport/rugbyunion/article-8751171/Englands-Joe-Marler-reveals-thoughts-ending-opens-depression.html

150 https://www.theguardian.com/sport/2021/jul/28/simone-biles-withdraws-from-tokyo-olympics-all-around-gymnastics-final and https://au.sports.yahoo.com/olympics-tennis-2021-naomi-osaka-staggering-confession-220037721.html

151 https://www.theguardian.com/sport/2021/jul/30/england-and-wales-cricket-board-and-cricket-australia-set-for-key-talks-over-families-making-trip-to-ashes

152 Setting the bar: athletes and vulnerability to mental illness, Hughes L and Leavey G *The British Journal of Psychiatry* vol 200, issue2, February 2012

153 In an Absolute State: Elevated Use of Absolutist Words Is a Marker Specific to Anxiety, Depression, and Suicidal Ideation, Al-Mosaiwi M, Johnstone T *Clinical Psychological Science*, 2018 July; 6(4)

154 Psychotic traits in comedians, Ando V, Claridge G et al *The British Journal of Psychiatry* 2014 vol 204, issue 5

155 Does comedy kill? A retrospective, longitudinal cohort, nested case – control study of humour and longevity in 53 British comedians, Stewart S and Thompson D *International Journal of Cardiology* 180C (2014)

156 https://www.theguardian.com/environment/2018/oct/18/uk-recycling-industry-under-investigation-for-and-corruption, https://www.theguardian.com/environment/2018/jul/23/uks-plastic-waste-may-be-dumped-overseas-instead-of-recycled, and https://www.theguardian.com/global-development/2018/oct/05/huge-rise-us-plastic-waste-shipments-to-poor-countries-china-ban-thailand-malaysia-vietnam

157 https://www.metro.news/scene-will-young-is-leaving-behind-his-gay-shame-and-tricky-pop-past/1594834/

158 http://communities.lawsociety.org.uk/junior-lawyers/news/jld-resilience-and-wellbeing-survey-report-2019/5067323.article

159 Occupations and the prevalence of major depressive disorder, Eaton W, Anthony J et al *Journal of Occupational Medicine* 1990 Nov 32 (11)

160 *Helplessness: On depression, development, and death* Seligman M (1975) WH Freeman/Times Books/Henry Holt & Co

161 Mourning and Melancholia, Freud S (1917). *The Standard Edition of the Complete Psychological Works of Sigmund Freud*, Volume XIV

162 Domestication Does Not Explain the Presence of Inequity Aversion in Dogs, Essler J, Marshall-Pescini S et al *Current Biology* 2017, vol 27, issue 12

163 Monkeys reject unequal pay, Brosnan S, de Waal F *Nature* 2003 (425)

164 Inequity aversion in rats, Rattus Norvegicus, Oberliesen L, Hernandez-Lallement J et al *Animal Behaviour* 2016 (84)

165 https//youtu.be/meiU6TxysCg.

166 https://www.theguardian.com/football/2018/jun/06/danny-rose-tells-family-not-travel-world-cup-player-racism-fears-abuse-england-football-team

167 The auditory hallucination: A phenomenological survey, Nayani T and David A *Psychological Medicine* 1996 (26)

168 https://www.theguardian.com/science/2018/may/16/living-in-an-age-of-anger-50-year-rage-cycle

169 Anger is More Influential than Joy: Sentiment Correlation in Weibo, Fan R, Zhao J et al (2014) *PLoS ONE* 9(10)

170 https://www.nytimes.com/2020/01/10/us/10IHW-female-rage-books.html

171 *Rage Becomes Her: The Power of Women's Anger* Chemaly S, 2018, Simon and Schuster, *Eloquent Rage: A Black Feminist Discovers her Superpower* Cooper B, 2018, St Martin's Press, *The Subtle Art of Not Giving A F*ck: A Counterintuitive Approach to Living A Good Life*, Manson M, 2016, HarperOne, *Everything is F*cked: A Book About Hope* Manson M, 2019, Harper Collins

172 *Spite…and the Upside of your Dark Side* McCarthy-Jones S, 2020, Oneworld Publications

173 *Difficult Women: A History of Feminism in 11 Fights* Lewis H, 2020, Random House

174 Mood Is Indirectly Related to Serotonin, Norepinephrine and Dopamine Levels in Humans: A Meta-Analysis of Monoamine Depletion Studies, Ruhe H, Mason N et al *Molecular Psychiatry* 2007 Apr 12 (4)

175 Neurobiology of escalated aggression and violence, Miczek K, de Almeida R et al *Journal of Neuroscience* October 2007, 27 (44)

176 Serotonin selectively influences moral judgement and behaviour through effects on harm aversion, Crockett M, Clark M et al (2010) *Proceedings of the National Academy of Sciences*, 107 (40), and Dissociable effects of serotonin and dopamine on the

valuation of harm in moral decisions making, Crockett M, Siegel J et al *Current Biology* July 2015 vol 25, issue 14,

177 Bad Is Stronger Than Good, Baumeister R and Bratslavsky E *Review of General Psychology* 2001, vol 5

178 Negative Emotion Enhances Memory Accuracy Behavioural and Neuroimaging Evidence, Kensonger E *Current Directions in Psychological Science* 1 August 2007

179 Differential effects of negative emotion on memory for items and associations, and their relationship to intrusive imagery, Bisby J, Burgess N *Current Opinion in Behavioural Sciences* 2017, 17

180 Prospect Theory: An Analysis of Decision Under Risk, Kahneman D, Tversky A *Econometrica* 1979, 47(4)

181 *Breaking Murphy's Law* Segerstrom S, 2006, The Guildford Press

182 A pancultural perspective on the fading affect bias in autobiographical memory, Ritchie T, Batteson T et al *Memory* 2015, 23;2

183 Dispositional Optimism and the Risk of Cardiovascular Death: The Zutphen Elderly Study, Giltay E, Kamphuis M et al *Archives of Internal Medicine* 2006, vol 166 (4)

184 Optimism and Recovery After Acute Coronary Syndrome: A Clinical Cohort Study, Ronaldson A, Molloy G et al *Psychosomatic Medicine*, April 2015, vol 77, issue 3

185 For example, Dispositional optimism as a predictor of depressive symptoms over time, Vickers K and Vogeltanz N *Personality and Individual Differences*, February 2000, vol 28, issue 2

186 https://ppc.sas.upenn.edu

187 Optimism and survival in lung carcinoma patients, Schofield P, Ball D et al *Cancer* (2004) 100 and Realistic acceptance as predictor of decreased survival time in gay men with AIDS, Reed G, Kemeny M et al *Health Psychology* (1994) 13

188 A longitudinal study of the effects of pessimism, trait anxiety, and life stress on depressive symptoms in middle-aged women, Bromberger J and Matthews K *Psychology and Ageing* (1996) 11

189 Predictions get tougher in older individuals: a longitudinal study of optimism, pessimism and depression, Armbruster D, Pieper L et al *Social Psychiatry and Psychiatric Epidemiology* (2015) 50

190 Is pessimism a risk factor for depressive mood among community-dwelling older adults? Isaacowitz D and Seligman M *Behavioural Research and Therapy* March 2001 vol 39, issue 3

191 Pleasure Now, Pain Later: Positive Fantasies About the Future Predict Symptoms of Depression, Oettingen G, Mayer D et al *Psychological Science* 2016, March 27 (3)

192 Positive fantasies about idealized futures sap energy, Kapes H and Oettingen G *Journal of Experimental Social Psychology* July 2011, vol 47

193 Optimistic expectations in early marriage, Neff L and Geers A *Journal of Personality and Social Psychology*, July 2013 (105)

194 The Power of (Non) Positive Thinking: Self-Employed Pessimists Earn More Than Optimists, Dawson C, de Meza D et al: IZA Discussion Paper No. 9242, July 2015, Institute for the Study of Labor

195 The Quest for Self-Insight: Theory and Research on Accuracy and Bias in Self-Perception, Robins R and John O in *Handbook of Personality Psychology* Hogan R, Johnson J et al (1997)

196 Anxiety Sensitivity and Opioid Misuse among Opioid-using Adults with Chronic Pain, Rogers A, Brooke M et al *The American Journal of Drug and Alcohol Abuse* 2019; 45(5)

197 Prescription Opioid Use among Adults with Mental Health Disorders in the US, Davis M, Haiyin L et al *The Journal of the American Board of Family Medicine* July 2017, 30(4)

198 Tools to tipple: ethanol ingestion by wild chimpanzees using leaf-sponges, Hockings K, Bryson-Morrison N et al *Royal Society Open Science* 2015, 2(6) https://doi.org/10.1098/rsos.150150

199 Alcohol discrimination and preference in two species of nectar-feeding primate, Gochman S, Brown M et al *Royal Society Open Science* 2016 Jul 3(7) https://doi.org/10.1098/rsos.160217

200 https://www.theguardian.com/society/2019/apr/22/exercise-helped-with-my-anxiety-but-i-became-obsessed-therapy-was-the-answer

201 Fear of Breakdown, Winnicott D *International Review of Psycho-Analysis* (1974) 1

202 A theory of thinking, Bion W *International Journal of Psycho-Analysis* (1962) 43

203 *The Noonday Demon: An Anatomy of Depression,* Solomon A, 2002, Vintage

204 Pattern and process in hominin brain size evolution are scale-dependent, Zipkin D, Hatala A et al *Proceedings. Biological Sciences* 2018, 285 : 0172738. doi:10.1098/rspb.2017.2738.

205 The social brain hypothesis and its implications for social evolution, Dunbar R *Annals of Human Biology* 2009, 36(5), and Ecological dominance, social competition and coalitionary arms race: why humans evolved extraordinary intelligence, Flinn M and Geary D *Evolution and Human Behaviour* 2005, 26(1)

206 Why Rejection Hurts: A Common Neural Alarm System for Physical and Social Pain, Eisenberger N and Lieberman M *Trends in Cognitive Sciences* (2004) 8:7

207 Why Rejection Hurts: The Neuroscience of Social Pain, Eisenberger N in *The Oxford Handbook of Social Exclusion* De Wall C (Ed.) 2013, Oxford University Press

208 Neural and Behavioral Correlates of Sacred Values and Vulnerability to Violent Extremism, Petrus C, Hamid N et al *Frontiers in Psychology* 2018 (9)

209 On the role of the pre-frontal ventromedial cortex in self-processing: the valuation hypothesis, D'Argembeau A *Frontiers in Human Neuroscience* 2013 (7)

210 This isn't an area to which much research has been addressed but, for what it's worth from a highly artificial laboratory setting and extensive reliance on questionnaires, there is evidence suggesting increased levels of resentment and aggression when it's harder for people to make realistic predictions about other people as a result of difficulties in thinking about other people's mental states. Spitefulness and deficits in the social-perceptual and social-cognitive components of Theory of Mind, Ewing D, Zeigler-Hill V et al *Personality and Individual Differences* (2016) 91

211 *Experiences in Groups and other papers* Bion W, 1961, Tavistock Publications Limited

212 Shared Experiences Are Amplified, Boothby E, Clark M et al *Psychological Science* 2014 vol 25 (12)

213 Fear and Loathing across Party Lines: New Evidence on Group Polarization, Lyengar S and Westwood S *American Journal of Political Science* 2014 vol 59, issue 3

214 The evolution of extreme cooperation via shared dysphoric experiences, Whitehouse H, Jong J et al *Scientific Reports* 2017 (7)2

215 For example, 'If feminist Linda Bellos is seen as a risk, progressive politics has lost its way: women and trans people alike are the targets of male violence – but gender issues are now so fraught that we're losing sight of what we have in common' https://www.theguardian.com/commentisfree/2017/oct/06/feminist-linda-bellos-women-trans-male-violence

216 The evolution of extreme cooperation via shared dysphoric experiences, Whitehouse H, Jong J et al *Scientific Reports* 2017 (7)2

217 https://www.theguardian.com/lifeandstyle/2019/sep/02/meditation-helped-me-drag-myself-out-of-self-loathing-and-failure
218 *On Death and Dying* E. Kubler-Ross E, 1969, Macmillan
219 *Bad Science* Goldacre B, 2008, Fourth Estate, *Bad Pharma: How Drug Companies Mislead Doctors and Harm Patients* Goldacre B, 2012, Fourth Estate, *I Think You'll Find It's A Bit More Complicated Than That* Goldacre B, 2014, HarperCollins UK
220 https://www.theguardian.com/society/2018/oct/18/one-in-three-young-people-suffering-mental-health-troubles-survey-finds
221 https://www.independent.co.uk/news/education/education-news/teenagers-mental-health-problems-emotional-wellbeing-action-children-a8589261.html
222 https://www.local.gov.uk/about/news/lga-responds-action-children-research-teenagers-mental-health
223 https://www.williamwragg.org.uk/news/william-wragg-supports-action-childrens-mental-health-campaign
224 Previously available at https://www.actionforchildren.org.uk/news-and-blogs/whats-new/2018/october/one-third-of-15-to-18-year-olds-are-suffering-from-mental-health-issues
225 https://digital.nhs.uk/data-and-information/publications/statistical/mental-health-of-children-and-young-people-in-england/2017/2017
226 *Mental health and wellbeing in England: Adult Psychiatric Morbidity Survey* 2014 McManus S, Bebbington P et al (eds) (2016) Leeds: NHS Digital
227 ibid
228 https://www.mind.org.uk/information-support/types-of-mental-health-problems/mental-health-problems-introduction/causes/#.XWz9dbfTV-E

229 The neuroactive potential of the human gut microbiota in quality of life and depression, Valles-Colomer M, Falony G et al *Nature Microbiology* 2019 (4)

230 Five Things to Know About Inflammation and Depression, Miller A *Psychiatric Times* 2018 (35)

231 The genetics of depression: successful genome-wide association studies introduce new challenges, Ormel J and Hartman C *Translational Psychiatry* 2019 (9)

232 Is there any association between *Toxoplasma gondii* infection and depression? A systematic review and meta-analysis, Chegeni T, Sharif M et al *PLoS One* 2019; 14(6)

233 For a review of a wide range of evidence of increased rates of mental health problems amongst privileged children see How the Wealthy are Disadvantaged, Kang S *Psychology Today* 2015 https://www.psychologytoday.com/gb/blog/the-dolphin-way/201512/how-the-wealthy-are-disadvantaged

234 Expressed emotion and relapse of psychopathology, Hooley J *Annual Review of Clinical Psychology* 2007 (3)

235 *The Child, the Family and the outside World* Winnicott D, 1973, Penguin

236 The Psycho-Analytic Study of Thinking, Bion W *International Journal of Psycho-Analysis* 1962 (43)

237 Objective and subjective experience of child maltreatment and their relationships with child psychopathology, Danese A and Spatz Widom C *Nature Human Behaviour* 2020 Aug; 4(8)

238 Psychological morbidity associated with hyperemesis gravidarum: a systematic review and meta-analysis, Mitchell-Jones N and Gallos I, *BJOG* 2017: 124 (1)

239 Anxiety and depression in COVID-19 survivors: Role of inflammatory and clinical predictors, Mazza M, De Lorenzo R et al *Brain, Behaviour and Immunity* 30 July 2020 https://doi.

org/10.1016/j.bbi.2020.07.037

240 Epidemiology and pathophysiology of Takotsubo syndrome, Akashi Y, Nef H et al *Nature Reviews Cardiology* (2015) 12 (7)

241 https://www.nhs.uk/conditions/post-traumatic-stress-disorder-ptsd/#overview and https://www.psychiatry.org/patients-families/ptsd/what-is-ptsd

242 Mental Health of the non-heterosexual population of England, Chakraborty A, McManus S et al *The British Journal of Psychiatry* February 2011, vol 198 issue 2

243 Prevalence of Mental Disorders, Psychological Distress, and Mental Health Service Among Lesbian, Gay and Bisexual Adults in the United States, Cochrane S, Greer Sullivan J et al *J Consult Clin Psychol* Feb 2003 71(1)

244 For what it's worth it's a similar picture in the National Survey on Drug Use and Health, which is probably the closest equivalent to the APMS in the US, except that respondents who identify as belonging to two or more races have consistently shown higher rates of mental illness than other demographics: US Department of Health and Human Services https://www.samhsa.gov/data/release/2019-national-survey-drug-use-and-health-nsduh-releases

245 Cross-cultural factorial validation of the Clinical Interview Schedule - Revised (CIS-R); findings from a nationally representative survey (EMPIRIC), Das-Munshi J, Castro-Costa E et al *International Journal of Methods in Psychiatric Research* 2014 Jun; 23 (2)

246 Statistics on Race and the Criminal Justice System 2018 - Ministry of Justice 28 November 2019

247 www.synergicollaborativecentre.co.uk - The impact of racism on mental health. The Synergi Collaborative Centre.

248 Detentions under the Mental Health Act: 2019: Gov.UK

https://www.ethnicity-facts-figures.service.gov.uk/health/access-to-treatment/detentions-under-the-mental-health-act/latest#by-ethnicity-5-ethnic-groups

249 Cultural Assessment and Treatment of Psychiatric Patients (updated 25 March 2020) Fogel A, Nazir S et al StatPearls [Internet]. Treasure Island (FL): StatPearls Publishing 2020

250 Is the General Health Questionnaire (12 Item) a culturally biased measure of psychiatric disorder? Lewis G, Araya R *Social Psychiatry and Psychiatric Epidemiology* 1995 (30)

251 Cross-cultural factorial validation of the Clinical Interview Schedule- Revised (CIS-R); findings from a nationally representative survey (EMPIRIC), Das-Munshi J, Castro-Costa E et al *International Journal of Methods in Psychiatric Research* 2014 Jun; 23 (2)

252 How the Wealthy are Disadvantaged, Kang S *Psychology Today* 1 Dec 2015 https://www.psychologytoday.com/gb/blog/the-dolphin-way/201512/how-the-wealthy-are-disadvantaged

253 The development of affective responses in infant monkeys, Harlow H and Zimmermann R *Proceedings of the American Philosophical Society* (1958) 102 and Total social isolation in monkeys Harlow H, Dodsworth R et al *Proceedings of the National Academy of Sciences of the United States of America* (1965) 54(1)

254 Analysis of Environmental Deprivation: Cognitive and Social Development in Romanian Orphans, Kaler R and Freeman B *Journal of Child Psychology and Psychiatry* 1994, 35(4) https://doi.org/10.1111/j.1469-7610.1994.tb01220.x

255 Problems Reported by Parents of Romanian Orphans Adopted to British Columbia, Fisher L, Ames E et al *International Journal of Behavioural Development* 1997 vol 20, issue 1 https://doi.org/10.1080/016502597385441

256 Developmental Catch-up, and Deficit, Following Adoption after Severe Global Early Privation, Rutter M *Journal of Child Psychology and Psychiatry* 2003, 39(4), and Effects of profound early institutional deprivation: An overview of findings from a UK longitudinal study of Romanian adoptees, Rutter M, Beckett C et al *European Journal of Developmental Psychology* 2007, vol 4, issue 3

257 Child-to-adult neurodevelopmental and mental health trajectories after early life deprivation: the young adult follow-up of the Longitudinal English and Romanian Adoptees study, Sonuga-Barke E, Kennedy M et al *The Lancet* vol 389, issue 10078, April 15, 2017

258 Local Brain Functional Activity Following Early Deprivation: A Study of Postinstitutionalized Romanian Orphans, Chugani H, Behan M et al: *Neuroimage* 2001(14)

259 Early childhood deprivation is associated with alterations in adult brain structure despite subsequent environmental enrichment, Mackes N, Golm D et al *Proceedings of the National Academy of Science of the United States of America* 7 January 2020, 117(1)

260 https://www.theguardian.com/society/2018/aug/10/four-million-people-in-england-are-long-term-users-of-antidepressants

261 Office for National Statistics – Overview of the UK Population: November 2018

262 *Mental health and wellbeing in England: Adult Psychiatric Morbidity Survey 2014* McManus S, Bebbington P et al (eds) (2016) Leeds: NHS Digital

263 Ibid

264 Ibid

265 The Five Year Forward View for Mental Health - A report

from the Independent Mental Health Taskforce to the NHS in England, February 2016 and https://www.hopkinsmedicine.org/health/wellness-and-prevention/mental-health-disorder-statistics

266 *Mental health and wellbeing in England: Adult Psychiatric Morbidity Survey 2014* McManus S, Bebbington P et al (eds) (2016) Leeds: NHS Digital

267 *The Gendered Brain – the new neuroscience that shatters the myth of the female brain,* Rippon G, 2019, The Bodley Head

268 Why Rejection Hurts: A Common Neural Alarm System for Physical and Social Pain, Eisenberger N and Lieberman M *Trends in Cognitive Sciences* (2004) 8:7

269 Belief in a just world is associated with activity in insula and somatosensory cortices as a response to the violation of norm violations, Denke C, Rotte M et al *Social Neuroscience* 2014, 9(5)

270 Pricing practices in the retail general insurance sector: Household insurance – Financial Conduct Authority TR18/4 October 2018

271 https://www.fca.org.uk/publications/policy-statements/ps21-15-general-insurance-pricing-practices-market-study

272 The role of low self-esteem in emotional and behavioral problems: why is low self-esteem dysfunctional? Leary M, Shreindorfer L et al *Journal of Social and Clinical Psychology*, 1995, 14(3), https://doi.org/10.1521/jscp.1995.14.3.297

273 *The Working Alliance: Theory, Research and Practice* Horvath A and Greenberg L (eds) 1994 New York: John Wiley

274 https://www.local.gov.uk/about/campaigns/bright-futures/bright-futures-camhs/child-and-adolescent-mental-health-and

275 *Mental health and wellbeing in England: Adult Psychiatric Morbidity Survey 2014* McManus S, Bebbington P et al (eds) (2016) Leeds: NHS Digital

276 https://www.bbc.co.uk/news/health-47740396
277 https://digital.nhs.uk/news-and-events/latest-news/iapt-2018-19
278 https://www.theguardian.com/society/2018/sep/11/mental-health-issues-in-young-people-up-sixfold-in-england-since-1995
279 https://www.bbc.com/news/health-47133338
280 The Mental Health of Children and Young People in England, 2020: Wave 1 follow up to the 2017 Survey, conducted during the Covid 19 pandemic, reported that rates of probable mental disorder in children aged five-16 had increased to one in six. However, since this survey relied entirely on self-reporting, online (rather than face to face structured interviews and trained assessors), used a different, narrower questionnaire to the 2017 survey, had a sample size approximately one third of the 2017 survey and discussed rates of 'probable' mental disorder it's probably best regarded as not being part of the same series for these purposes. As the authors themselves said 'direct comparisons with the MHCYP 2017 are not advised'
281 Mental Health of Children and Young People in England, 2017 – NHS Digital 2018 https://digital.nhs.uk/data-and-information/publications/statistical/mental-health-of-children-and-young-people-in-england/2017/2017
282 Mental health and well-being trends among children and young people in the UK, 1995–2014: Analysis of repeated cross-sectional national health surveys: Pitchforth J, Fahy K, et al *Psychological Medicine* 2019 (49) doi:10.1017/S0033291718001757
283 https://www.ons.gov.uk/peoplepopulationandcommunity/birthsdeathsandmarriages/deaths/bulletins/suicidesintheunitedkingdom/2018registrations https://

www.ons.gov.uk/peoplepopulationandcommunity/
birthsdeathsandmarriages/death/bulletins/
suicidesintheunitedkingdom/2019registrations

284 https://www.parliament.uk/business/publications/
written-questions-answers-statements/written-question/
Lords/2018-07-12/HL9500

285 https://www.ncbi.nlm.nih.gov/pubmed/21901675 and
Acupuncture and Counselling for Depression in Primary Care:
A Randomised Controlled Trial, MacPherson H, Richmond S
et al *PLOS Medicine* 2013, 10(9): e1001518

286 https://www.nhs.uk/news/medication/big-new-study-confirms-
antidepressants-work-better-placebo

287 See for example *The Politics of Experience and The Bird of Paradise*
Laing R 1967 Penguin Books

288 Fear of Breakdown, Winnicott D *International Review of
Psycho-Analysis* (1974) 1

289 Objective and subjective experience of child maltreatment and
their relationships with child psychopathology, Danese A and
Spatz Widom C *Nature Human Behaviour* 2020 Aug; 4(8)

290 https://www.health.harvard.edu/newsletter_article/new-
insights-into-the-nocebo-response 0

291 Sham device v inert pill: randomised controlled trial of two
placebo treatments, Kaptchuk T, Stason S et al *BMJ* 2006, 332:391

292 This is an article about GPs telling children to exaggerate
mental health symptoms if they want NHS treatment:
https://www.telegraph.co.uk/news/2018/03/08/gps-telling-
children-exaggerate-mental-health-symptoms-want. This
is a piece by the American Sociological Association arguing
that sociological research has greatly over-estimated rates of
mental illness in community studies: The high percentages of
depression have been greatly exaggerated: The Methodology of

Community Surveys leads to an overestimate of mental illness, 6 March 2006, American Sociological Association https://www.eurekalert.org/pub_releases/2006-03/asa-thp030306.php. This is an article by a doctor warning about medicalising everyday mental experience: https://www.theguardian.com/commentisfree/2019/jun/24/medicalising-mental-health-illnness-nhs. This is a letter in the BMJ by a Professor of Psychiatry about 'the exaggerated claims of the mental health industry' *BMJ* 2012; 344 doi: https://doi.org/10.1136/bmj.e1791. This is a book devoted to the subject by a clinical psychologist and mental health researcher: *Losing Our Minds: What Mental Illness Really Is – and What It Isn't* Foulkes L 2021 Bodley Head

293 https://www.standard.co.uk/news/crime/driver-accused-of-killing-man-in-127mph-crash-was-overcome-by-mania-a4197021.html

294 The Predictive Value of Risk Categorization in Schizophrenia, Large M, Ryan C et al *Harvard Review of Psychiatry* 2011 (19)

295 Violence and Mental Health – Mind Fact Sheet 2014 and https://www.time-to-change.org.uk/media-centre/responsible-reporting/violence-mental-health-problems

296 Perpetration of violence, violent victimization, and severe mental illness - balancing public health outcomes, Choe J, Telpin L et al *Psychiatric Services,* 2008 , 59(2)

297 Violence and mental illness: what is the true story? Varshney M, Mahapatra A et al *Journal of Epidemiology and Community Health* 2016 (70), and Schizophrenia and Violence: Systematic Review and Meta-Analysis, Fazel S Gulati G et al *PLOS Medicine* 2009 (6)

298 Violence and mental illness: what is the true story? Varshney M, Mahapatra A et al *Journal of Epidemiology and Community Health* 2016 (70)

299 In an Absolute State: Elevated Use of Absolutist Words Is a Marker Specific to Anxiety, Depression, and Suicidal Ideation, Al-Mosaiwi M, Johnstone T *Clinical Psychological Science*, 2018 July; 6(4)

300 Me, Myself, and I: self-referent word use as an indicator of self-focussed attention in relation to depression and anxiety, Brockemeyer T, Zimmermann J et al *Frontiers in Psychology* October 2015, and A meta-analysis of correlations between depression and first person singular pronoun use, Edwards M, Holtzman N et al *Journal of Research in Personality* 2017 (68)

301 Risk for recurrence in depression, Burcusa S and Iacono W *Clinical Psychology Review* 2007, vol 27, issue 8

302 Ibid

303 Predicting recurrence of depression using lifelog data: an explanatory feasibility study with a panel VAR approach, Kumagai N, Tajika A et al *BMC Psychiatry* 2019, 19, 391 https://doi.org/10.1186/s12888-019-2382-2

304 *Toward a Unified Criminology: Integrating Assumptions about Crime, People and Society*, Agnew R 2011 NYU Press

305 https://www.theguardian.com/stage/2019/apr/22/sofie-hagen-fat-is-a-neutral-word-i-want-us-to-reclaim-it

306 Lifetime prevalence and age-of-onset distribution of DSM-IV disorders in the National Comorbidity Survey Replication, Kessler R, Berglund P et al *Arch Gen Psychiatry* 2005 Jun; 62(6)

307 Mental health statistics: children and young people – Mental Health Foundation https://www.mentalhealth.org.uk/statistics/mental-health-statistics-children-and-young-people#:~:text=50%25%20of%20mental%20health%20problems,and%2075%25%20by%20age%2024

308 *Triumphs of Experience – The Men of the Harvard Grant Study* Vaillant G 2012 Belknap Press

309 Adult mental health disorders and their age at onset, Jones P published online by Cambridge University Press 2 January 2018 https://www.cambridge.org/core/journals/the-british-journal-of-psychiatry/article/adult-mental-health-disorders-and-their-age-at-onset/13F1A156235E5FF0D904F2CE2FDC053F

310 *Mental health and wellbeing in England: Adult Psychiatric Morbidity Survey 2014* McManus S, Bebbington P et al (eds) (2016) Leeds: NHS Digital

311 Confusion of the Tongues Between the Adults and the Child – (The Language of Tenderness and of Passion) – Ferenczi S (1949) International Journal of Psychoanalysis 30 (originally produced as a paper at the Twelfth International Psycho-Analytic Conference in 1932 and published in translation in 1949)

312 *Relational Concepts in Psychoanalysis* Mitchell S (1988) Harvard University Press

313 Vacillation in *The Winding Stair and Other Poems* - W.B. Yeats 1933

314 https://www.theguardian.com/music/2020/jul/23/song-of-the-summer-2020-our-writers-pick-their-favourite-tracks

315 *Triumphs of Experience – The Men of the Harvard Grant Study* Vaillant G 2012 Belknap Press

316 https://www.theatlantic.com/magazine/archive/2009/06/what-makes-us-happy/307439/

317 *Friends – Understanding the Power of our Most Important Relationships* Dunbar R 2021 Little, Brown

318 Valiant attempts have been made to ground these conclusions in data but the use of variables as opaque as students' free form recollections of childhood experiences allocated scores using researchers subjective ratings decades later, subjective ratings decades earlier of 'soundness' of personality as undergraduates and retrospective assessment of the maturity of defence

mechanisms employed by participants many years earlier tended to undermine their foundations as science. In addition, since the parameters used to define a successful life, included a number to do with social relations (in a good marriage between ages 60 and 85, close to adult children and friendship outside family) the exercise had something a little self-fulfilling about it

319 https://www.theguardian.com/uk-news/2013/nov/26/nigella-lawson-cocaine-charles-saatchi

320 https://www.theguardian.com/music/2019/apr/12/people-who-sing-it-want-the-world-to-know-they-exist-50-years-of-my-way

321 https://www.theguardian.com/us-news/2019/mar/31/sandy-hook-shooting-suicide-parents-fake-news-conspiracy

322 https://www.ons.gov.uk/peoplepopulationandcommunity/birthsdeathsandmarriages/divorce/bulletins/divorcesinenglandandwales/2017#what-percentage-of-marriages-end-in-divorce

323 *Mental health and wellbeing in England: Adult Psychiatric Morbidity Survey 2014* McManus S, Bebbington P et al (eds) (2016) Leeds: NHS Digital

324 Mental Health Foundation – Fundamental Facts about Mental Health 2016

325 Health Survey for England – 2005, Health of Older People: Volume 4, Mental health and well being: NHS Digital https://digital.nhs.uk/data-and-information/publications/statistical/health-survey-for-england/health-survey-for-england-2005-health-of-older-people

326 https://www.theguardian.com/society/2018/aug/10/four-million-people-in-england-are-long-term-users-of-antidepressants

327 Changing prevalence and treatment of depression among older patients over two decades, Arthur A, Savva G et al *Br J Psychiatry* 2020 (216)

328 Mourning and Melancholia. Freud S (1917) *The Standard Edition of the Complete Psychological Works of Sigmund Freud*, Volume XIV

329 Cumulative adversity and depressive symptoms among older adults in Israel: the differential roles of self-oriented versus other-oriented events of potential trauma, Shmotkin D and Litwin H *Social Psychiatry and Psychiatric Epidemiology* 2009 (44) https://doi.org/10.1007/s00127-009-0020-x and Evolutionary Theories of Depression: A Critical Review, Hagen E *The Canadian Journal of Psychiatry* December 1, 2011 https://doi.org/10.1177%2F070674371105601203

330 *Cognitive Therapy and the Emotional Disorders* Beck A (1976) International Universities Press: New York

331 *Evolutionary Psychiatry: A New Beginning* Stevens A and Price J 1996 Routledge, and Social rank theory of depression: A systematic review of self-perceptions of social rank and their relationship with depressive symptoms and suicide risk, Wetherall K, Robb K et al *Journal of Affective Disorders* 1 March 2019

332 Automatic activation of self-discrepancies and emotional syndromes: when cognitive structures influence affect, Strauman T and Higgins E *Journal of Personality and Social Psychology* 1987 Dec 53 (6)

333 Therapeutic Alliance and Outcome of Psychotherapy: Historical Excursus, Measurements, and Prospects for Research, Ardito R and Rabellino D *Frontiers in Psychology* 2011; 2: 270

334 https://www.family-institute.org/behavioral-health-resources/importance-relationship-therapist

335 Me, Myself, and I: self-referent word use as an indicator of self-focussed attention in relation to depression and anxiety, Brockemeyer T, Zimmermann J et al *Frontiers in Psychology*

October 2015, and A meta-analysis of correlations between depression and first person singular pronoun use, Edwards M, Holtzman N et al *Journal of Research in Personality* 2017 (68)

336 *Paradise Lost* - John Milton

337 *Mindfulness and acceptance: Expanding the cognitive-behavioral tradition* Hayes S, Follette V et al (Eds.). (2004) New York: Guilford Press

338 Ego distortion in terms of true and false self, Winnicott D in *The Maturational Process and the Facilitating Environment: Studies in the Theory of Emotional Development* 1960 New York, International Universities Press

339 Association between physical exercise and mental health in 1.2 million individuals in the USA between 2011 and 2015: a cross-sectional study, Chekroud S, Gueorguieva R et al *The Lancet Psychiatry* September 01, 2018, vol 5, issue 9

340 Setting the bar: athletes and vulnerability to mental illness, Hughes L and Leavey G *The British Journal of Psychiatry* vol 200, issue2, February 2012

341 https://www.health.harvard.edu/newsletter_article/sleep-and-mental-health

342 The neuroactive potential of the human gut microbiota in quality of life and depression, Valles-Colomer M, Falony G et al *Nature Microbiology* 2019 (4)

343 Relationship Between Diet and Mental Health in Children and Adolescents: A Systematic Review , O'Neil A, Shae E et al *American Journal of Public Health* 2014 October; 104(10)

344 Relationship between Diet and Mental Health in a Young Adult Appalachian College Population, Wattick R, Hagedorn R et al *Nutrients* July 2018

345 Five Things to Know About Inflammation and Depression, Miller A *Psychiatric Times* 2018 (35)

346 https://www.sciencedaily.com/releases/2012/04/120402162546.htm
347 *Biophilia* Wilson E (1884) Harvard University Press
348 https://www.mind.org.uk/information-support/tips-for-everyday-living/nature-and-mental-health/how-nature-benefits-mental-health/, and https://www.mentalhealth.org.uk/campaigns/thriving-with-nature/guide
349 The relationship between greenspace and the mental wellbeing of adults: A systematic review, Houlden V, Weich S et al *PLoS One* 2018 Sep 1;13 (9)
350 Results from an 18 country cross-sectional study examining experiences of nature for people with common mental health disorders, Tester-Jones M, White M et al *Scientific Reports* 2020 10 (1)
351 https://fullfact.org/health/mental-health-spending-england
352 Thriving At Work – The Stevenson/Farmer review of mental health and employees: October 2017
353 https://www.england.nhs.uk/2018/02/mental-illness-recovery/#:~:text=49.3%20per%20cent%20of%20people%20completing%20IAPT%20treatment%20for%20anxiety,starting%20treatment%20within%20six%20weeks

INDEX

A

Absolutism: defence against feelings of inadequacy 93-96
    textual analysis and absolute terms in language 95-96, 235
Advertising 81-83, 205, 245–246, 280
Antidepressants and medication: number of prescriptions 9, 17, 50,
    204, 218, 220, 304
  other medical uses 23, 70, 153, 304
  how they work 50, 57, 143
  effectiveness 52, 54-55, 216, 228
  side effects and potential for harm 53-54, 59
  and serotonin 50, 143
  use amongst elderly 304-305
  place in mental health treatment 314-315
Anxiety disorders: 23, 27, 61, 68, 70, 170, 285
  neurological features in common with depression 71
Autism spectrum disorder
  (ASD) 47

B

Bereavement 31, 176, 185, 186, 191, 193, 203, 288, 303

C

Co-dependency 135
Coronavirus 13, 191, 192, 267

D

Deep brain stimulation 50
Depression 23, 32, 46, 51, 56, 58,
  66, 67, 68, 82, 84, 85, 112, 124, 125, 136, 138, 175, 186, 187, 191,

192, 193, 198, 204, 223, 236, 237, 238, 241, 244, 248, 294, 314, 315, 321, 322, 323
statistics 9-17, 59
DSM-5 diagnostic criteria 33, 34, 72, 123, 320
ICD-10 diagnostic criteria 33, 34, 72, 123, 320
and neurological evidence 46-47
and serotonin 50, 142, 143
co-morbidity and association with other mental disorders 68-72, 117
and self-esteem 65-68, 72-75, 117
textual analysis and absolute terms in language 95-96, 235
experience of unfairness and aggression 143
textual analysis and use of first person singular personal pronouns 235, 311
and optimism and pessimism 145-146
amongst the elderly 16, 304-305
Diet 321
Dunbar's number 259

E

Eating disorders 69-70, 82, 83
Elite sports 92-93, 319
Ethnicity and mental health statistics 182, 184, 195-198
Exercise 151, 225, 319-320
Expressed emotion and family relationships 188-189

G

Gender 28, 53, 82, 106, 107, 154, 160, 162, 194, 195, 203, 210
Grant Study 248, 259
Greenspace and nature 322-323

H

Hot sauce experiments 36-37
Humour 100-101, 147, 262, 275, 290
Hyperemesis gravidarum 191

I

Inflammation 187, 192, 223, 322

M

Maladaptive Self Focussed Attention 235, 311
Marshmallow experiments 38
Mental health statistics 9-20, 33, 84, 182, 194, 196-198, 217, 221, 247, 248
Mindfulness 148, 317-318, 321, 323

N

Narcissism 29, 73, 146, 155-158, 187
Neuroscience 45-51, 73, 76, 153, 156, 209-212

O

Obsessive compulsive disorder (OCD) 23, 47, 68, 70, 132, 171, 285

P

Perfectionism 90, 91, 319
Post-traumatic stress disorder 23, 68, 70, 193
Psychiatric diagnoses 24, 82-35, 41, 51, 61, 70, 72, 73, 75, 155, 251, 325
Psychological research 12-20, 25-28, 32-33, 36, 39-41, 46-49, 51-53, 59, 61, 75, 117, 179-181, 247-249, 304, 307
Psychological questionnaires 13, 24, 25-28, 61-62, 181, 198
Psychotherapy: place within mental health treatment 21-24, 314

different forms 21, 41-45
effectiveness 43, 55-56
provision of in NHS 216, 218
and idealised states of mind 251, 253
and the positive aspects of negative emotions 282
and self-assertion 240, 286

R

Remorse 291, 294, 297-299, 310, 312, 313
Romanian orphans 201-202

S

Serotonin: and depression 50, 142-143
  and aggression 143
Sexual orientation 82, 106, 154, 162, 194, 210
Single child syndrome 188-189
Sleep 33, 34, 61, 320, 321
Social media 69, 83, 84-86, 87, 115, 140, 147, 182, 199, 205, 264
Sociometer theory 212

T

Takotsubo cardiomyopathy 193
Toxoplasmosis 187
Transcranial magnetic stimulation 51

www.ingramcontent.com/pod-product-compliance
Lightning Source LLC
Chambersburg PA
CBHW020240030426
42336CB00010B/552